I
AM
THE
REFEREE

Ian John-Lewis

Written

By Mark Heffernan

BERFORTS GROUP LTD

I am the referee

ISBN 978-1-908616-87-6 Softback
ISBN 978-1-908616-88-3 Hardback

First Published 2014
Publishers Berforts Group Ltd

Printed and bound in Great Britain by
www.berforts.com
Berforts Information Press

I

AM

THE

REFEREE

Ian John-Lewis

Written

By Mark Heffernan

Dedicated to

Les Roberts

Mentor, manager, friend.

I Couldn't have done it without you

Foreword by Barry Hearn

As a fight fan I have watched lots of boxers during their careers and one of the most pleasing to the eye for action packed bouts was Ian John-Lewis.

He began his career and ended his career with back to back losses, but in the middle part he was involved in tough crowd pleasing bouts against good fighters and mainly ended up in the winning corner.

I promoted his last two losing bouts against Mickey Hughes and Darren Dyer and both of these contests showed why Ian was the man he was... tough, unrelenting and a never giving up type of boxer, carved from the old school.

When he asked me for my thoughts about him becoming a boxing referee, I gave him some very simple advice... always be your own man, always be in charge, always think of the boxer's welfare and be totally honest. In my opinion, Ian has never waived from these recommendations.

I am proud to say that I was the man that suggested to Ian that he always introduce himself to the boxers as 'I am the Referee', therefore making sure they knew from the outset he was in total charge of the bout and until this day there has never been anyone left in any doubt of this particular man's authority in the four cornered ring... the toughest place on earth.

Barry Hearn

A note from the author: Mark Heffernan

The hardest thing about writing this book was convincing the world class referee, Ian John-Lewis, that he'd already achieved enough in his life to warrant a book being written about him.

Having arranged a meeting to discuss the book, it was only when I agreed that he would be able to halt the process at any stage that he was happy to embark on the project.

Ian is a modest man, humble and not open to displays of show. He has worked hard in all areas of his life and is well thought of by the people he comes into contact with… just look at the tribute section!

The book finished, Ian turned to me and said,

'I really like it… but do you really think I've achieved enough?'

World Boxing Council

Jose Sulaiman: (1931-2014) Former President of the World Boxing Council (WBC).

'Referees have in their hands the safety of the sport and the protection of the health of the boxers, as well as the control of the fight for strict respect to the rules, cleanliness and impartiality.

There are several different styles, attitudes and basic guidelines. The WBC's first priority is to train and give opportunities to those who can do the best performance possible, as safety is in their hands.

Ian John-Lewis is, without doubt, one of the very best referees in professional boxing. When I want someone who I can absolutely trust, Ian John Lewis comes immediately to my mind.'

Mauricio Sulaiman: President of the World Boxing Council.

'We thank you very much for your kind support and we are very proud of your great performance representing your commission and WBC with absolute confidence, integrity, competency and dedication to make the sport and our organisation proud of your exemplary manner.'

Tito Gonzales: World Title Fights Coordinator (WBC).

'The World Boxing Council is a big family within the boxing world. Working for the most prestigious boxing organization has given me the opportunity to meet many important boxing people, some of them are my friends, Mr. John-Lewis included of course. He lives an interesting life as one night he can be refereeing a WBC world title fight and the following morning he can be back working in the Police Station. Ian is a humble and level headed human being and perhaps why he is such a successful referee.'

Sam Hadfield: Caris Boxing Club. carisboxing@hotmail.com

'We are a boxing club for the homeless and we are so pleased to have Ian's support. Ian gives us his time for free. In our conversations he told me he had not been far from the guys at the gym, the ones who feel it is safer to sleep on the streets as they think it is less dangerous than staying at home. Ian is an amazing guy.'

Trevel Henry: Chairman of the Kent Minority Ethnic Police Association.

'Ian is one of the most generous, enthusiastic and humble persons I have known. It is only when pressed to talk about current topics within boxing that you suddenly realise that this fairly quiet unassuming guy, has just returned from far afield overseas having just refereed a world class boxing match! He has the respect and admiration from many of his friends and colleagues at work. As now, when the name Ian John-Lewis is mentioned, I am left with a good feeling…respect!'

Wendell Henry: KMEPA and NBPA executive.

'When I first met Ian there was nothing to say 'famous referee'. He is known as the quiet man of custody and his importance begins to show as he takes command of confrontation. He is the perfect role model for the black community and always has time for people. He is the consummate champion and a pleasure to work with.'

Tributes

Adam Smith: Head of Boxing/Boxing Commentator for Sky Sports.

'Ian is a fabulous guy, boxing to the core – a dedicated referee and his smile lights up all around ringside. One of the sport's true characters – and the friendliest of faces.'

Adam Booth: Respected World-Class Trainer of Former World Heavyweight Champion David Haye.

'Ian is one of the most recognisable and respected Referees and Judges in world boxing today. He has always been able to personally relate to fighters and coaches whilst maintaining his authority in the ring. He is a 'fighters favourite!!'

Alan Pughsley: Chief Constable Kent Police.

'During the past 18 years as a Detention Officer in Medway, Ian John-Lewis has routinely utilised many of the same skills that he uses as a boxing referee. He has a unique and rare ability to build an instant rapport with everyone that he meets, building trust and confidence in both prisoners and the public that he meets in the course of his daily duties. His continued passion for the police service is a credit to him and a much valued asset to the Force.'

Barry Mcguigan: World featherweight champion.

'Ian John-Lewis is one of the most enthusiastic and passionate referees in the business. It's not surprising that he has quickly risen to the top of the A star referees in the U.K. What's more IJL is an absolute gentleman and I'm pleased to call my friend.'

Bernhard Hart: (past MD and founder of Lonsdale)

'Ian John-Lewis was one of the best value for money fighters of his time, followed by a career as a distinguished referee. A true gentleman of his time!'

Bob Lonkhurst: (Author and BBB of C inspector).

'Apart from regarding Ian as a friend, I have great respect for his professionalism and the way he has dealt with adversity over the years. A thoroughly nice guy, a fair and honest official, he is a credit to boxing and I wish him every success with this book.'

Darren Dyer: Commonwealth/ABA Welterweight Champion and Ian's last opponent as a boxer.

'When preparing to fight IJL I trained really hard as I knew he was a danger. I had to be at the top of my game and came properly prepared. As a referee he is the top man and shows all of us that it can be done.'

Dave Still: Best mate

'I have known Louie since we were 4 years old…we grew up together, went to the boxing gym and disco. Our lives may have taken us down different paths but we are still and always will be the best of friends.'

Domonic Negus: Former Southern Area/WBU Champion and Boxing Security Consultant.

'The best referee in the game. He looks after the boxers, cares about us all. He's been a fighter, a good one, and knows how important it is to us who pull the gloves on.'

Duke Mckenzie: World Champion at three different weights.

'The man in the ring needs to have good experience and he has the best. He has boxed to a very good standard so has walked the walk and because of this you know his decisions are correct.'

'The best referee we have and anyone thinking of becoming a referee, just look at IJL, he is the man to follow.'

Eddie Cotton: World-Class Referee from the USA.

'I had the pleasure of working with Ian in Kazakhstan. I could tell he loved the sport and wanted to learn all he could. I simply reminded him to relax and enjoy his fight. Since then we have talked at many conventions. Ian still has the fervour the sport has given him and he works hard at being a top official. I am happy to be his friend and associate.'

Gary Jacobs: Former WBC International/European Welterweight Champion.

'... one tough guy... exciting fighter... world class ref.'

Harry Holland: Former Promoter/Manager/Match maker & Trainer.

'IJL is the type of man and boxer you'd like your son to take after. A genuine man of high integrity, unswayable in his decisions. He calls the result as he sees it. I am proud to know him.'

Ian Learmonth: Chief Constable (retired) Kent Police

'On a daily basis in the course of his work as a detention officer, Ian demonstrates his commitment to making Kent's communities a safe place to live and work. He has the unique ability to instantaneously establish a great rapport with everyone that he meets, whether they are a prisoner or a member of the public. He has boundless energy, enthusiasm and a passion for his job, making him an excellent ambassador for the Force.'

James Cook: European Super Middleweight Champion. (MBE)

'IJL... very high standard boxer in his day. Not many boxers reach the top in refereeing like he has... Plus he is a top man in my Cricket team!'

Johnny Armour: Former ABA/WBU Champion and stable mate both amateur and professional.

'Ian has such integrity. If he's the referee you know it will be fair, that he will look after both boxers equally and that you'll be able to display your ability. Top guy, top referee.'

Kellie (Frank) Maloney:
'Ian has shown the same dedication to refereeing as he did as a boxer. He may have missed out, narrowly, on the British title but as a referee he has reached the ultimate level. Deserved.'

Kendall Webb: Work Colleague.

'It's not just because Ian is the 'boxer bloke' that he gets respect from people held in custody. It is because he is firm and fair, treats people with respect. He trained my two boys at boxing and they have nothing but respect for him. I am proud to call him my friend.'

Kim Matchas: Work/former school colleague.

'Working with Ian is a dream. He will always back you up, no matter how difficult or dangerous the job can become. A real gent.'

Lee Minshull: Professional footballer. Newport County.

'Ian's dedication to his sport is an inspiration. He still trains as if he was fighting in the ring, not refereeing. I am sure this will help him to stay at the top for many years to come!'

Mark Willougby: Former employer and long-time friend.

'It would not have mattered what Ian would have ended up doing, he would always have given it 100 per cent and been the best he could be. Hardest worker I ever worked with and a genuinely nice guy.'

'Nathan':

'Been locked up by Ian on many occasions... He always treats you with respect. Top bloke who really does care. We all respect Ian and why wouldn't we. If he catches me with stuff on me I know he is going to do his job. I know a lot of us prisoners would go to his aid if he was in trouble. When given this tribute he said to me... 'Nathan, appreciate your kind words but when are you going to turn the corner and do something for yourself fellah?' He makes you think.'

Paul Brandon: Deputy Chief Constable, Kent Police.

'Ian is highly respected across the Force as an experienced Detention Officer. There is no doubt as a former professional boxer he is more than capable of handling himself when confronted with a hostile situation within the custody arena. That said, he has consistently demonstrated the ability to calm such situations down by establishing a good rapport with prisoners, as he also does with members of the public and other officers and staff. He has enormous passion for his job and is an excellent ambassador for Kent Police.'

Paul Lynch: Friend/Former tough Middleweight from Sevenoaks ABC.

'IJL… good boxer, brilliant referee, lovely fellah. True grit!'

Richard Steele: Former World-Class Referee from the USA.

'IJL is a strong referee with commanding and decisive techniques, which are great attributes inside the ring. Referee Lewis is a skilled official and I am proud to call him a colleague in the sport of boxing.'

Ricky 'Hitman' Hatton: Former IBF/WBA Lt-Welter/Welterweight Champion.

'In many ways the job of a referee is impossible as they don't have the benefit of an action replay when making their decision then and there on the spot. Depending on who the fans are supporting they can sometimes turn the referee into the bad guy and I don't envy them their job.

The referees appointed by the British Boxing Board of Control are amongst the best in the world and Ian John-Lewis is at the top of the Star Referees appointed by the Board. He delivers very clear instructions but still lets you know, without being overbearing, that he is the boss in the ring. I had the pleasure of Ian refereeing me for my fights with Vince Phillips and Joe Hutchinson and he also judged my fight against John Baily. My style of boxing was very physical and I wasn't the easiest to ref but Ian seemed to breeze through it like the true pro that he is.

Ian is a Gent both inside and out of the ring and he is one of the nicest guys you could wish to meet.'

Simon Block: Hon Secretary Commonwealth Boxing Council 1980 – present day.

'…If I had to sum Ian up with five qualities I would say; honesty, heart, enthusiasm, dedication and ability to learn. If more people had these qualities what a better world this would be. I am proud to call him a friend.'

Steve Holdsworth: Eurosport Commentator.

'Whenever I knew IJL was on the bill, a sense of excitement coursed through me, knowing I was about to witness Mr. Excitement. Ian was never in a bad fight and always gave 100% unlike so many who just turn up for the money. Ian was a real warrior in the ring.'

Sean Naylor: Work Colleague.

'Always kept an eye on Ian's career from the 80's. Ian is a people's man, he is loyal, trustworthy and I know at work my back is always covered'.

Acknowledgements

First to thank of course is my wife. Could not have followed my refereeing career and lived the dream without the support of Julie. We are a team, a very good one.

Thanks to everyone in boxing, from all around the world. From fans to promoters, thank you for your hospitality. It is a great sport, the hardest game, a way out and up for many, myself included.

Thanks to the guys behind this book, team 'John-Lewis' as they call themselves. Maggie Langley www.officehounds.com, Chris 'clubber' Langley(cboxing.co.uk) and Mark Heffernan (m_heffernan@talktalk.net). Maggie, you are a genius and generous. Thanks to you and Chris for your support and help in getting me into this century regarding 'twitter', websites and Facebook. Thanks to Linda Weeks for proofreading the book and brilliant young photographer Charlie Stanhope www.charliestanhope.co.uk, for his advice regarding what we should be looking at for a book cover. Thanks again to 'click click' Mick Smith, a lifelong friend.

Thanks to Action Images for the front cover, David Haye and Amir Kahn photos.

To Derek Rowe for the back cover and Herol Graham pictures and Tony Fitch for the photos of the Micky Hughes fight.

A big thanks to Dale Burgess and Sandie Ball of Berforts Information Press for all their help in getting the book pulled together.

Thanks to the writer, (also my physiotherapist), Mark Heffernan, a man obsessed, for the thousands of hours he devoted to the book. Thanks for your constant questions, re writes, and re writes of re writes! For the thousands of miles travelled meeting with people in the boxing world and for showing me that so many people want the best for me. Thanks to all who were more than willing to give their time, write tributes, share memories and be interviewed and of course to all you good people that will make it a success. Hope you enjoy reading it as much as I enjoyed living it!

Ian John-Lewis

Chapters

I

AM

THE

REFEREE

Ian John-Lewis

Written

By Mark Heffernan

'I am the referee.

I spoke to you both in the dressing room.

Obey my command at all times.

You both know the rules.

Watch your heads and keep your punches up.

When I shout 'Break!' break clean,

... and remember ...

defend yourself at all times.

Shake hands.'

Ian John-Lewis

' Star-Class' Referee

The Promise

Cut eye… nothing serious, but the referee kept looking at it. Was boxing well; winning; wasn't expected to on Micky Hughes' home turf, Bethnal Green, in the East End of London. York Hall, 'the venue', was and still is a hot, deafening, intimidating place and the Mecca of British boxing.

Even Les Roberts, my mentor, when I asked him about taking this British Welterweight final eliminator with Hughes, said he'd knock me out! But he hadn't and didn't look like he would, as he couldn't see me too well.

Gary Nickels, my trainer, calmly told me as I sat on the stool between rounds eight and nine, 'Six minutes of the same John L, you'll be fighting for the British Title.'

I'd trained for 14 years to get to this and was just two rounds from my dream. The referee looked at my eye again but was waved away by Mick 'the rub', my cuts man.

'Nothing to worry about here ref,' Mick 'the rub' told him.

'How bad is it Mick?' I asked.

'Nowhere as bad as Micky's. You've shut it nicely with that jab of yours!'

The referee didn't even glance at Micky's eye. Although to be fair it couldn't be seen through the closed lid, shut tight under the swollen, still swelling, misplaced eyelid and brow. Knew it wasn't good for Micky, he wouldn't be able to judge what distance I was from him. So to win and get a title fight, I just had to keep boxing. Stick, move, in and out, deliver hard stinging jabs to keep him on the back foot, but most importantly, move, and keep Micky moving. Don't let him plant his feet; that way he can't drop the big bombs which have knocked out 21 of his 24 opponents. His body shots bloody hurt and in the dressing room, after the fight, I pissed so much blood, the toilet water looked like a bloody

Mary. Didn't want one of those punches to my chin. Micky Hughes was the toughest and strongest guy I ever fought. During the fight when we got into a clinch, he would just throw me off as if I weighed nothing.

Jim McDonnell, one of the commentators for Sky Sports that night and long-time friend of Micky from the same boxing stable, had turned from saying the fight should be a formality to, 'If he doesn't knock him out soon, Micky's in trouble. He's getting frustrated in there because he can't land the big bombs.'

The bell sounded the start of round nine. I was off the stool quick, eager for the two rounds to pass.

'Same again John L… box and move… keep moving!' was the order as I left my corner and went to the middle of the ring.

Was in the best shape of my life for this. Knew I'd have to be to get a shot at the British title. Lung busting runs up Chatham hill that left the taste of metallic blood in my mouth. Denial of alcohol and food that was no good for me. The first date with Julie, now my wife, ended at 9.45 p.m. when I told her I had to go, as I had training in the morning. For some strange reason she wasn't impressed and told me later I was lucky to get a second date! All this and the training would be worthwhile… if I got my shot. Ninety seconds into round nine, the referee ordered us to stop boxing.

'Bout bloody time!' I thought, knowing that he should've looked at Micky's eye long ago.

You can imagine the shock when he came to me, took my face in his hands and said, 'Sorry son, it's all over.'

'What!… nah!… nah!' I stuttered the words out, couldn't believe what I was hearing.

Pulled away from him, walked around the ring with my arms outstretched as if pleading to the booing crowd to overturn the ref's decision. They couldn't, no one could; the ref's decision was final.

My eye was no different than when the ref had been waved away by Mick 'the rub' but for some reason he felt he should stop the fight. He didn't look convinced at his decision, but even less convinced were the hundred plus fans that had come up from the Medway towns to cheer me on, along with a large section of the East End crowd, Micky's fans, who booed loudly. That's the thing about East Enders, they're a loyal, proud people, the backbone of London, born out of being the underdog and an underdog can win them over and I had.

Frank Maloney, my manager, a man not to mince his words, found his way up onto the apron of the ring and yelled at the ref, 'You've taken a fucking liberty!'

Micky's eye was far worse than mine, so bad in fact that he couldn't do the post-fight interview with Sky because he had to be seen immediately by the doctor.

On leaving the ring, Les put his arm around my shoulder, said he was proud of me, that it was the best he'd seen me box... and that I'd been turned over! Les being proud of me would have made me float for days normally and although nice to hear it, it didn't lift me. I knew I wasn't fancied to win, with most thinking Micky would beat me easily. He didn't, but the ref did. His decision hurt me more than Micky's bombs, and they really did hurt. I was shattered by his decision, not physically as I was really fit, but mentally. Something inside me had gone. That hunger, the fire, the will and desire you need to be a boxer had diminished immediately. My career was over, the title shot gone. I would never fight in the big arenas and never fight for the British title. Should've retired there and then; it would've saved me a lot of pain.

Couldn't remember the long walk back to the dressing room, but found myself sitting on the massage table getting my bandages cut off by a quiet and disappointed trainer. The tatty old dressing room was like a morgue. We all felt cheated and down after having fought a near perfect fight. Frank Maloney was the only one who had any energy left and paced the room. Obviously pissed off, he stated, 'That was a disgrace to stop you... I'll be putting in an official complaint to the Board.' (British Boxing Board of Control). Frank added some expletives to drive the point home.

The tactics for the fight that my new trainer, Gary Nickels and I had agreed on had been right. Our first meeting had been in the gym of the Henry Cooper pub in the Old Kent Road. I looked at his baby face, thought he was a bit young and wondered what he could teach me. Turned out he was four years my senior, a former ABA Flyweight Champion in '78 and a top pro with the Terry Lawless camp. Good apprenticeship. We hit it off straight away and after a good session on the pads, he told me what my biggest failing was: he said that when my opponents want to fight, I fight and when they want to box, I box. He added that because I was a really good boxer/fighter and could mix it up, I shouldn't let the fighters drag me into war and the boxers dictate the tactics, style or pace. After all the years of being told the same thing and it not getting through, the way he said it made perfect sense, especially for the upcoming fight against the knock out specialist Micky Hughes.

In the dressing room, I looked at Gary, Mick 'the rub' and Frank and realised that it wasn't just me that had been turned over. Anybody can celebrate the highs with you but these guys also felt the lows. It was a great team and we should all have been celebrating a win and a shot at the British Title.

Wanted some alone time, so changed slowly and timed it so everyone had gone from the dressing room. Sat slumped on the massage table and avoided taking deep breaths as my ribs ached from Micky's ferocious body shots. Thought of what Les had said to me as I got out of the ring, *'You were turned over son.'*

Felt numb but prepared myself for the meeting with Julie, who I knew would be bitterly upset with what had happened. Wasn't wrong, but she wasn't the only one unhappy. There were at least two coaches full of supporters for me, who had spent their hard earned cash on tickets and travel up to London to see my fight. They'd come from 'The Napier

Arms', Gillingham and 'The Bounty' in Bligh way, Strood. Might have only numbered one hundred but they sounded like ten times as many.

Julie, with tears in her eyes, told me straight, 'He robbed you Ian... the bloody ref robbed you! You know that don't you!' Wasn't a question and yes, I knew it.

On the drive home, lay in the back of the car, not asleep but with my eyes closed, escaping being talked to.

Julie, by now my partner of three years (second date must've gone well!) sat in the passenger seat crying, saying, through sobs and nose blowing, 'Look at him Chris, just look at him, he's battered and bruised and for what? That bloody cheating ref!'

Chrissy Hallett, my mate who drove me to fights, stayed quiet, unsure of what to say: probably awkward as men tend to be when a woman is crying her heart out.

I knew we'd entered the Blackwall Tunnel, because even though my eyes were shut, it became very bright and white. I heard some more of Les's wise words, the ones he'd said to me after he told me Micky Hughes would knock me out.

'*After this fight, quit boxing Ian... you go reffing... you'll be a really great referee.*'

Felt myself nodding as if we were having a real conversation. Thought it strange but made a promise to myself then, one that I have kept and will continue to keep for the rest of my days in boxing:

'*John L, when you become a referee, be fair, call it as it is, as you see it, whatever the consequences.*'

Being on the receiving end of a very questionable decision really hurts. I didn't like it... and to be honest... over 20 years later... still don't.

1968... And Black Ain't Beautiful!

I was just five years old, surrounded, scared, with everyone staring at me. One of the girls in the crowd stepped forward, her curiosity getting the better of her fear, shyness, or whatever it was that kept her and the other fifty kids six feet away from me. She rubbed the skin on the back of my hand, then began to touch my big, afro hair. I didn't react in any way, which is probably why the rest of the kids followed her and soon I was engulfed with them all now touching my afro and stroking my skin. They seemed to be checking that their eyes were telling them the truth.

Just a few minutes earlier my dad had taken me to the local primary school for my first day. He joined the other parents, mainly mums, some fighting back tears, some in floods as they said goodbye to their children. Dad just told me to be good and learn.

When all this attention got too much for me, I discovered two things that day: first, I was naturally fast, as I sprinted around the playground away from them; second, I was the only kid in the school wrapped in black skin. Although only five, I can remember thinking, '*Why me? Why do I have to be different?*' This is my first memory of school.

113 Darnley Road, Strood, Kent, in a really cold council house, is where I was born. Ask any copper or criminal in the Medway area, they'll know the road. Had notoriety then, still does now. The area was full of South-East Londoners, who'd headed down the A2, leaving behind London's dirty air but bringing the accent and culture with them.

In '57, my dad came from Dominica, one of the islands of the West Indies, to Strood in Kent, after his mate Delaney settled there. At that time in England work was plentiful and like many invited over from the islands, Dad accepted the invitation, left home, got on a massive ship and sailed to England to graft and earn money. Dad didn't want a hand-out; just work and the cash that went with it. He was soon to find out that although jobs were plentiful, the streets were not paved with gold and the money earned, you worked very hard for.

The job he found, digging holes for pylon foundations, was hard, heavy and very cold for a man used to the heat of the West Indies and when he first saw snow falling, he couldn't believe his eyes.

As a small boy sitting on his lap, Dad often told me, in that lovely West Indian accent of his, how he looked at the big ship that was to bring him over and thought, 'Yah trow ah laaarge pebble in da sea and it sink, sa ow com dat boat float?'

Mum's family were born and bred in Strood and white. Her dad had died of tuberculosis when she was two, and, when old enough, she found herself the carer of her disabled mum and brother. She was timid, quiet and shy, and, because of this, a target for bullies.

Dad first saw her in the local grocery shop and heard that she was a week behind with the shopping bill. They were always a week behind as many in the infamous Darnley road and the surrounding roads were in those days. When she left, Dad asked the shopkeeper what this type of 'credit' was about as he was strictly a 'no debt' type of guy.

The following week she went to the shop to pay the bill but found it already settled. The shop owner told her it had been paid for by my dad who was at the back of the store waiting for her. Mum thanked him and they got talking. She went home and told her mum what had happened and was ordered to give the money back. She tried, but Dad wouldn't take it and instead asked her to the Cuxton Cricket Club's dinner and dance. They married soon after in January 1962. Mixed marriages were not a regular occurrence in those days and were frowned upon by some, although Mum told me that no one ever said anything negative to her about it.

I was born and named Ian John-Lewis on November 28th 1962, just before the winter turned white, snowing for twelve weeks and resulting, for the first time ever, in the River Medway freezing over. Mum often told me, through a warm smile as if she was there at that moment, that the two bar electric fire was continually on, facing my direction, keeping me warm against that bitter winter. Must have cost a small fortune as those fires weren't cheap to run.

Early life was uneventful and I soon found myself with a younger brother and sister who, like me, were born at home. I was nearly five years old when my sister was born and can remember the screams coming from Mum's room as she brought her into the world. I put my hands over my ears and hoped for the screams to stop and for my mum to be alright.

This uneventful life would change when I went to school and as early as day two it appeared that school meant fighting, with some of the older kids wanting to see if they could beat the black boy. The only black people they had probably seen in those days were in the films about Tarzan, the white man who was, strangely, king of the jungle. I was probably, in fact I'm sure I was, the first black boy they'd seen in person.

Abuse, by a vocal minority, was plentiful and racial, and when I ran into my house crying one day because of the name calling, Dad chased me out and told me to fight them! So at the age of six, found I could fight and when I beat the 'terrible' twins in the school sandpit, throwing sand in the eyes of one, and then smacking the other, everyone else knew it too.

There was a girl, older than me, who lived a few doors down. She may have been a little on the slow side and bit of a scruff bag but her greatest gift was kindness and that kindness was shown to me. She'd suffered abuse by bullies, knew what it was I was feeling and would really defend me against the boys and girls my own age, telling them not to call me names. I still think of her and her bravery, she really stuck her neck out for me on many occasions.

When I told my mum about the name calling she'd just say, 'Sticks and stones can break your bones but names will never hurt you.' But names did hurt and if left unchallenged led to more bullying and violence. Tried to walk away when possible, knowing Mum didn't like me fighting, but she really didn't know what I was going through.

Tried making friends with these kids and it worked with some; others weren't interested but wouldn't leave me alone either. They followed me, pushed me, thinking that my walking away meant I was a coward. The name calling would become more personal and even gang members so low down on the food chain that an amoeba would spit them out, would join in the abuse. The laughter would get louder, more fake, more cutting and they'd begin to insult my family. Humiliation was the name of their game and if unchallenged, the next day when I saw them again, the abuse would get even worse.

Didn't take long for me to work out that I wouldn't be allowed to walk away: so I fought. Had to. Turning the other cheek just meant I'd get slapped twice! In an ideal world, it shouldn't happen, but Darnley road was not an ideal world, though no different from anywhere else I have been. Abuse had to be dealt with, but I gave them a chance and never started anything. I soon learned that just grabbing the collar of the leader of a gang would shut some of them up. Occasionally it didn't, but because I could fight, I would back it up; always did. Won most, drew some, lost some, mainly to older boys. I didn't want to fight but had to. They didn't have to but chose to; so even after me losing, they weren't so quick with the abuse any more. No one likes pain and even the winner of a fight, if hurt, will think twice before they make that choice again. I made sure that even if I lost, they all got hurt.

So hated being different that, in school, I was quick to tell others my mum was white. They didn't believe me! Wanted to get on with these kids, be accepted, make friends, and telling them my mum was white would give us some common ground; I hoped. They'd come to my house, knock and ask my mum if I was home, but it wasn't me they wanted to see; it was to see if my mum really was white!

Dad would probably have said he was a disciplinarian, but even in those days, when it was an acceptable national pastime to hit your kids and hit them hard, the punishment he dished out would have had social services taking a very close look. 'Wait till your father gets home.' was a cartoon series on TV at the time. Those words would haunt and panic me for all of my childhood.

This particular evening I lay in bed, door open, dreading the turn of the key in the front door. On hearing him, I felt sick and the terror grew as I heard his boots stomping up the stairs. He yanked me out of the top bunk, yelled in my face and then laid into me. I thought he was going to kill me. The bedroom window was getting nearer and nearer and I thought he was going to throw me out of it. He shook me like a rag doll and I was screaming with fear. My mum, hearing my screams, came upstairs and shouted at him from the bedroom door, 'Stop John. Please stop John, or you'll kill him!'

That was the only time she ever raised her voice to him and it pulled him up sharp. He threw me into the corner of the room and headed downstairs, cussing as he went. The beating he dished out was for the terrible crime of losing my jumper. Dad took me to school the next day and it was found in 'lost property'.

He was always harder on me than my younger brother, who would always drop us in it if we'd done something wrong, like going to play round the big block of flats behind Darnley Road. This was where most of the naughty kids hung out and so was always more lively round there.

When we got home, my Dad would ask me what we'd been up to and I'd lie and tell him we'd been playing down the park, where we were allowed to go. This was a park at the bottom of Darnley Road with swings, roundabout, seesaw and an old steam engine us kids could climb on. Boring it was. He would then turn to my brother, give him 'the look' and ask again. My brother would try and lie but would start to blubber and tell him the truth.

'You little shit!' I would say under my breath because I knew I'd soon be feeling the full force of Dad's anger and be buckle belt beaten. Once finished with me, his temper would be lessened and he would deliver a few, very measured hits to my younger brother.

Happy days? No, they weren't.

My brother was two and a half years younger than me and just when I thought I no longer had to be fighting all the time, he started school. Once, when he came home crying, saying an older boy had beaten him up, Dad grabbed me, marched us to the park and told me to fight the boy. I did, I won, but now had to protect my brother as well. Even though I did this for him, we were never friends. Don't think he knew or appreciated what it was I was doing and don't think he ever realised that my reputation as a fighter meant that kids in his year left him alone. As I got older I realised that in some black families the eldest boy is almost revered. Not me – I was more like my brother's protector and whipping boy.

So at ten years old, tired and scared of the abuse from Dad's belt and boots, I decided it was time to scarper. It was three in the morning as

I sneaked downstairs and got my stuff together. On looking up I spied my younger brother sitting on the third step down, studying what I was up to. He never made a sound, didn't ask where I was going, what I was doing and didn't try to stop me either.

Soon my duffle bag was full of clothes. Pulled my blue anorak on and opened the door. Would love to say that when I looked at my brother, thought I couldn't leave him, or that he broke down crying and pleaded with me to stay, but that wasn't the case. We weren't close, never would be.

Looking out of that house through the open front door, could see it was dark and felt the cold, neither of which bothered me. What did pull me up sharp was the thought that if I ran away and the Police found me they would bring me back and when they left, my Dad would definitely kill me, no doubt! Closed the door, hung up my coat, emptied my duffle bag and made my way upstairs to find my brother already tucked up in his bed asleep. I got into my freezing bed and lay there thinking and hoping that life would get better.

God that house was cold. Getting into bed at night the sheets were stiff, and in the morning were warm, so didn't want to get up. The net curtains would freeze against the window overnight and I made sure not to touch them in the morning in case I tore them. Breathing out I could see my breath and would try to make shapes or pretend I had just had a puff on a ciggy, which was strange because I thought smoking was disgusting. Would put off getting up as long as possible and snuggle under the heavy warm blankets with only my eyes showing. Eventually, my feet would have to touch the ice cold lino, something I dreaded and wanted to avoid but knew I couldn't. My mum would be up, getting Dad his breakfast after starting the coal fire in the living room. Once I'd decided to get up, I'd run as fast as I could down the stairs to get dressed in front of the fire.

Dad insisted the clothes were folded in a certain way and laid on the threadbare sofa at night. How to fold and place these clothes was taught to me through another session of 'discipline'. Plus side; to this day I've never forgotten how to fold my clothes!

Dad loved sport and was a very good all-rounder at cricket. His speciality was fast bowling but he was tasty at batting too. He and John

Shepherd had trials for Kent and both were selected to play for the county. Shepherd accepted, but Dad was working for Seeboard and had three kids, a wife and bookie to support. The money in cricket then was poor, and he couldn't take care of a family on it, so he had to give it a miss. At the time, Tony Gregg, Alan Knott and Derek Underwood played for Kent, and he would've played alongside these England cricketers. It must have been frustrating for him not being able to follow his dream.

He was well known in Kent for his cricketing prowess and on a warm Sunday afternoon, down at Cuxton, I remember a man coming up to him with his teenage son by his side, shaking Dad's hand and telling him he was proud that his boy was playing on the same pitch as him. He really was a very good cricketer.

On the fireplace were Dad's cricket trophies and cigarette lighter. A little radio, tuned to Radio 1 and Tony Blackburn, lived on the small black and white telly. Round, brown, patterned, council wallpaper lined the room and worn lino was our carpet. Best described as sparse, but to me it was home.

School began to slowly improve. When people realised I could fight, it was easier to be accepted and make friends. If people didn't like me, or were not allowed to play with me, they just ignored me now, keeping their thoughts to themselves. Worked well for me, didn't care what they thought, just what they said.

I had three great mates by now and the four of us hung around together: David Still (best mate to this day), Ian Chambers, Alan Burchell and me. Knew I'd been accepted because my mates invited me into their houses. This was nice but was just another shock as I realised how poor we were in comparison. They had carpet, not lino in the living room, gas fires and big colour televisions, much bigger than our black and white TV; lovely furniture, ornaments and pictures everywhere. When I found this out I would never invite people back to mine, embarrassed at our lack of these everyday items.

We didn't have a fridge, which didn't matter so much in the winter, as the milk probably would have warmed up in there! To stop it going sour in the summer heat, the milk bottle was placed in a bowl of cold water. At one of my friend's houses, during a heat wave, I was given a cold drink with ice cubes in it. It was so good, thought I'd died and gone to heaven! They also had games and toys like Tonka, Action Man, Subbuteo and the Number 1 game at the time, Mouse Trap. I could only dream of stuff like that. We only had old fashioned games like Snakes and Ladders and Ludo, which my mates would snigger at, but my Dad had this great ability to make the games really funny and would have us laughing our heads off.

I became really fit during these early years as my three mates had bikes. Dave had the 'Chopper', Ian and Alan, Racer's, me, well, to keep up with them in the summer holidays and at weekends, I used to run alongside them. By the end of the day I was exhausted and had no trouble sleeping at night. This could explain why I was so fast at running because all through primary and junior school I was unbeaten at the sprints. Every time a new kid came to our school I'd challenge and beat them, it felt really good because even though I was small, this was something I was best at.

Secondary school loomed and we all wanted to go to Temple, which was further away, as we had heard so many bad things about Rede School. I thought starting the new school would be hard enough without having to find new best friends. It caused a lot of worry but we were all told that we had to attend Rede school as that was our nearest one.

Dad took me to buy school uniform and whenever he saw the price of a shirt, blazer or trousers he sucked his teeth or cussed under his breath, or did both. With the new uniform on I stood in front of him and he told me he expected me to come in from school looking just like that. I didn't think he was serious... I was wrong.

We felt the angst that everybody feels when they go to secondary school but settled in very quickly, which was great, with Dave, Alan and me in the same class. There were five non-whites in the school and by now all the kids that had grown up with me had seen black faces so no curiosity was left. Our gang of four stuck together and knew we could rely on each other. We liked to move around as one, so I hated free school dinners and that I had to stand in a different line away from my mates to get them.

I'd been playing football in the playground and had marked my uniform. When I got home Dad inspected my clothes and then marked me far worse.

Now knowing he was serious, I had a choice to make, stand around in the school playground looking like a 'tool' so I wouldn't dirty my clothes, or play sport and get a beating.

At home I found a long handled light blue clothes brush and cut the handle off it. It fit in my left hand blazer pocket and would come to school with me for the whole five years. My schoolmates would laugh when they saw me brushing my clothes on the way home from school. They quietened down when they realised the reason why I had to do it. That brush saved me a lot of hurt.

It was as easy a transition as I could've wished for. Sometimes the older boys would push things a little far and violence would break out, but the biggest shock came at the end of my first year in school. It wasn't abuse or a fight; but sports day. I'd never lost a sprint race up to then and expected to win with ease. Third! That wiped the smile off my face. I kept thinking… *How'd that happen? Did I slip? Did they false start?* No, I just found two kids that were faster than me. It was a weird feeling seeing two people in front; thought I was having one of those nightmares when you're running in treacle or have lead boots on.

Exams – was not a natural and, like a lot of the kids there, found formal education dull. Could read, write and count, loved sport, with P.E. lighting my brain up. The teachers really liked me because I tried to learn. Never once did I truant or try to get out of a sports lesson, like some of the other kids who faked notes, colds, forgotten kit and injury. Saw no point in standing on the side line, shivering; might as well get running and warm up.

Mr. Cramp, a really nice, quiet guy, loved cricket and because I was a good cricketer he made me Captain. Mr. McCabe was a short, hard-looking Scot who seemed to have no neck and looked like a Toby Jug. He loved athletics and rugby and because I was good at these too, he always had kind words for me. Then there was Miss Dunn, who married and became Mrs. Blood. We gave her some stick for that. She was our teacher for CSE in P.E. It was the first year they brought the exam into the curriculum and I got a grade 2. 'Mrs. Blood, you know that it should have been a grade 1!' They were good people, trying to make a difference.

Although there were only five non-white people in my secondary school, not too many problems came my way. I was friendly to all, popular and tried to make friends, not by being the butt of the joke as some young blacks felt the need to be in those days, but by being myself. There were still times when I'd wonder why I had to be different, generally when I was standing on the corner of a street, getting rained on, while waiting for a white girlfriend. That was the norm for me in those days as it wasn't common for a white girl to date a black lad, so they had to keep it hidden. One girl playfully called me her dark secret. Her parents wouldn't have felt they were being racist but would've felt that it wasn't right. Heard often at that time that people should stay within their own race, but there is only one race... the human race. Get used to it.

On our first school trip we went to the Cutty Sark in Greenwich, South East London. That was the furthest I'd been up to then and I really loved that outing; still remember walking round that old ship. I only went on two school trips; the other was to Hampton Court, which wasn't that good.

My world was really small, but it got a bit bigger when one of my brother's mates got a new bike for his birthday, and his dad gave me the old one. When he presented it to me I could've cried. It was such a kind thing to do, and I really appreciated that he'd thought of me. I could now cycle with my mates and would not be out of breath all the time running alongside them!

Being streetwise was something I'd learnt early; always looked further up the road than any of my mates, checking to see if the people we were about to meet were friend or foe. One afternoon, when walking home from the very popular Rochester swimming pool, I saw in the distance two trouble makers from school but couldn't do anything to avoid them as we had to pass them to get home. Told my brother to keep his head down, his big mouth shut, walk fast and ignore anything said. The guy I was trying to swerve was a local hard man from Strood; no one messed with him. He was in the fifth year and I was in the third. He was a lot bigger than me, as was his reputation. His side kick was a little wannabe hard man who reminded me of a pilot fish which swims next to a shark, picking up leftovers from what the shark devours. As the small one saw me he nudged his big mate, nodded in our direction and began to egg him on.

'*Oh shit!*' I thought as they crossed the road, outside Woolworths in Strood, to be on the same side of the street as us. I just hoped they'd ignore us. They didn't. Pilot Fish started the trouble when he grabbed hold of the bag, my mum's, that my little brother was carrying. He then hit my brother who started to cry. Before Pilot Fish could laugh, he found himself on his arse looking up at me. There were three reasons I hit him: one, he started the trouble; two, he hit my brother and three, I knew very soon I'd be fighting the bigger one which would be difficult enough without having his tiny, piss ant mate kicking and punching me as well.

The bigger one got my mum's purse out of the bag. He looked at me and said, 'You want it, here, go and get it!' and with that he threw it up onto the roof of Woolworths.

There was no way I was going to be able to get that back and knowing that when I got home, a bloody good hiding was coming my way, I steamed right into him with no fear, just rage. He was so shocked, the look on his face let me know I'd caught him by surprise and so had him on the back foot; not for long as he was too big, too strong, too good. Although he soon got the better of me and was beating me up, I just kept on going, getting up from the pavement time after time to punch him again and again, as tears of anger ran down my face. He kept telling me to leave it and give it a rest as I ran into him, throwing wild fists again and again. The guy said I was nuts, crazy; but he didn't know what I was going home to. His little side kick stayed on the floor, shocked at the ferocity of my attack.

When home, obviously battered and bruised, I explained what had happened and where mum's purse was. The explanation was met with me having my forehead smashed into the kitchen wall a number of times. I was screaming in pain and Dad stopped. A shocked look appeared on his angry face. He went to the tap, ran the cold water and soaked a flannel, which he pressed onto the bump that had appeared. His face showed worry as he continued to try and reduce the size of the lump that was still growing out of my forehead. That lump, smaller now, still survives today.

In the following months, whenever I saw Pilot Fish on his own at school, he would scuttle off scared, and I'd smile at his cowardice. When I saw him with his hard man mate, he would almost hide behind him.

Another game of football and another jacket for a goalpost was put down. Colin, my mate Alan's brother, two years older and a good fighter, thought it would be funny to pick my jacket up and dump it in some mud. I was so angry, I knew my blue brush wasn't going to get it clean, so there'd be more 'manners' dealt out to me when arriving home. We threw punches at each other, but I was losing as he was bigger. His hand came close to my face, so I bit it, hard, justifying it by thinking I shouldn't be getting in trouble when I got home, for something that wasn't my fault. Colin screamed in pain, calling me crazy as he jumped about, swearing, like he had a bad case of Tourette's. Did my best to remove the mud with the blue brush but couldn't do a good enough job. Once home, the inevitable came my way.

Just before boxing found me, I was in school and bumped into an older boy. Before I could apologise he snarled, 'Wanna fight, you black bastard?'

Before I could think about it, tapped my left pocket to make sure my brush was there; it was, so I answered, 'Yeah, all right!'

'Outside then!' he barked.

Had come to my senses by then and realised that I didn't want to fight, but the wheels were in motion and there was no way of backing down when I heard my school mate, Derek Johnson, shout, 'Cor! Louie' (my nick name back then) 'is gonna have a fight!'

School kids ran towards us as soon as they heard the shout, 'Bundle!' and made a circular ring. Worried about another beating once I got home and not wanting to have my watch (bought for me by my Dad's mate Delaney) broken, I said, 'Let me take my watch off.'

What a fool I was. As I was removing it, I took my eye off my opponent, didn't protect myself at all times, and he smacked me full steam on the chin. It bloody hurt. I ducked down but felt blows raining down from all angles on me like the guy had four arms. I felt surrounded.

I was now a popular and respected guy in school, the crowd were pro me and were chanting, 'Louie! Louie!' and I hadn't even landed a punch yet!

He then caught me a peach of a right hook to my left cheek, which really hurt, and I reacted by swinging and delivering a big left hook with the word bastard attached to it. It caught him square on his chin, wobbled him and changed the tide of the fight, with him now trying to throw punches as he went backwards. I smacked him all over the place with the crowd still chanting my name. Then I grabbed him around his neck and forced him down to my upcoming knee again and again. It was now a street fight which back then suited me. A teacher appeared, broke the fight up and next day we were in front of the headmaster who told us off, royally. That fight was the talk of the school for weeks. My reputation, not only intact, had grown. My opponent was older, bigger, stronger and a good fighter. Later I found out that he was in fact a boxer.

Summer arrived and a school trip to Brighton had been planned for the whole year, and we were really excited about it. Everyone in the year was going except for four poor souls and one of those poor souls turned out to be me. I pleaded with Dad to let me go, telling him that all my mates were going. He just replied that he couldn't afford it. I wanted to tell him it was such a pity he could afford betting on three legged donkeys, but didn't fancy another beating. It was one of the lowest times in my school life. The coach pulled out and I sat in the class room for the whole day, bored senseless. My mates had talked about it for weeks before, saying how brilliant it was going to be; then talked about it for weeks after, telling me just how brilliant it had been.

It hurt.

Life Changer

The night that would change my life came with no warning, no fanfare, or near death experience. It came via an invite from my mate John Harris, who, at seventeen, was two years older than me. He wanted me to go to Strood Youth Club to do some weight lifting. I didn't think my dad would let me go as I wasn't allowed out past eight o'clock in those days and the club finished at ten. Amazingly he said yes, but I had to be home before ten which would mean running home through the streets of Strood, on my own, to get in before the curfew – even Cinderella was allowed out 'til midnight.

Four of us went to the club and were met by, what we thought at the time, was an old, black guy. Sam Mercer was really welcoming and from the good shape he was in at 50, had obviously done a lot of sport in his day.

Sam came from Antigua in '54 to box, and the guy who was meant to meet him quayside, never turned up and never would. A kind, Christian, English woman let him stay rent free for three weeks while he got sorted. He made ends meet by fighting in the boxing booths, living off 'nobbins': money the crowd would throw in the ring following the fight. It got him through those difficult first months.

In 1960, while living on the Isle of Dogs, working and walking between three churches in the area, he took a course to become a youth club leader. Later he told me he moved to the Medway Towns to get his kids away from the persistent, 'Conflic', conflic', conflic', on der streets ahh der Isle ah Dogs!'

We gelled immediately because he showed interest in me and I showed interest in what he had to teach. This was sport and the stuff in life that hooked me. I hung on every word he said about weight training and why we did certain exercises. These weight sessions continued for a few months with Sam always keeping an eye on our lifting form and making sure no one messed about and injured themselves. At the end of one session, just before I had to leave the club and run home to beat the curfew, he asked me to come to the boxing training that he was starting on Friday evenings. Soon as he said boxing, I recoiled as if he had swung a hook at me and quickly said, 'Thanks, but no thanks, Sam. Like the way I look.' Shouted bye as I left the gym and ran home, getting back just before the ten o'clock deadline.

The next Tuesday, went to the youth club as normal and Sam asked me where I'd been on the Friday.

'Friday?' I replied, knowing what he meant but pretending I didn't. Thought I'd made it plain to him that I wasn't coming to get punched!

'Yessss, der buxing Ian! Der buxing!' he replied in his really keen, deep West Indian accent.

Obviously I felt a bit embarrassed as he'd given me a lot of time and didn't want him to feel let down. He was a good guy.

'Thanks, Sam, but don't really want to be a boxer.'

'Look… Ian… if yah com' ta der buxing, sum' o' yah mates will com' aahs well. T'is only a bitta trainin' ta go wid da lifting.'

Sam was such a likeable guy, didn't know at the time that he'd been such a quality boxer and champion in the West Indies, just thought he was an old guy trying to make a difference for us, but because I respected what he was trying to do, I told him, 'Okay… I'll give it a go… have to ask my Dad first, though.'

What I said to Sam didn't sound convincing and I wouldn't have minded my Dad saying no, as it would give me an excuse. When I did talk to him, he surprisingly said yes. He reckoned I would do it for a while but soon pack it in. His reasoning was that I had tried Karate after seeing the Bruce Lee films and the series "Kung Fu", but after jumping around in the dojo for a few sessions, found it boring and quit.

First night training with Sam, he got me to put on these big black gloves and told me to punch him! Seemed wrong to throw punches at someone I respected and admired so much. Began to land a glove on him, but turned my face away as I didn't want to be hit. Sam beckoned me to stop punching and said, 'Like da way ya mooove, ya mooove well... an' fas', natcheraly.'

Once my 'cockney' brain deciphered what Sam meant, the words had me hooked. It was another sport I was naturally good at but now someone would guide me. Settled quickly into a training regime with Sam and learnt everything he tried to teach. Loved these training sessions, had no idea where we were going with them or that they'd have to end at some point.

After a few months and another good training session in the bank, he sat me down and said, 'Tyme fer ya ta mooove on Ian... shone ya awll aah know... tyme fer propah buxing gym... yah got talen' der bwoy.'

Wasn't exactly the part in Kung Fu when the blind master says to his subject, 'When you can take the pebble from my hand... then it will be time for you to leave the temple.'

It meant the same though; would be leaving Sam and moving on. Scared and excited at the same time, I looked forward to seeing the inside of a proper gym for myself. Would it be just like the Rocky film?

Sam trained me hard, saw to it that I was fit enough to stand the rigours of a boxing gym. Told me, years later, that I was everything he wasn't, said he liked the way I walked the 'wrong' way round the ring and how I trained so hard. Sam tried to teach me to keep away from the opponent's gloves but said he knew from the early days that I was a warrior and would always like a good tear up.

We were to meet at St Mary's Amateur Boxing Club in Chatham, the other side of the River Medway, on a Wednesday evening. I grew more nervous and excited in the days leading up to it, shadow boxing around my bedroom whenever I felt the butterflies in my stomach. Was shadow boxing a lot.

When with my mates, would proudly tell them that Sam had said it was time for me to move on, that he said he couldn't teach me anything more. When on my own, would be nervous about walking into a proper boxing gym with proper boxers. What if Sam was wrong and I ended up looking stupid, or humiliated, or worse, stupid and humiliated! Consoled myself with the thought that I was across the river and if humiliation occurred I wouldn't have to return to St Mary's and no one on my side of the water would be any the wiser. I could just tell my mates that it wasn't for me.

With my face-saving plan worked out I walked the hour journey to the Chatham boxing club. I was on the other side of the river now, well away from the 'safety' of Darnley Road. The hour walk gave me a lot of time to get nervous and wonder if this boxing thing was a good idea. One thing about tonight was I had a very high chance that I was going to be punched, and the way some of the local kids looked at me as I walked to the club, thought I might not have to wait to get into the boxing ring to receive that punch.

I got there before Sam, so I could have a peep before I went in. Looked through the dirty windows of this old, cold looking, spit and sawdust place: it was just like Rocky's gym. There were lads using the well-worn equipment, pounding the bags. Speed balls, used to improve timing, were expertly being hit, making a rat a tat noise as they hit the wooden backboard. The skipping was so fast that I could hear the whoosh of the rope as it went round and round in a blur. One guy was shadow boxing; looked so good that I didn't even want to box his shadow! Although intimidating and my legs like jelly, something in the pit of my stomach told me I was home.

Sam arrived, and before I could panic, said hello, opened the door and shoved me in. It was the noise that hit me first; the sound of worn soft plastic on worn soft plastic at speed. Then that smell of effort, fresh and stale sweat mixed, hit my nose. If you bottled it; it wouldn't sell.

One by one, heads turned, eyes focussed in on me and the room became quiet. I felt like I was the black Sheriff, in Blazing Saddles, turning up at his new town. It was probably quiet for about two seconds, and not really that quiet but seemed like a lifetime to me. Almost said, but managed just to think, *'Fuck this, I better turn round and fuck off!'*

Before I could turn and run, head trainer, Freddy Ludlow, who was in the ring with a young guy training him on the pad mitts, called over to Sam and shouted, 'Hi Sam... who you got there?'

'Gotta good kid 'ere Freddy,' drawled Sam.

'Yeah? Well show 'im the changing rooms, then get 'im in 'ere.'

'Great! First time in a proper gym, straight into the ring with a boxer...ohhhh shhiiitttt!' I thought.

There was no, 'Come on in, Ian, meet the 'friendly' looking lads. Here, come on, punch this bag, skip with this rope. Don't worry, won't hit you today, we'll just pretend and have you box with your own shadow.'

No, none of that, just: get in, get changed, get in the ring, get moving or get punched by the smiling opponent from Chatham who wants this Strood boy's blood!

If looks could kill, I would've been dead. Nothing to do with colour or race, because the black kids there were giving me just as evil stares as everyone else! Was because they found out I came from Strood, the other side of the Medway River and they were Chatham boys. Different postcode, big local rivalry, that's all, and the rivalry between the Kentish Boy and the Boy of Kent is still alive today.

In the small ring, designed to make the boys fight, not run, my sparring partner stared at me. I delivered a stare back that probably wasn't that convincing. Didn't want him to look away though, especially down, because my knees were knocking so badly that I thought he'd see them! The lad I sparred with – I say sparred, but he was definitely trying to remove my head from my shoulders – was trying to give me a baptism, in my own blood. Every punch he threw was designed to flatten me. He was trying to show off to his mates, who were leaning on the ropes wanting to see the Strood boy beaten. Yeah, he beat me because he could box and I was doing my best just trying to survive and fight, but Sam had disciplined me well because at no time did I think to resort to a street fighter's mentality, even when hurt, and I was hurt a lot. I did manage to throw a good punch of my own that found its way to his nose; bloodied it and pulled him up a bit sharpish. I got a lot of satisfaction from that.

Fred signalled for us to stop and although my sparring partner had won, Fred pulled a face of interest, nodded and said, 'Like what I see Sam… leave him with us.'

And Sam did. He smiled, nodded in my direction and was gone.

What I immediately liked was the instant respect and acceptance due to proving myself in the ring. The lad, who'd been trying to flatten me, put his gloved hand on my shoulder and nodded at me. Others nodded in my direction and began talking to me. It didn't matter to them that I was a Kentish Boy, from Strood, or black. I was now a boxer; one of them, no different. I belonged.

Despite being hurt from the sparring, Freddie's comments and the look he gave me made me think I had potential. I wanted to take that talent as far as I could. Strange, but this cold, cobwebbed, smelly place felt like it was where I was meant to be.

Up to then I'd never read much, was a stranger to the library, but the next day borrowed a book about boxing written by Harry Carpenter. Its title, 'The Hardest Game', is a perfect description of boxing. This reading was so much easier and more interesting than formal education.

The following Sunday morning I walked the hour to training and met the founder of the club, Ernie Magog. He'd opened St Mary's in the 1930s.

'So you're the new boy… What's your name, son?' Ernie asked.

'Ian John-Lewis,' I answered.

'Wot's that then?' he replied.

'Ian John-Lewis,' I repeated.

'Naaaaah, that's toooo long… John L will do for me, okay with that son?' he barked.

'Okay,' I said.

He asked me if I was left or right handed.

'Does it matter?' I thought.

Yes it does. If you're left handed, you lead with your right, and then throw the left (Southpaw). If you're right handed, you lead with your left, and then throw the right (Orthodox). So told him I was left handed and he put me in the southpaw stance. After thirty seconds of testing me on the big pads he told me, 'Naaaah, 's all wrong. Change round… Lead with the left,' he ordered.

I did, and boy it just flowed.

'That's better son, you're what's called a converted Southpaw.'

This meant my lead hand (left) was my strongest, so had a powerful jab which would soften up opponents for a big right hander. I didn't have much of a clue what he was on about at this stage but I felt comfortable, was punching well, so got on with it.

Ernie had never boxed but was a marvellous coach and once said to me, 'You don't have to be hit to know it hurts! So get hit as little as possible.' Good advice.

At the end of the first week, I was coming down the stairs in the club and spied Keith Kirby shadow boxing. He looked great and I was in awe. Ernie saw me staring and said, 'Bet you'd like to be as good as him, wouldn't you?'

I nodded and replied a long, 'Yeahhhhhh!' and that was my first aim. It took two years!

At this time I was sparring with Jamie Duff, a good junior lightweight, who beat many a good fighter with his no nonsense approach and all action style. His fast blurring punches, when they hit me, blurred my vision. He was tough, real tough and was the same on the streets too. Jamie fought on the front foot, kept coming after me; relentless he was. Sparring with him taught me how to fight while on the retreat and to take a punch. He was the first guy to make me see stars after copping a big right hander of his. Fred said I would learn a lot from this kid. I did. Learnt how to run in a small ring, learnt how to fight in close, which was the whole point of the sparring. Jamie was beating me up with regularity due to his experience and speed. This is when new fighters will quit or get good. I took the pain; learnt fast; got good.

Training was going well; was fit from running the two paper rounds from two different newsagents each morning, and the circuit training was making muscles pop out of places I didn't know they could pop out of. Sparring was tough and with every session I learnt something.

Even with all the preparation, I was still really nervous when my first bout came up in Deal, Kent. I would be matched against another first time boxer. A nerve wracking experience for both of us, I'm sure.

Lenny Smith, another coach at St Mary's would be in my corner that night along with Freddy Ludlow. Deal was miles and miles away from Strood, a long drive in the St Mary's mini bus. It gave me a long, long time to get really nervous before that bell sounded. Saw the road signs, Deal: 15, 10 then 5 miles. The closer we got, the more scared I got. When we arrived, thought I'd never empty my bladder. As soon as I left the toilet I had to go back in!

In the changing rooms I pulled on a pair of football shorts and my running trainers, as I couldn't afford the proper boxing kit. Felt a bit embarrassed but noticed I wasn't the only one under dressed.

Climbed into the ring and was surprised at how big it was in comparison to the one at St Mary's. Ding, ding. Round one. Out I went on rubber legs, trying to think of everything I'd been taught but remembering nothing. As the first minute passed, the strength came back to me, I settled and remembered what I did on the pads. Then it clicked, became natural and I was in full flow. In round three, the last; caught him with a corker of a left hook and then pinned him to the ropes. As I hit him with a barrage of punches he made the noises of someone hurt, so I backed off and looked at my corner, confused as to what to do next. Lenny sorted out the confusion when he screamed at me from the other side of the ring, 'Don't stop, Ian! Finish the bloody job!'

Was lean, felt mean but was definitely green, the learning curve in boxing can be sharp, as it was for my opponent who was also having his first fight. After such a baptism, I wonder if he boxed again?

My win was rewarded with a trophy and I smiled all the way home. Dad answered the door and when he saw the trophy, was obviously pleased with me. That night, I went to sleep with it by my pillow and woke several times in the night to check it was real and not a dream. I would smile and drift off into the happy sleep of success. I couldn't wait for morning to come when I could take the trophy to school and show my P.E. teachers. This was the first time that I'd something to share. I showed everyone and felt really good about it.

A lot of respect, probably some fear as well, was shown to me now. No one needed to fear me as I was willing to be friends with anyone. Boxing, fighting, loved it, but it was to be saved for the shows. Freddy impressed on me that being a good boxer meant discipline; save the fight for the ring, nowhere else.

I would go on to win my first 10 fights: first three on points, the next seven by stoppage or knockout. As my wins began to climb, my reputation grew and at 16 years of age, coming home late, tired, but floating with trophy after trophy, I felt I had a future.

Life was getting better, had a bit of money in my pocket from the paper rounds, felt I had a purpose, a gift that would need training, lots of it. Dad became more interested and seemed pleased for me after I began to box in tournaments and won. On fight nights the door would be opened by him, always keen to know how the fight had gone, and I'd be proud to tell him that I'd won. As he turned away I could see the beginnings of a smile on his usually stern face. Never went into great depth about the fights, but these were the times that there was some peace between us. Dad saying, 'well done' meant a lot, and I knew he was proud when he made two shelves for my trophies to live on. He never announced that he was going to put them up. I just found them completed one day. My Mum would polish my trophies with pride. They were always glistening, and she never minded me getting another one.

Boxing was in my heart, my blood, was my waking thought, and what I fell asleep to. I would continually shadow box round my house, punching out at flying insects that had been unlucky enough to have found their way into our lounge. At night in bed I would mentally rehearse the moves taught to me in training, as I drifted off to sleep, exhausted but happy from the training. I always slept well.

Dad even came to see me a few times as an amateur but got frustrated as I wouldn't always get a match due to my growing reputation. He came to Sheerness, Ashford and Sevenoaks, and I never got a fight because I was bowling my opponents over. One kid looked at me at the weigh-in and refused to take me on; Dad was fuming! When he did get to see me fight he was over the moon. It really lifted me having him there.

In comparison to some of the abuse thrown my way as a young boy, what I was to get next was mild. It lasted as long as the series 'Roots' did: the brilliant program about black people stolen from Africa and forced into slavery. As soon as the first episode was finished I thought, *'Oh fuck! Am I in for some stick tomorrow.'*

Wasn't wrong as it seemed everybody in school had developed a bloody limp with my mates asking me how Kizzie was. I heard the names Kunte Kinte, Toby, Chicken George, shouted my way from little gatherings of school kids. Another favourite was, 'Toby… How's your sister?' It wasn't really a question.

Would always wake up on training days excited, couldn't wait to get the gloves on and get sweaty. Never missed a session, training always came first and everything else had to be fitted in around it. Sunday, Monday, Wednesday and Thursday were training days and I walked there and back, come rain, shine or snow, saving the bus fare to spend on a pair of boxing boots. The pair I wanted, white with blue trim, looked the business and when I had enough money to buy them, I took them home, put them on and danced like Ali around my bedroom! Couldn't wait to get into the ring and see what they felt like on canvas.

There was no pocket money for us. So the two paper rounds were my source of income. Ran them, delivering so quickly that I would finish the two rounds before the boys who had one did; even the ones who had bikes! Twice as much money for doing the job quick. Having to work hard for my money taught me the value of it; not to squander it. My customers liked me as they got their papers early and at Christmas they would tip me well. Also on those cold, dark mornings, running my rounds kept me warm and fit. Used those rounds as road work. I'd always arrive first to training and was always the last to leave, taking a wash at the gym from a shower that dribbled out tepid water in front of a lukewarm stove. I loved that gym.

At one of the ex-boxers' gatherings (always a good laugh and I highly recommend attendance to them) I met a guy who'd trained at St Mary's back in the '40s who claimed that a lukewarm dribbling shower was luxury compared to the shower they had… which was a watering can poured over the boxer from a mate standing on a chair! He could be right.

Once back home from training, would eat my dinner, wash up, thank my mum and fall into bed exhausted, knowing that 6.30 a.m. would soon arrive and the paper rounds would have to be run again.

Also at 16, I joined a football team, JFC Cuxton and played well. The trainer contacted my dad from the club and asked if I'd be coming to the Football League awards evening. Dad insisted I attend and wear my suit. I was picked up from my house by the club Chairman in his nice car, so nice, in fact, that I was scared to move in case I dirtied it. Once there, thanked him for the lift and joined the rest of the team in the hall. The presentation began with the youngest age group getting their awards first. I sat there looking at them with their shiny trophies thinking, *'Lucky little sods.'*

Then it came to the Medway league 'Player of the Year' under sixteens award. It was quite a shock, as they read my name out. Kept looking round at people who were smiling at me and telling me, 'well done'. I had only played half a season but scored a lot of goals. They voted me not just best player in the team but the whole of the Medway league! Another trophy!

My natural pace made me a good player, I flew down the left wing creating chances and seemed to be able to score for fun. Football was just a friendly game in comparison to boxing as the physicality of most sports is nothing to you when you've stood in a boxing ring.

At the end of the awards evening, a photo was taken of us with our trophies. I was so proud to have made it into the local paper again. Another photo and report to put in the scrapbook. It was exciting waiting for the paper to come out, knowing that someone had taken the time to write about my success. I didn't mind delivering those papers to my customers, not one bit.

On the way home from that awards evening, the Chairman of the club offered me a job; told me to turn up at 'Turner, King and Shepherd' in Cuxton when I left school, which would be in a few weeks. Once home, told my Dad about the offer, and he was more than interested. I was busy making my way in the world of Strood, Kent, and boxing, so didn't feel the need to know what was going on in the cities and wasn't aware how difficult it could be for young people to get jobs. This was

1979; the country was not in a good way now. There had been a three day week, power cuts and in the city, just up the A2, the National Front were stirring up trouble between disenfranchised whites and blacks. Also, not in my favour, was that I wasn't academic. Tried my best, but books weren't for me. I was practical, a grafter. You wanted bricks carried up the top of the ladder; I was your man, quick and hardworking.

The qualifications I gained at school, 'O' level in Art and a grade 2 CSE in P.E., wouldn't get me much in the workplace. Could read, write, count, box, paint, had ample common sense and had learned to be streetwise. Now, I also had a job; was one of the lucky ones.

Although finding that I was good at football, not once did I think that I could, or would, take it further, and so I quit after one of the boxing coaches said I couldn't concentrate on both and to make a choice. There was no choice; boxing it was. A strange place to find a bit of peace, but that is what I found at St Mary's boxing gym. Boxing was my every thought, and I wanted to be a British Champion.

Arrived at Turner, King and Shepherd and thought I'd be working on the shop floor of this paint factory, so turned up for work on the first morning wearing a donkey jacket and work boots. They kept me in the office and showed me some clerical stuff. Some of my old school mates were working there and they would put their thumbs up to me from the shop floor saying that I'd be out with them soon. But it never happened and so on the second week I turned up for work, smartly dressed.

Found out later that Bert Self, Chairman of the football team, was also high up in the business and had told Ernie Tucker, my immediate boss, 'Don't put Ian in the shit outside. Keep him in the office.' He obviously liked me, and I was, and still am, grateful for the job he gave me. Thanks Bert.

Amateur

They lied! Training didn't get easier. Never would, as I always tried to run my route quicker, do more press ups or sit ups, and skip faster. Was trying to be the best I could be and would always train like this. It had to be to the maximum, and it wasn't until the end of my career that I realised training didn't always have to be eyeballs out! Made me very fit though and even today, may have slowed the training down a tad, but it's nice to know I can eat and drink whatever I like.

Because of the new job in the paint factory I was able to quit the paper rounds, so instead of running the streets delivering papers seven days a week, now only had to get up four mornings to run. The extra sleep on the other three days was bliss, especially when the wind and rain hit that rattling bedroom window. Would lay there, smiling, revelling in the fact that I could stay in my warm bed for an extra hour. Simple pleasures.

Sixteen years old, and a bit too sure of myself, when I fought Michael Gaunt, at the winter Gardens, Margate. This was my last fight as a junior as I would soon be seventeen, and because I'd won all my fights, was starting to think I could beat everybody. Before the fight started, Fred Ludlow told me to watch out as my opponent had broad shoulders, so may be a big hitter. In the first round I knocked him all over the place, got overconfident, bordering on flash, and in the second round he returned the favour. I was pleased when the bell sounded for the end of round two and went back to the corner a bit shell shocked, but was soon woken up when Fred Ludlow slapped me hard around the face.

'Right! Now I got your attention. Listen to me. What's up with ya a?! You let him back in the fight and made him look good. Cut the crap. Start boxing the way I taught ya. Go out there and remind him who's boss!'

After that talking to and slap from Freddy, I couldn't wait to get out of the corner and face the punches. Went out in the third; took it to him, and battered him so much that the referee stopped it. That was a tough learning curve, for both of us boxers.

In the amateurs, once seventeen, you become a senior, meaning I could fight anyone up to the age of thirty five, which is a big step up for a youngster. I've always thought that another age group, maybe under twenty two, should be put in there. At seventeen, was strong, fit, but not fully developed, as that occurs around the age of twenty one. The invaluable advice given to me by Freddy Ludlow was to box; don't get dragged into wars with older, stronger, more experienced guys who would lead you into fighting the kind of fight they wanted.

Fought a twenty three year old guy, S. Williams, from Romney Marsh. Out boxed and out foxed him in the first, and Freddy told me that the guys chin was open to a right hander. In the second round, I came out, threw some left jabs and then a fierce straight right hand, bang on his chin. It landed beautifully. I felt good about the shot but when it appeared to have no effect on him, felt shocked and thought, *'Shit! That had no ...'* Two seconds later, to my relief, he collapsed in a heap and was counted out. Beautiful punch.

Boxing shows came thick and fast, just like my next opponent. It was at a contest in Bexhill, where I fought a lad who really upset Ernie. Had never seen Ernie upset. It just wasn't his way. After the weigh-in, Ernie (also known as Ginger) came to me with a face as red as his hair and said forcefully, 'John L, knock this kid clean out, will ya!'

'I'll try Ginger,' I replied.

'No!' he replied even more forcefully, 'I want you to knock this kid out and shut his filthy mouth!'

Bell went for round one and knowing the kid upset Ernie and that Ernie wanted me to knock him out, I went to the middle of the ring with that in the back of my mind. Had to stay focussed because the point was to win it, not get knocked out trying to settle a score. My opponent flew out at me, did his best to catch me cold and chin me. He was just a no style brawler, so just like a bee at a picnic, I teased and tormented him, delivering spiteful jabs to his reddening face. He swatted and swung telegraphed punches but I was long gone, having shifted to a new position. He was getting very frustrated and before the end of the two minutes his mates, who'd been shouting for him, went quiet. The bell sounded the end of the round and we headed to our corners.

'That boy's chin is open to a right hand, John L... when you throw the left, chuck in a quick right,' suggested a relaxed Freddy Ludlow.

Ernie just said again, 'Knock him out, John L! Knock him clean out!'

Didn't know what had gotten into Ernie. Normally a composed and controlled guy; something really had upset him.

'Seconds out! Round two!' Carried on where I left off: stinging, annoying jabs that can bring tears to a grown man's eyes, making each second feel like a life time. Sting, move, jab, sting, torment, frustrate, and now that I've lined him up, jabbed a fast left and then delivered a beaut of a right which landed flush on his nose and broke it. As the Irish say, 'It was a good crack'. Felt it through the glove. He fell to the canvas like a dropped sack of spuds and the referee stopped it. I jumped for joy, another win, another knock out, another trophy. Ernie's' lips wore a very big smile as he shouted,

'Nice one, my boy!'

My opponent's trainer came to our corner complaining, saying there was no way that this was only my eighth fight. It was, so I smiled, took it as a compliment and thanked him.

This boxer was the only boy who never shook my hand in all the fifty three amateur fights I had. It was unheard of back then. On getting back to the dressing room, found out what had upset the now beaming, much less red faced, Ernie.

'Why'd you want me to knock him out, Ginger?'

'Because when the little shite found out he was fighting you, he mouthed off to his mates that he was fighting a nigger and that he was gonna do you bad!'

Just hearing the word brought back some 'happy' childhood memories. My opponents name was Eastwood. He thought I was a punk. Don't think I made his day though as most of it was spent in casualty getting his broken nose attended to!

Next, won the Kent Championships, the first of a run of five years and was very proud of knowing I was the best fighter in the county and of the trophy gained. To win the first Kent Champs I had to box three times. First, I beat the favourite on points from White Oaks, Swanley; a very useful fighter named T. O'Brien. In the semi-final I knocked out Ian McCarthy, from Margate, with a good left hook in the third round. Then in the final I beat tall, Glen Lowther from Faversham, a right tough nut. I was so determined to win that title that I threw everything I had at him. Backed him up against the ropes in the last round: hooks, uppercuts, lefts and rights were all landing.

Glen then became the first boxer to speak to me during a fight. It wasn't the type of talk Muhammad Ali was famous for when he took a good shot, like, 'My mother can hit harder than that!' Or, 'Is that the best you got, man!' No, it was talk that told me he wasn't enjoying himself while against the ropes under my heavy bombardment.

He loudly announced, 'Fuck this!'

Quite took me by surprise!

All seven of our St Mary's boxers reached the finals and we won five. We would've won more but two of our boxers got to the final in the same weight category, such was our dominance. That was some coaching set up and was why St Mary's was one of the most feared clubs in the county.

A big test for me came next, a fight with the junior ABA Champion, S. Payne, on his patch, East Ham, London. Looking at him from the other side of the ring and feeling confidently cocky I thought, *'I'm gonna give you some pain alright!'*

What actually happened was that he boxed my head off! In round two I caught him with a cracker of a right hand which made his knees buckle, but he didn't even have the good grace to go to the canvas! He just carried on, completely out boxing me. At the end of the fight I checked to see that he only had two arms!

That was my first loss and some of the boys felt I might quit; thought I may take it hard when realising that I wasn't as good as I hoped. Didn't even think about taking the easy option and quitting. Learnt more from that loss than all the wins put together and realised that to change that result I would have to train smarter, learn more, get better.

More wins, another loss, then some more wins. It was quite an apprenticeship and occasionally being beaten was to be expected as the opponents were older with more experience and strength. As long as I had given 100 per cent, I could handle being beaten by a better guy. Losing happens to everyone, how it's handled and how badly you get beaten is the problem. Some fighters are never the same after a bad loss. Seems to be the mental side that causes the problem. Bruises heal, broken jaws knit together but if another boxer is able to get inside your head, into that deep pain centre, there may be no recovery. Bouncing back from a defeat really shows the character of an athlete. You have to work hard, run the miles, spar the rounds, jump the rope. Even then you're only guaranteed to be the best you can be, and if you meet someone who's better, then it's going to hurt. Losing a 100 metre race hurts mentally. Losing a boxing match hurts physically as well.

With a wage coming in, saved hard and as soon as I reached seventeen, took driving lessons and quickly passed the driving test. Continued to walk to training to save the bus fare and was able to pay cash for my 'brand new' used car. Loved it, cherished it because I earned it through hard work, even harder saving and not going out some nights when my mates did. Paid cash for the car, much to the surprise of the dealer who thought I'd need 'hire purchase', which even at the age of seventeen, I knew was another word for debt.

'Freedom!' I thought, until my dad insisted I still be in by eleven p.m., even at weekends. If I weren't in, I'd be locked out.

'But Dad, I won't be late as I got training, but don't wanna come in at eleven!' I pleaded with him.

'Dats da rules under dis roof son. If yah don't like it yah know what yah carn do,' was his reply.

I thought he was joking, but after coming home from the Old Ash Tree pub (a very popular place) at 11.30 p.m., I found out he wasn't. Tried my key in the door but it was bolted from the inside. When my mum got up to let me in, Dad told her to leave me outside, which she did.

Spent a few nights sleeping in that car, but so I wouldn't miss my early morning run, always packed a bag of training kit and put a blanket in the boot. Would be freezing when I woke, but it didn't feel that much colder than the house. Would get into my kit, run, and by the time the run was complete I'd be warm, the front door, magically unbolted, and I'd be able to get in for breakfast and a shower.

One day my car wasn't running right so I popped the bonnet. Didn't have a clue what I was looking at, so asked my dad to take a look. I stood back from the engine and was lucky I did because a big, hard, unhappy looking, lump of a geezer, was walking toward us with a purpose, carrying a white plastic bag in his hand. Whatever was in that bag wasn't a present and looked heavy.

I gathered he wanted my dad and warned him, 'Dad!'

Dad looked up and saw where I was looking. The big bloke scowled, and through gritted teeth and screwed up face, growled, 'I'm gonna fuckin' kill ya!'

He swung the white bag at my dad, who dodged out the way.

'Go on dad, 'ook him!' I shouted.

The guy raised his right arm again, preparing to bring it down with power on my dad's head, but then clasped at his own chest. His face changed from rage to shock, then contorted in pain. The bag dropped from his hand to the ground and landed with a heavy metal thud. Both his hands grabbed at his failing heart and he fell to the floor and died.

The neighbours came out of their houses and the whispers started immediately. The street was packed with everyone wanting to know what had just happened. To be honest it was horrible, people shouting, sniggering, whispering. I was so glad my mum was at work because she'd not have taken this attention well.

The police and ambulance crews arrived, as did an investigation team. They assessed the sight, spraying a white outline around the body that would last for weeks! Every time I went out to my car, there it was… horrible; a man's life had ended there. Dad drove to Rochester Police Station with me in the passenger seat and fortunately an elderly neighbour from across the road was a useful witness, telling the police that my dad hadn't touched the deceased. If he had then Dad would have been facing a manslaughter charge at the very least. The stories that went round were unbelievable, such as my dad had kicked this poor guy to death, punched him in the head or strangled him. The list of ways my dad was meant to have killed this guy were endless and untrue.

I was seventeen, fit, fast, disciplined and it would be the last time my dad would raise his hands to me. It was a big slap around the face that I didn't see coming; the type of slap more humiliating than hurtful. Freddy Ludlow and Ernie Magog had done a great job in honing my discipline as I was a good boxer by then and could've dropped my dad easily, but chose not to, not wanting to stoop to his level of violence. The coaches at St Mary's had made me a thinker and although stung by the slap I didn't retaliate because I'd been trained to analyse, not react. If you're a reactor in boxing, you can get battered as you become a brawler trying to dish out the violence seen in a pub fight. My dad looked at me that night, after he slapped me, and realised I was now a man; his equal. He never hit me again.

Soon after that he left the family home. I was now eighteen and had been making plans to leave myself. It was upsetting for Mum and I was sad to see her so hurt, but for me it meant I wouldn't have to live in bedsit land or crummy rooms. No, now I was the man of the house and enjoyed the new found freedom but respected my mum's rules which were far more liberal.

It was a good time without him in the house, until I found my brother had been bullying my mum. If his dinner wasn't on the table he'd belittle and growl at her. My poor mum would panic, apologise and cry. Found this out by accident when I came home early from work one day and heard the way he spoke to her. Couldn't believe the lack of respect. Where'd that come from? Tried to talk to him but he wouldn't listen, waving me away like I was nothing. Wasn't happy with him to start with but his bad attitude and the way he was disrespecting our mum meant I ended up delivering some manners to him. It quietened him down for a couple of weeks but found him doing it again. Tried to talk sense into him and with not much warning, he picked up a kitchen knife and went to stab me with it. Fortunately for me, he didn't know how to use it and I took it from him. As we shared a bedroom, that night, I slept with one eye open!

The boy I protected against bullies when he was growing up, the boy I tried to show that bullying was wrong, had turned into one. Never really liked him but felt a loyalty to him because he was my brother. Now my dislike of him would be permanent. After our fight he gave me a wide berth, we rarely spoke and he behaved himself better.

Eighteen, man of the house, no curfew, no sleeping in the car, but was always quiet if coming in late so as not to wake my mum. Along with this freedom came more responsibility. Money was tight and I had to help out by putting more cash in the house. It's a big step up for an eighteen year old to go from paying keep to making sure the roof is kept above our heads.

This new responsibility might explain the no nonsense attitude I displayed when fighting Steve Kendell, on his club show in Maidstone. He was a good boxer and really tall for a welterweight. Hadn't noticed his height until I saw him from the other side of the ring. God that boy was long. When the bell went and we got closer, I almost stopped to check what my eyes were seeing. Accepting that he was as tall as he seemed, went about my business in a clinical way. He covered up his jaw but his chest seemed exposed and so I caught him with a vicious jab to the solar plexus which had the desired effect of knocking the wind out of him. Before he could even register what had happened and knowing I'd caught him well, followed up with two stinging flick jabs to the face. Now knowing where his chin was, dropped a bomb of a left hook that knocked him clean out. Never even hit him with the right. That was the quickest and easiest fight of my whole career, all over in thirty seconds, including the count!

With Dad having moved house, bookies, and unavailable for comment or cash, we lived a reasonably quiet life in Darnley Road. My brother found work and took some of the financial burden off me, so we coped. Two years passed with no contact from Dad, then out of the blue, he made an appearance and introduced me to a woman called Joan, a really nice lady. We got back on talking terms and he took a keen interest in my boxing. It was nice to have him at the fights and I could hear him cheering loudly and proudly for me.

The opponents matched to me were getting better. I fought Roy Connor, from Fitzroy Lodge on his club show at the Porter Tun rooms in London. He had the distinction of going to East Germany, as it was back then, with an England squad. He was the only British boxer to win both his fights at that show. Roy was world class and to be honest, the best opponent I faced as an amateur.

Considering it was my first fight of the season, I acquitted myself well but he was too classy, experienced and moved beautifully. I may have lost but he'd known he'd been in a fight as I was relentless, chasing him all round the ring. His class meant he picked me off and was gone like the wind. Boy, this guy was good, and to his credit, Roy came to my dressing room after the fight and asked me what I'd won in my boxing career. I was proud to be County Champ but up against this guy's achievements it was nothing. Puffing up my chest I said, 'Kent Champion!'

Roy was genuinely shocked at the answer, 'Is that it?!' he said, while he shook my hand and kindly told me I would get much further in boxing. I liked that.

Next fight was to defend my Kent Title at Greenways night club, Maidstone. The Challenger would be S. Williams, the older brother of the guy I beat a while before. I was in the toilet getting rid of the pre-fight nerves when a judge said to me, 'You got a toughun tonight Ian. That lads a goodun.'

64

I replied quickly, 'Yeah, but so am I.'

He nodded in agreement.

Once the bell sounded I found out the judge was right and from the off he was giving me a real beating. Shouldn't take these things personally but as his younger brother was in the audience, couldn't help but think there was a bit of rough justice being dished out to me. The first round ended, not soon enough for me, and I gladly headed to my corner where Fred Ludlow calmly said, 'Just like his younger brother, Ian... open to right hands. Throw in a quick left and then a right... that'll do it.'

Round 2: we carried on where he left off. As his punch landed on my nose, I felt it crack and it bled a goodun. In measured desperation, threw in a quick left and the straight right that Fred had suggested. It had the desired effect of sapping his energy and putting him on the back foot. I then delivered some of my own rough justice, battering him with no reply. Seemed like that right hand was a family weakness and soon after, the referee stopped the fight and declared me winner.

Me and Dave Hutchings (a big middleweight who was a right hard man in and out the ring) went down to Ramsgate as opponents for their top fighters. The venue was Nero's 2000, a big night club at the time.

Dave fought 'the Animal' who at the weigh-in, gave Dave 'the stare'. It did him no favours as Dave bashed him into submission in a round! After the fight, when they both came in the dressing room, Dave said to him, 'What was all that staring about earlier?'

'Yer sorry mate, I tried to psych you out... Didn't bloody work though!'

It was my turn now and I fought Lee Greenidge, a flashy boxer who thought he was 'Sugar' Ray Leonard. He wasn't.

I out boxed and dropped him quite a few times forcing the referee to stop it. He never worried me at all that night, but the person who did was his mum. She was in the audience, obviously loved her son and really unnerved me as she paced up and down outside that ring. She pointed and sucked her teeth, then shouted at me in a scary West Indian accent, telling me what a bad man I was because I'd beaten her son up. Was glad I didn't have to pass her on the way back to the dressing room. Might have run!

It was another good St Marys double, keeping up our fierce reputation.

Winning the Southern Championships proved a lot harder than winning the county trials, and so it should, but I did make hard work of it. In '82 I was beaten by Frankie Lyons, a really good southpaw. Ernie said to me that Frankie's the favourite; let's get him out early. Gave him a hard fight but his experience beat me. It was the first time I had boxed three rounds of three minutes, up from three rounds of two minutes. This made a difference, not so much physically as mentally. Came in at the end of round two feeling the fight was over and kept thinking, '*But I've boxed for 6 minutes.*'

In round three I wasn't concentrating, couldn't get my head on it and so lost on points. Frankie was class.

Later that year, I was booked to fight Dave Tomsett from Brighton. He concerned me so I made sure I had my boxing head on before I even got out of my house and was prepared to box/fight for the full 9 minutes. I was 19, he was 27, and Ernie Price had bought him along with the belief that he would beat me. There was an atmosphere before the fight and looking at Dave when he arrived, I knew he meant business. Fight night was at the Corn Exchange, Rochester, our St Marys show. I was really popular there as I'd won 'fight of the night' the previous year and runner up the year before that. I looked at the trophies that were up for grabs. I liked the bronze statue and noticed that Dave was eyeing it up also and heard him say to Ernie that he really wanted it.

I met Dave recently at the ex-boxers gathering in Brighton and was given a great reception by all when my arrival was announced. A great day was had and then Dave arrived. We hugged as only two people who have been in a 'war' can. It was great to see him. We'd both put on a few pounds but his memory of the fight was as if it was yesterday.

We'd both been warned about how good the other boxer was by our trainers and I was left in no doubt that Dave was a great boxer. His record on retiring after our fight was 87 fights and 80 wins. That is a very good record. He was class, one of the many tough Irishmen from County Cork, Ireland and one of sixteen kids. With that many siblings about, you know he'd have been fighting from day one!

In the ring he looked short, but wide. I didn't need Freddie to tell me he could bang, he just looked like power.

As soon as the bell rang, we went to the middle, touched gloves and all hell broke loose. For three minutes we went toe to toe; there was no need for ropes as we never went near them. It was war. Dave told the story of our fight to a group of us:

I came back in from round one and told Ernie Price I didn't want to go out for round two! Ernie was shocked, as I'd never said it to him before this fight. He told me I was winning, and I said – 'I don't know what fecking fight you're looking at mister but it ain't dis one!'

He got me off my stool telling me no one has ever quit on him and to go out and knock John's head off.

Another 3 minutes, another war, I managed to back John up to the ropes and Ernie was screaming 'Hook him!' Every time I tried to land the hook the fecker had gone. He was so slippery... fast. I went back to my corner at the bell and told Ernie again I didn't want to go back out. He didn't listen and I thought if I was going back out then I might as well get up early and get it over as soon as possible!

I looked across at John and found we were both off our stools. I took a look at him and realised I couldn't wait to get to it. The crowd were yelling and screaming. I called over to him asking him if he wanted some.

He replied, 'Yeah, how about you?'

'Yeah!' I replied and we both shouted to each other about coming to get some.

We met in the middle, tapped gloves and world war III broke out. We knocked lumps out of each other, but John had knocked a few more lumps out of me than I had of him. The bell went for the end of the fight and we hugged each other as if we were long lost brothers. It was such a sign of respect. Normally a hug is for a couple of seconds but this was for much longer. Money from the crowd came into the ring. The referee broke the embrace and we waited for the result. I felt John had won so wasn't surprised that his arm was held up in victory. We were both proud of our work that night.

We went to the trophies and as John had won he had the pick. I knew he wanted the bronze statue that I wanted and realised I would have to make do with an inferior trophy.

John being the kind of guy he is, turned to me and said, 'Dave, after that display of boxing, you choose mate... I know the one you want!'

What a gentleman, sportsman and top bloke. I picked the bronze statue and felt quite emotional. We had just battered each other for 9 minutes and here he was, not 9 minutes after, giving me 'the winners' trophy!

It was 20 years later on the anniversary of that fight that I handed it back to John. I had looked after it for him and felt it was time for him to have it in his trophy cabinet.

Couldn't believe it when he gave it back to me, was quite emotional. I offered him the trophy I had taken that night, to which he replied – as only an Irishman can – 'Feck off John… I don't do losers trophies!'

In the Southern Counties Championship of '83, lost to Dean Frankham in the semi-final. Nice boxer, from a lovely traveller family. His dad was a great guy who always, at shows, came up to speak to me and shake my hand. He liked the fact I knocked a lot of boxers out and told me so, but came up to me before this fight and said, 'No knocking out my boy now, Ian!'

I didn't. I lost to Dean, on this occasion, but would beat him a couple of times later in my career. To his credit, he always went the distance.

'84: I was the favourite. In boxing, favourite can mean nothing if you get caught with a good punch and that's exactly what happened in the semi-final. First round; a big right hand gave me stars and a fog in my head, which stayed with me for two rounds! Third round I was all over him. Too little too late.

In '85, finally won it! I beat the classy, J. Laundon from Portsmouth. I was winning easily but he got disqualified when he tried to head butt me. Champion at last. Knew I was getting better because both the semi-final and final were stopped through head butts as that was all they had left in their locker. It was seven years later, when working on the door of the Globe pub in Bow Street, Covent Garden, two guys with their girlfriends came up to me and one said, 'Hi Ian.'

'Who are you?' I said with a puzzled look on my face.

'It's me, Laundon. You beat me in the Southern Counties final in '85!'

'Well I never,' I replied. We hugged, had a nice chat and they went on their way.

To be honest, thought I was going to win the ABAs that year and was winning the quarters no problem, having put Steve Kyriakides on the floor three times in the first round. Really it should've been stopped but as it was on his home ground in Ipswich, it was allowed to go on.

To his credit, he tried to fight back and after the third knockdown, when he rose, threw a straight right that caught me bang on the left eye. I felt a sharp pain I'd never felt before and then the bell went. I was cut; first time ever as an amateur, in my 50th fight! The cut was bad and Andy Kidd, my corner man, told me I had to knock the guy out quick. Soon as the bell went, I rushed in, threw a couple of big shots but the exertion made my own cut bleed heavily and look worse than what it was. The referee had no choice but to stop the fight. Steve went wild with celebrations.

In '86 got to the final of the Southern Counties again. Steve Smith from Gravesend, a very experienced fighter, beat me on points; so I didn't make the ABA's that year.

It was a good amateur career, winning 40 out of 53 fights, but decided to go professional after Speedy Mitchell suggested it was time to move on. Talked it over with Freddy and the other coaches and they reckoned I'd take to it because of my fitness and endurance. It was an exciting time for me and my goal was to be British Welterweight Champion.

Speedy, Bernard, Les

'Professional,' I kept saying to myself. Had a ring to it, implied excellence at something. Felt proud about being a 'pro' and wanted to make my dream of becoming a British Champion come true. Pictured myself often with that belt around my waist or held above my head. Having a healthy amount of self-belief I felt that, with a lot of hard work and some luck, I could achieve my dream.

By now I was aware that some boxers are brilliant in the amateur game but can't make it in the professional arena. The increase in rounds means the mind and body must be able to ignore pain for a much longer time.

My heart for boxing was not in question and I was obsessive about training. The people I trusted told me fitness was never going to be an issue, my chin was strong and that turning professional would suit me. Fred Ludlow would always say to me, 'John L, you are always fit. You're so easy to train.'

What a compliment to get from someone you admire so much, and on those dark, rainy mornings, when I could've done with just knocking the alarm clock out and taking the extra hour in bed, I would think of Fred's words. Not wanting to let him or myself down, I'd leave my warm blankets and just like Rocky, pound the pavements, only mine were in Strood, Chatham and Gillingham.

Being obsessive about my training meant I would never cheat on myself. If I felt I miscounted the sit ups or press ups, would always do a couple more just to make sure I'd hit the target set by the coaches. A couple of extra sit ups are not so bad, but if I thought I'd missed a whole set of them, would do an extra set just to make sure. If I wasn't happy with the training session, wouldn't be able to settle; the nagging little accusing voice in my head, calling me a cheat, would just gnaw away at me all day. Liked to keep that voice quiet.

The guy who was now my trainer was Achille 'Speedy' Mitchell. Top class guy. Got to know him personally through Robert Xavier, his cousin, who was the top heavyweight that trained out of St Mary's. Speedy lived in Coventry, occasionally came down to see Robert and train in our gym. Although retired, he was still in good shape, with a laid back West Indian manner, until, that is, he put on a pair of boxing gloves.

Xavier and Speedy 'sparred' some hard rounds and would knock lumps out of each other. We would all watch closely at ringside because Robert was a classy boxer with knockout power in both mitts. He took no prisoners in the ring and hit his opponents with all his power. But this guy Speedy (a lot smaller) not only took all his big shots, he gave it back with interest. The way they went at each other, you'd never have believed they were related. I liked the way Speedy conducted himself and he got my respect from the off.

A welterweight in his day, Speedy fought 'the gifted one' Kirkland Lang three times, twice as an amateur and once in a final eliminator for the British Title which he lost by majority decision. When I turned pro, Kirkland was still the British champion.

Speedy saw me sparring at St Mary's, stopped to watch and when I'd finished, told me I was good. To have that said by someone who had been number two in the country to Kirkland Lang made my week.

A couple of years after I first met him, Speedy came back to our gym and put the idea into my head of turning professional and him being my trainer. Talking with Speedy, found we had a lot in common. He came to England from Dominica aged 10, was the only black kid in the school and suffered a lot of racial abuse from a minority. Out of his depth with learning and the culture, he struggled to find his feet and acceptance in Coventry. Speedy just carried on being himself and eventually clicked with his neighbours who looked beyond his black skin.

One of these neighbours was Les Allen who'd been a professional boxer and didn't care that Speedy was black. Les welcomed him into his home and his son, Mason, was Speedy's best mate. Les guided Speedy, took him under his wing, and his son, Mason, a huge guy, was protection for Speedy. They had great fun in secondary school but for Speedy, just like me, school was difficult for learning but not for sport.

In Les's basement was some boxing equipment that Speedy and Mason started to work out on. Les came down, spied Speedy on the bag and said to him, 'Didn't know you were a boxer Speedy.'

Speedy wasn't; was quite a timid guy at the time, an easy target for bullying racists when Mason wasn't around. Les told him he was a natural and before Speedy knew it, he was at a boxing club training three days a week. He was hooked. The noble art gets you like that.

Speedy watched me train, told me we were from the same mould. Neither of us would miss training and both gave 100 per cent. He knew I was a good distance runner; said the transition to pro would be smooth and that I'd got what it would take.

Speedy's manager had been Dave Roden, who is, at time of writing, a Steward of the British Boxing Board of Control. Speedy was generally avoided in England because he really was that good, just a thin slice below Kirkland. Because he couldn't get the fights on home soil, he fought in Europe with the best. It was well paid work, but he lost more than he won as the step up between British and European boxing can be huge.

At that time, Speedy felt that to get the decision in these fights and the fights he had in the 70s, he'd have to knock his opponent out as rarely did the home referee decide in his favour. For Speedy to develop to his full potential he needed more home grown fighters to box, so he could practice honing his immense talent. The jump from number two in Great Britain to fighting the best in Europe was too much of a leap.

Speedy was laid back with a voice, just as chilled. He seemed to have the attitude, 'why rush?' and was an excellent coach. His plan was to get me to box more, less war, as he was not impressed with the windmill arms and off balance punches that were thrown during a fight that descends into a brawl. He was quite a purist, saying that boxing is about skill and warring was for the street fighter.

'Why war when you don't have to? Box... Use your brain... don't lose your brain,' Speedy would say.

Training was in Carnaby Street, London, in the Lonsdale gym. Worked out harder than ever before, knowing that to succeed I'd have to be the best I could be. Speedy soon realised that he couldn't beat me in the gym and even announced, following one of the many gruelling sessions, that he was impressed.

The training was made harder because at the time my job was as a 'Hoddie' on a building site. My day would start with a run in army boots while holding hand weights; then home, shower, breakfast, cycle to work, all day getting bricks and muck up and down ladders, cycle home, bit of a lie down; then off to the evening training session for two hours of speed ball, bag, skipping and sparring. Once home; big drink, bed, out like a light before my head touched the pillow, then back up in the morning and same again.

Speedy saw I could handle the training necessary to progress in pro boxing and spoke to Bernard Hart, the creator of the world famous Lonsdale brand, about my chances. Bernard had seen thousands of boxers and Speedy valued his opinion.

Bernard and Speedy gave a lot of time to charity work, through Lonsdale, for the Boxers' Benevolent Fund and got on really well. Bernard loved the sport and was concerned for the boxers' welfare. He named his company Lonsdale after the 5th Earl of Lonsdale who was responsible for making the sport fairer and safer. Bernard was, and is, a real gentleman.

Speedy arranged it so that we would spar in front of Bernard. A nerve wracking experience, but to be honest, I wanted his opinion, good or bad, as he really knew his boxing.

We sparred three good rounds to show what I was capable of. Bernard said he was impressed and Speedy asked him if he would manage me as he was aware that there were a lot of 'shark' managers in the pro game. Bernard didn't have the time to do the management job properly but knew someone who could help me. He rang Les Roberts.

Didn't know at the time who this Les Roberts was and only found out later that the guy who was to take me on had been involved for many years, 1950-73, with the National Sporting Club, Café Royal. Les was the matchmaker and had been involved in many big fights. He was then linked with the St Andrews Sporting Club in Scotland, 1973-87, and was instrumental in the Ken Buchanan/Jim Watt fight that Buchanan won on points.

Speedy arranged a meeting with Les but due to a wedding that I'd agreed to be at, told Speedy I couldn't make it. He wasn't happy, telling me I may miss a great opportunity and told me to ring Les and explain.

Phoned Les, ready for him to say that I was messing him about and was I really serious about turning pro? Les answered; we talked and I explained the problem and that I knew the meeting was important but felt that it would be bad manners to not turn up at a friend's wedding I'd been invited to. No questions came from him, reprimands or power plays, he just said, 'I agree, so let's make the appointment for the following Saturday. Can you make it?'

Later, Les would tell me that my explanation and the fact that I was obviously loyal to my friends and true to my word, made him interested to meet me. He added that Bernard had given me such a good reference, saying that I was a 'no nonsense' type of boxer who trained hard, was aware of my limitations and wanted to and had the potential to be a British champion.

We met at a café in Beak Street, London, and we got on really well. Les asked what my goal was and told him I wanted to be a British Champion to go with my few titles I'd won as an amateur. He said it was a shame I'd not met him five years earlier because back then he was the secretary of the St Andrew's Sporting Club and had more contacts in the world of boxing. The reason he'd left was because he'd become disillusioned with boxing there and thought it was time to step aside for new blood to take the reins.

The papers at the time called Les outspoken but from my point of view he was just truthful. Les was a typical Yorkshire man; said things as he saw them, honest to the point of seemingly being blunt, but still honest. What I like about these rare people is there is no mistaking what they mean, as they mean what they say, stand by it and will stand by you.

Les said we'd make a good team with Speedy on board. He drew up a manager's licence, told me that he could take up to 25 per cent but said he'd never take a penny off me. Les was generous and true to his word. To be honest, it cost him money to be associated with me as he paid his own way to fights and was never in the queue to get his entitled percentage. I owe that man so much.

Later in my career he told me that Bernard had been right when he said I wouldn't be a boxer he would need to chase to get hard work out of. Les would always say to me, 'Conditioning rules the day, Ian J!'

He was, and still is, right. There are no shortcuts in this game. Fail to prepare… prepare to be bloody hurt.

Speedy was a clever coach, a thinker, had his own training ideas and one of them that I'd never seen (let alone done) was when he gave me the pads to hold and he punched them. First of all I questioned this – in my mind, not verbally – but soon found that this really developed my reflexes and also had the effect of me using my hands to protect my jaw better. After many hours of this, my hands were kept higher and I found I slipped punches that would normally have connected.

My professional debut wasn't the best start. This was a big bill to have my pro debut on, and I wanted to impress. It was in Dudley, Birmingham and headlining the bill was Horace Notice, the unbeaten British and Commonwealth Heavyweight Champion. He defended his

Commonwealth belt against the massive, Proud Kilimanjaro, stopping him in the fifth round.

My fight was a six rounder. I may have boxed neatly, picked my shots and moved well, just as Speedy had shown me, but the result in the records showed that I lost. At the end of round two felt everything was going to plan, then in round three: disaster. After landing a few good shots and coming on to my opponent, I got an unintentional thumb in my eye. That really hurt and felt worse than any of the punches my opponent had landed. It was a sharp electric shock pain, like a fractured jaw, which later in my career I'd know all about. At the end of the round, my eye had shut tight; couldn't see a thing. The referee came over and stopped it straight away. I was gutted.

Next up: fight number two in Weston Super Mare. I boxed well but came second in a close points decision that left me and Les fuming. I had stuck to the task of hitting and moving and we felt I'd boxed his head off. As we all know, in boxing, second is nowhere. Didn't matter to me how close it was; I lost and wasn't happy about the start to my career.

'Keep going, Ian. You've talent, just need a little luck, that's all.' Les calmly told me.

Les arranged my third fight in Glasgow, Scotland using his contacts there. Before the fight Speedy Mitchell did his best to wind me up and his best worked. We arranged for him to pick me up at 8.00 a.m. but he turned up at seven, making a real racket knocking on my door, shouting through the letter box and up at my window. His noise really upset me, waking me up when I thought I was going to get an extra hour's kip! Once in the car, still bleary eyed and shell shocked by his carrying on, we headed up to Euston station, London for the long journey north to Glasgow. On the train I glanced to my left and see this guy who looked familiar.

'Excuse me mate,' I said, 'You look like that Phil Cool fella!'

He pulled all these weird faces and said, 'What makes you think that pal?'

We fell about laughing. Had a great time with him; very funny guy. He got off at Preston where he was doing a gig and wished me all the best for my fight. The laughter over and somewhere just north of Preston, Speedy told me as he saw it, laying it out plain, simple and straight, so I'd make no mistake about what he thought.

'Lose the next fight... may as well quit!'

He may have said it in his laid back, cool, West Indian way, but the way he said – 'quit!' – got right under my skin and wiped from my face the smile I usually wore.

That really, really, pissed me off and whether he meant to or not; didn't matter. In my eyes I was unbeaten, just a bit of bad luck that's all. Nice Ian disappeared for the rest of the day and when the bell sounded for the fight to begin, I came out of that corner with a purpose, ready to war, determined that I'd return home with a victory. As I laid into this unfortunate Scot with punch after punch, Speedy was busy shouting at me from the corner, 'Box Ian, box!'

'Box Ian, box!.. fuck off Speedy!' I thought as I laid into this guy who, although a lot taller than me, was quite happy to trade punches. A big mistake! He should have used his reach advantage.

Even as I was moving around the ring looking for the money shot, could almost feel that it was going to be a bomb. The power seemed to be building as I searched for a way in. Occasionally my opponent's chin would show itself and then hide away. Told myself to be patient and then there it was, full view for a micro second, but when you're in the zone that tiny amount of time seems like you have an age to deliver any choice of punches that could complete the task of turning the opponent's legs to jelly and his lights off. Before I threw it, knew it was over and when it connected, knew he'd be out for the whole count because I'd thrown it from the floor. Unfortunately it was never filmed and because Les was so pleased for me, he made sure that in the future, Steve Holdsworth, a great guy with a face that belongs behind a camera, was always there to film my fights.

My opponent had been a useful, tough Scot from Glasgow. Am convinced the Glaswegians are born ready to take on the world! His dad came to my dressing room after the fight and although disappointed for his son, kindly – I say kindly, but the accent is one that always sounds to me as if they're having a go – congratulated me and told me no one had ever done that to his son before. His generous words were the icing on the cake and gave me an added lift to my self-belief.

When I returned to London, Bernard asked me to take part in advertising some Lonsdale kit. I was to be photographed with the world class Herol 'bomber' Graham who fought for a world title and lost to Julian Jackson. What an honour for me. It boosted my profile, as the picture was above the counter in the famous shop in Beak Street for years. Had many people mention that photo to me.

Les had no problem getting me another fight in Glasgow and I won that in similar style. My reputation and confidence were growing and the contests were being won with this exciting fighting style. Speedy still insisted that I was a good boxer and needed to concentrate on boxing/fighting/boxing rather than warring to win fights. In that third fight he'd unleashed the warring part of my brain and was going to have a hell of a job getting it under control.

With this style I was winning, so didn't feel like changing back. The crowd, who know boxing, then expect you to war and the commentators like your style because it is edge of the seat stuff. Putting a smile on the paying public's face is nice to see. The back slapping on the way to the ring is always welcome, as are the ones when you go back to the dressing room.

Speedy was trying to get across to me, in his way, that good boxing is about getting hit as little as possible, not trading blows because you know you have a strong jaw and iron abdominals. He was also worried about me getting cut, saying that they don't heal like the real thing and are a weakness forever. I was 23, winning, felt indestructible and did not take it on board.

My next opponent was Roy Callaghan, at York Hall on his own turf. He was, like me, on his way up. This was going to be a tough fight as there was a lot to lose for both of us. Speedy insisted that the fight needn't be hard for me, and told me to, 'Box, Ian... Box!'

'Box, Ian... Box!' I thought, parodying his words.

Training for the fight went well. Thought I was boiling down nicely to the weight. Felt fit, fast and ready to rumble. Speedy had to do his day job but would join Les and me later that evening in Bethnal Green.

At the weigh-in, at the Lonsdale gym, I jumped on the scales expecting to hear the customary shout of, 'Ian John-Lewis…10 stone 8lbs.'

What I actually heard was, 'Ian John-Lewis…10 stone 10lbs.'

Got off the scales and said to Les, 'What happens now?'

'You've got to get the 2lbs off… within an hour… or you'll be fined,' he answered.

'Fined!' I thought. As if money wasn't hard enough to come by; was going to have to pay a bloody fine. That set off a mixture of panic and paranoia as I began the job of shifting 2lbs of weight in sixty short minutes when I should've been eating, drinking and resting up.

The one good thing was that Speedy wasn't there. He'd have told me exactly what I was thinking about myself, and at that point I didn't need anyone else beating me up mentally.

Before this, I had always been spot on the weight and found it fairly easy as I'd always kept myself in shape between fights. Eleven stone was the absolute maximum I'd allow my body to climb to. As soon as 11 stone 1 pound showed itself on the weighing scales, it was time to train a little harder and eat a little less. Within a few days the weight would be off. Always believed, still do, that it's easier to make the weight if you keep yourself fit between fights. Obviously you can't keep to your boxing weight all year round, the diet is just too strict and you feel irritable all the time.

Julie would tell me that my moods during the final few weeks coming up to a fight were awful. 'Arsehole!' was the term of endearment used by my better half to describe my mood. But what she hated more than this was the fact that four films would continually be on the video recorder. Between work and training, Rocky 3, Rocky 4, First Blood and Enter the Dragon would be playing in those last three weeks.

So, just one hour to lose 2lbs. No kit with me as the fight is at the famous York Hall, Bethnal Green – the weigh-in at Carnaby Street, London. Luck was with me as they knew me well in the shop. They provided me with a tracksuit and allowed me to use the gym and sauna. Was definitely having trouble mentally. Was finding it hard to stop beating myself up and tried to focus on the job I'd have to do on Callaghan later that evening.

Losing 2lbs in an hour means only one thing, the workout is going to be a tough one. Just hours before I get into a ring with a professional who has just won four on the bounce, I am going to sweat out 2lb. At this point I agreed with Julie.

'Arsehole!' I thought.

Les didn't panic, curse at me or say anything negative. He just got me skipping, shadow boxing, then into the sauna, with the tracksuit on. It didn't take too long before the light grey material went dark grey around the neck, arm pits and waist. As I continued to work-out, the patches migrated towards each other and soon it was all dark grey.

In my mind I'm weakening, going dizzy but unable to even sip water, and all the time Callaghan is sitting, relaxing, watching me work out hard.

'Is that bastard smirking at me?' I thought, wondering if it was just my dehydrated brain playing tricks. Soothed myself with the thought that later on that evening, I'd wipe that smirk off his face.

Roy waited for thirty minutes to pass, when they would reweigh me. He stayed to make sure every ounce of that 2lb was off. Must admit, would've done the same to him. My paranoia filled in what he was thinking and they weren't pleasant thoughts. No one wants to enter the ring on fight night feeling weak, mentally or physically. You can't have a bad one in boxing, too dangerous.

Thirty minutes passed. Stripped off, dried off, back on the scales.

'Ian John Lewis... 10 stone 9lbs.'

Pound still left to lose. Roy smirks again, or does he? Is he playing mind games or is it my mind playing games? Back on with the now cold, sweaty tracksuit: disgusting! Into the sauna, feeling weaker, dizzier and knowing that I am losing goodness from my body. As the sweat poured out, dehydration kicked in, thinking became difficult. Can see I'm losing fluid but my brain was telling me that the sweat is muscle burning and to make the weight I will be losing power.

As Roy kept looking at me, thought he looked relaxed, almost smiling and probably thinking that I was an insult to the profession, that I couldn't even be professional enough to make the weight. Mind's a mess now and can't think with any clarity. It was like having a nightmare with my eyes open! Back in the sauna, out, more skipping, shadow boxing, Les keeping me moving. Roy slumped in his chair, looking at me jumping up and down like Zebedee, while he decided if he wanted to slump on his left side or his right side. He was growing in confidence while mine disappeared out of my sweat pores as I punished my body to make the weight.

They announce that the hour is up, it's 2 o'clock. I remove the tracksuit that is now 2lb heavier and that no one will ever want to buy. I dry myself of every spot of moisture that could add to my weight, breathe in – like that will make me lighter – and step on the scales.

'Ian John-Lewis… 10 stone 8 lbs.'

Breathe out, relieved but drained. Mind is a dizzy mess. Les gives me water and tells me to drink deep.

'Get that fluid down you John L… the brain will clear. You'll feel better soon.'

Les utters more wise words to help me regain the lost confidence and kill the embarrassment I was feeling.

That was the first and last time I'd get my preparation wrong and not boiled down to the weight needed. Not a pleasant experience and one that would, in future, make me always be smack on the weight.

Never did feel the effects of that hard training session just six hours before the fight. Just as well as Roy came out thinking it would've weakened me. Certainly wouldn't advise it's done, but Les said the reason I got away with it was because I was so fit.

Again it was a war: a war I won. Les congratulated me. I was ecstatic with the win, still lapping up the applause when Speedy said to me, 'You're such a good boxer, could've beaten him by just using your left hand. Why'd you have to war all the time?!'

He wagged his head, turned to the ropes and leant on them. Speedy looked frustrated as he took his hat off and then put it on again for no purpose. I felt the timing and tone of his comment, poor. Bet he was sucking his teeth at me but couldn't hear it because of the cheers of the crowd.

A win was a win, and in the style that I'd just shown, would make me an exciting TV prospect. Speedy told me later that evening to take a break… a holiday… to recover. He had the face of a trainer whose fighter had just got beat. It was a really tough fight, so that pissed me right off.

Took Speedy's advice and went on my first trip abroad. Never ever been on holiday before, so it was exciting stuff but became real nervous when looking out at the plane. I was 25 and had never seen a plane that close. Remembered what my dad had thought when he had looked at the boat that brought him over to England from the West Indies, *'Dat's big… dat boat 'll never float!'*

I looked at the plane and thought, *'That's big… that'll never get off the ground!'*

It did, and more importantly… it landed.

Fight of the Year!

My next fight was meant to be against Chris Blake, the former Southern Area Light-Welterweight Champion and British title challenger. It would be, literally, a home venue for me as the Black Lion Leisure Centre, Gillingham, was only around the corner from my house in Saxton Street. I'd have a full home crowd to cheer me on, so was really disappointed when Blake pulled out the week before. The promoters, Gary Davidson (owner of the famous Thomas A Beckett pub) and Tony Doodney, wanting to save the show, offered me a fight with substitute, Lloyd Lee, aged 34, from Wales.

'Old bloke! No problem!' I thought.

My confidence was growing and I felt I could fight anyone. The danger with this type of confidence is that you might feel you can fight anyone but the truth is you can't. This is when you need good people advising you, putting the reins on you, so this was definitely a time to talk to Les, who, as always, gave me some words of wisdom:

'He may be getting on Ian, but the last thing you lose in boxing is the punch and he does have a big punch. Don't take the fight. You're on the way up. More to lose than gain.'

Les's reasoning was that Lloyd Lee had once dropped the superb Colin Jones, the former British, Commonwealth, and European Champion, who'd been good enough to fight for the world title twice against Milton 'Ice man' McCrory and Don 'the Cobra' Curry.

I phoned them back and turned it down. They offered me double the original purse but I'd never been in boxing for money. Was on a good run, working toward the title, so again said no. They were not amused as the show had to be cancelled. Gave the ticket money back to the people I'd sold tickets to, and because I wasn't fighting at the weekend, enjoyed a good meal with the biggest bar of chocolate I could find.

My next fight would be at Woodville Halls, Gravesend which was only 12 miles away from my house. Considering I'd been travelling all over the Country, felt this would be a home fixture as it wasn't too far for friends and family to travel. Was really looking forward to the fight and to hearing the crowd cheering me on. They might even drown out the support I always had from my good mate, and ex St Mary's boxer, Chris King (Kingie), but I doubted it.

My opponent was Tony Britland. I nearly blew him away in the first round, such was my onslaught. Kingie was screaming with delight, telling me to finish it, but Tony was a tough guy; survived and gave me quite a tussle for me to win on points. The promoters Gary and Tony were so pleased with the full house, they put on another show a month later, where Nick Meloscia would be my opponent.

As soon as the Meloscia fight began, I could hear Kingie, above the rest of the crowd, willing me on. Round one was fairly uneventful with me keeping out of harm's way because I knew Meloscia was a step up in ability, and a real handful. Sure enough, second round, he gave it to me: unloading bombs, trying to take my head off.

'Keep them bloody hands up Louie!' Kingie shouted. I did, but then he attacked my body and landed two almighty right hooks that sunk right into my rib cage. They hurt, and he knew it; pouring it on, backing me up against the ropes. I was glad to hear the bell sound and went back to my corner, winded.

'You've got to back him up. He's a bully and you're letting him take control. Back him up,' ordered Les calmly.

I sucked up the pain and went after him. It took him by surprise. He backed off and I caught him with a big right. Now I was doing the chasing with my home crowd going wild. The bell sounded and I accidentally hit him. Before I could apologise he gave me a dig back, so I dug him again, which is ridiculous because where does it end? He dug me for digging him, so I was going to dig him again for digging me, for digging him. The referee stepped in, stopped the nonsense and prevented it from becoming a childish brawl.

In round four, Nick appeared to be running out of gas and I was definitely getting on top. I continued to follow him around the ring, preventing him from catching a breather.

Round five: obviously losing, becoming desperate, and without trying to hide it, he went to head butt me. The referee missed his first attempt, but about five seconds later he did it again. The crowd jeered, the referee jumped in between us and instantly disqualified Nick. He protested his innocence and as he trudged off to the dressing room we exchanged unkind words and hand gestures which couldn't be seen as we had boxing gloves on. We never shook hands.

About a month later, my training partner, Mark Pellett was in the Thomas A Beckett gym. Normally I'd have been with him but this particular Saturday morning I was working. In walked Nick Meloscia, who recognised Mark, walked up to him and said, 'You're mates with that Ian John-Lewis aren't ya?'

Mark thought that Nick was going to say something negative about me and was ready for a verbal war.

'Yeah, he's my mate.' Mark replied.

'Well, when you see him, tell him I had to get disqualified. I was running out of gas and knew he was going to knock me out! Tell him he's a good fighter and wish him all the best for the future from me.'

Was really surprised but pleased to hear it and respected Nick for it.

Around this time I was contacted by Steve Jenkins, a businessman from Hoo, near Strood. His brother in law had showed him the tape of me fighting Meloscia and he immediately contacted me and sponsored me a fair few quid. He told me that I was a fit guy and wanted to help me out as I obviously worked out really hard and that as a self-made businessman he understood all about hard graft. It really helped me buy the gear I needed and also freed up a few quid to enjoy myself with.

Next fight was at Greenwich Town Hall. There was a lot of betting going on from the Strood boys. They'd paid out enough already on tickets and travel and I thought they might break even if I won.

Johnny Nanton was my opponent and from the off we knocked lumps out of each other. The crowd were enjoying the battle as much as we were. Then, in round four Nanton landed a beaut of a left hook to my chin. I felt something that I hadn't felt before. It was just a click, no real pain to scream about, but it did feel odd. I gathered I couldn't feel the pain because I was in the zone but thought, *'Shit, my jaw's broke!'*

Wasn't really sure if it'd broken or not and knowing I could do nothing about it, got on with the job in hand. The fight went the distance and I won the decision. With my arms aloft in victory, money came showering into the ring from the very pleased spectators. One of the bucket men put a towel on the canvas of the ring and gathered the money together. Johnny and me split the 'nobbins' money and got over £100 on top of our fee.

Back in the dressing room, the ache in my jaw turned to pain. Told the doctor and after a brief assessment, he diagnosed bruising. I believed him, well he was a doctor, but only believed him until the pain really broke through. After thinking about that punch Nanton delivered, I suspected the worst. It was, after all, a cracking punch – literally. Next morning, after a poor night's sleep, went to Medway Hospital to be checked over. Sure enough, a fracture was confirmed, and I was sent to East Grinstead Hospital to have my jaw wired together.

Once wired, they handed me some wire cutters, just in case I needed to be sick! Was told to liquidise my food and that my jaw would stay wired for three weeks. It was December the 9th which would mean my Christmas dinner would have to be blended!

Because of that injury, I didn't fight for a few months, making sure that it was fully healed. At the time of having my jaw wired, the doctor assured me that it would be as good as new in a couple of months. Even in training I hadn't really had it tested and it was still on my mind as I entered the arena on fight night. I also discovered they'd mentioned it in the programme, stating I was recovering from a broken jaw: was not happy.

'Nice trunks!' I thought as Jim Beckett got into the ring, wearing pink shorts, *'Go very well with the highlighted blond hair.'*

Well, it was the 80's! He might not have looked like your typical 'hard man' boxer but he was.

Jim and his trainer must have seen the write up also, as from the off, Jim targeted my jaw.

After three minutes in the ring with Jim testing its durability with some really heavy shots, I stopped thinking about it. It hadn't turned to glass; was strong again, 100 per cent. The doctor, this time, was right.

After a couple of rounds I got into a great rhythm and then delivered a body shot that sent Jim to the canvas for a full 30 seconds. Once he recovered and was on his feet, the crowd again threw money into the ring.

As Jim climbed out of the ring, my next future opponent was brought in and introduced. Tony Baker it was to be, who had also beaten Jim by a body shot in three rounds. We shook hands and as we did he said, 'I'm gonna knock you out!'

'Yeah? We'll see.' I answered.

Tony was a dangerous journeyman, in his thirties with a lot of boxing experience. The promoters were happy with my fights as the fan base was growing, so they knew I'd sell well in my home town. This contest would be a home fight for me and I mean, a home fight, as it would take place at the Black Lion Leisure Centre in Gillingham. I'd be able to walk there in less than five minutes.

This was the first time in 20 years that professional boxing had been held in the Medway Towns and it would be televised. The crowd was great and the roar they gave me when I entered the ring was spine tingling. Could hardly hear the music I'd picked, "Hard Times" by The Human League. I was so up for this fight, wanting to give the crowd their money's worth. In the dressing room Steve Holdsworth (Eurosport commentator) asked me my prediction and I told him I'd knock my opponent out in the fifth.

Nearly did get him in five and landed some beautiful shots, but he was durable. As I hit him I could hear him wincing above the noise of my cheering home crowd. As I laid in with another powerful body shot, I was thinking, *'Just fuckin' go down will ya'. I 'ave a crowd to please!'*

In the sixth, I switched from warring to boxing so I could take a breather. In the seventh, I began trying to bomb him out again and in the eighth, continued on and delivered a punch that finally rocked him to his boots. Had been looking for that one all night. The referee, Dave Parris, stepped in and stopped it. The crowd went wild, and so did I, jumping, screaming, hugging Speedy and some of my real close mates that dived into the ring. That's how much it meant to me – what a night!

When home, found it really difficult to sleep with the excitement running through my veins. It had only taken me five minutes to reach my house, so was still buzzing when I got there. Even thought about going out for a run to wear myself out.

Was then matched with another dangerous journeyman called Paul Seddon. Not a boxer to be taken lightly they told me. Journeymen keep themselves in good shape all year round. Obviously can't be 100 per cent fit all of the time, it's impossible to maintain, but they have the mental and physical ability to be able to fight at a few hours' notice if needed. How they do it, I don't know, but think that for them to make the weight, most journeymen probably fight in a weight class above what they would be if preparing properly for a fight

The nearest I came to being a 'journeyman' was when I'd been offered a fight after I rang Barry Hearn's 'Matchroom Promotions' office for tickets for a show that very evening.

I'd just got back from a weekend away in Plymouth, where I'd broken my normal training routine. I'd finally met up with my future brother-in-law Mark, a no nonsense hard man and his wife, Alison. We went out for a couple of beers at their local pub, the Blue Monkey. It was a right 'spit 'n' sawdust' pub and with the amount of weed being puffed in there it should've been called the 'Blow Monkey'. I spent most of the evening escaping the sickly sweet smelling smog, by taking trips to the toilet to get some fresh air by the open window!

Anyway, the voice on the end of the phone said, 'Hang on Ian,' I then heard him say to Barry Hearn, 'Got Ian John-Lewis on the phone here.'

The phone switched hands and Barry said, 'You want tickets? Better than that Ian, why not be on the bill yourself and earn a few quid?'

'Who'd I be fighting?' I asked.

'Micky Hughes...' Barry replied.

'*Fuck off Barry!*' I thought with lightning speed but came out with, 'No thanks, Barry.'

(Gary Jacobs, who was meant to fight Hughes had pulled out.)

Barry continued, 'Ian... Give you £3000 to do it.'

Julie was nearby, heard £3000, became interested and got closer to the phone. I turned the offer down and Barry raised it,

'£4000.'

Julie was now looking like a Meerkat in shock, staring at me as if I were mad not to accept.

'It's not right for me, Barry. Out of my normal routine.'

'£5000, Ian... Five thousand pounds. That is a good night's work!'

'Take it! Bloody take it!' hissed Julie.

'Thanks for the offer, Barry, but I'm not in shape for it.'

If I'd not broken my normal training regime, I'd have taken it. But two late nights and a couple of beers had done enough to me to know I wasn't 100 per cent.

Julie argued with me, saying it was all in my head, that I was always fit, and a couple days out wouldn't make much difference. She told me I was crazy to turn it down, that we could have done a lot with that money. Yeah, maybe we could have bought a nice headstone for my grave with it or maybe she was right, but Micky Hughes was getting a name for himself as a knockout specialist and if I were going to get in a ring with him, I'd be properly prepared. Later that night, Micky fought Nick Meloscia and took him out with a wicked body shot; first round. Nick earned his money – painfully.

Paul Seddon, the journeyman, had knocked out fighters he wasn't meant to. I really wanted to beat him in four rounds as Chris Blake had won in five, and he was in my sights being ranked highly in the division.

Don't underestimate Seddon, was the advice that my team kept giving me.

'Box, Ian, box!' insisted Speedy, knowing I was excited about the home fixture and trying to keep me under control without damping down my fighting spirit.

I was buzzing, as I was fighting at the Black Lion in Gillingham in front of a one thousand strong, home crowd. Mates I went to school and grew up with, people I worked with, family, new friends and old, would spend their hard earned money to come and support the Darnley Road kid. They packed the place and everywhere I looked were people I knew. Felt quite emotional and had to fight to keep it under control.

So wanted to put on a show and knew that could be dangerous! Can lose your discipline, get cocky, trade punches, show a bit too much chin, lose concentration and see a little too much ceiling or worse, the inside of your eyelids! A good corner will do its utmost to keep a lid on you, calm you down, help focus you, and if they see you're not concentrating, or listening, a sharp slap across the face will get the attention. Strange that, you take a massive punch to the jaw and it hurts but nothing like a sharp slap to the face.

Steve Holdsworth, the commentator told me that he was really looking forward to the fight, adding he loved the pace I fought at; liked my heart and style. With people telling me this, no wonder it was difficult for Speedy to keep me on the leash. He wanted me to box, play hit and run… I wanted war and Seddon out in four.

Mum & Dad Marry in Jan '62.

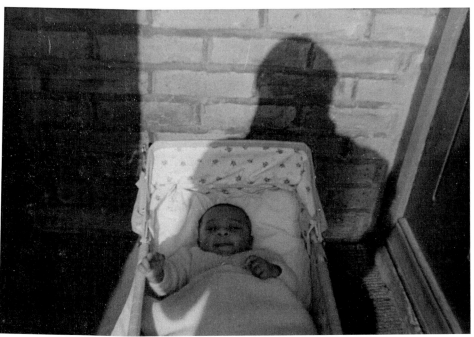

First pictures of me in '62.

As a toddler.

Me & little brother I always protected!

U16 Player of the Year '79 Gravesend League JFC Cuxton.

St Marys how I remember it.

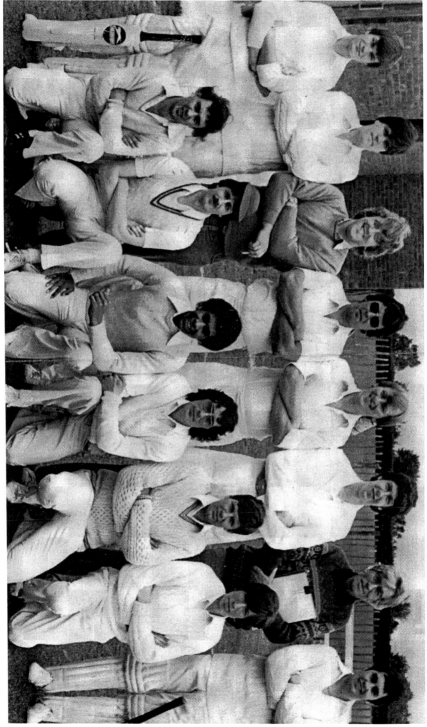

Cozenton Cricket Club 1980.

16 year-old lean mean fighting machine.

Another opponent just about to be KO'd.

Proud with my trainers Fred Ludlow & Harry Shannon.
Been voted 'Best Boxer' by Terry Spinks Kent v Navy.

Spar Wars with 'hard nut' Chris King.

Another one bites the dust.

Paying attention & taking advice from Fred.

Another good win.

Working my way up the rankings as a Pro.

Me & 'Bomber' Graham advertising for Lonsdale.

Me & 'Bomber' Graham advertising for Lonsdale.

One tough battle with Hughes.

Trading with Hughes.

I fought Hughes all the way to the untimely end.

My face says it all after a tremendous battle with KO artist Mickey Hughes.

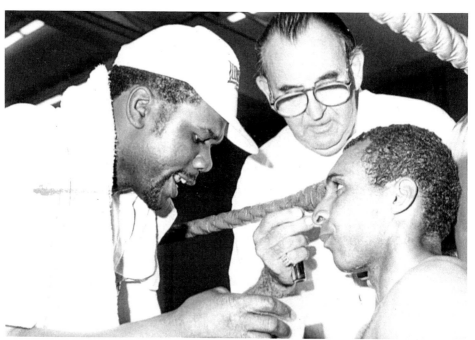

Paying attention to Speedy while Les attends my cut eye.

Great win at the Black Lion Centre.

MIKE BARRETT

Presents

THE SOUTHERN AREA WELTERWEIGHT CHAMPIONSHIP

TREVOR SMITH
(Harlow)

v

IAN JOHN-LEWIS
(Gillingham)

★ *PLUS FULL SUPPORTING PROGRAMME* ★

LATCHMERE LEISURE CENTRE
SHEEPCOTE LANE, BATTERSEA, S.W.11

W.B.C.
Ratings
Enclosed

TUESDAY
24th JANUARY
1989

Souvenir
Programme
£1.50

Programme of Fight of the Year '89.

Was a great battle, with Seddon catching me with more than a few good shots. Knew he would and with my desire to beat him in four rounds, knew I'd have to take a few chances. Overcame his ferocity, trapped him against the ropes where I unloaded a barrage of punches to the head until referee Roy Francis dived in and stopped it in the fourth round. I jumped for joy, soaking up the adulation of the local fans. We congratulated each other and I headed to his corner to shake the hand of his trainer.

'You're never 10 stone 8 lb!' he shouted above the din of the echoing hall.

'Smack on the button, always am!' I replied, briefly thinking of the Roy Callaghan fight, as I turned away to receive more cheers.

Was a hard battle with Seddon, me winning a round sooner than Chris Blake had disposed of him. Paul was everything I expected, took a lot of good shots and delivered a fair few, too. A very tough opponent, I wondered just how good he could have been if he'd prepared 'properly' and fought in the right weight category.

Paul told me in the dressing room that he was getting married next week. I looked at his battered face and as we shook hands I wished him all the best on his upcoming nuptials and said, 'Hope them bruises are gone by then, buddy.'

After the fight, Les sat me down and made the night even better, telling me I was ready to fight for the Southern Area title. It would be against the up and coming, unbeaten Trevor Smith at the Latchmere Leisure Centre Battersea, South West London. Even though Smith came from Harlow, Essex, he'd fought most of his fights in London so this was his back yard. But I wanted this title so much I would've fought him in his kitchen.

In 1989, it was a title worth winning and would be voted 'small hall' fight of the year. A bloody and bruising encounter till the end, the cheering crowd would get more than their money's worth. Years later, Ambrose Mendy, one time Nigel Benn's manager, told me that he thought it was the fight of the year... even better than the Nigel Benn /Michael Watson fight!

Now that's what I call a compliment.

Was so up for the fight because if I won this, a British Title shot would not be far away. First though, was this unbeaten, short, powerful guy who seemed to be built like a V from his shoulders to his toes. He had a face the shape of a photo fit and a square chin made of granite. This would not be easy… for either of us.

As preparation for Trevor, Speedy got some good amateurs in for me to spar with. One of these sparring partners was really trying to rough me up, which is what Speedy had asked him to do. I mistook it for him trying to prove something and when he caught and really hurt me, I delivered some bone crunching shots and basically beat him up. Speedy wasn't happy, sucking his teeth and cussing, telling me he'd wanted me to box my sparring partner into submission, not get into a war. He felt I'd need to and should use my boxing skills to beat Trevor Smith. Speedy must have said this many times to me during my career and it was only years later I realised what it was he wanted from me. While I was a boxer, the message just never got across. Don't know why; just didn't.

On fight night, the atmosphere was electric and although on Trevor's home ground, I had great support from the Medway towns. They nearly took the roof off the place when my name was announced. It sounded more like I was the home fighter. May have been his back yard, but didn't sound or feel like it.

Standing in the corner I thought, *'Win this one and the British Championship belt is in reach.'*

The announcements made, Speedy gave me the usual talk but I was already in fight mode so couldn't hear him. I was totally focussed on my opponent and just wanted to get on with it. Can remember feeling like I was moving really well as I went to the middle of the ring to hear the referee's instructions.

Went back to the corner and Speedy wanted me to tap his hands but I was so psyched up, just wanted him out the way.

The bell sounded: war broke out. We come out blazing and I used my height advantage to keep away from the big right handers Trevor loved to throw. Another shot he was very good at was short, sharp, counter punches. Took me about ten seconds to realise this wouldn't go the distance. Round one was a real trade off, trying to soften each other up with will sapping punches.

Once back in my corner, Speedy told me to keep boxing, but just as Speedy feared, and as much as I tried not to lose discipline, I was allowing Trevor to pull me into a brawl; a real pier 6 type tear up. Trouble was, I was enjoying it, and so were the crowd who were on their feet, screaming us on, in a contest of their own, seeing who could chant the loudest for their boxer. They appreciated the show we were putting on and expended a lot of energy showing it!

Round three: Every time I landed what I thought was a good shot, Trevor countered with a punch that was equal. We knew each other well by now and it's time to up the stakes. He hurt me which was a mistake for both of us as now I was willing to brawl and go toe to toe. I caught him a peach of a shot, that made his legs rubberise and forced him to hang on to me. It felt like he was starting to flag and he held on to me to catch his breath. Knew I could go the distance: was superbly fit. Knew I had to be, against unbeaten Smith.

End of round three; we patted each other, a sign of respect in the middle of battle. We knew we were giving the crowd a treat and in that short glove touch we let each other know it. The fight would have to continue that way, the crowds' excitement was dictating the pace and I was willingly being swept along. Just talking about it now sends the hairs on the back of my neck upright.

Round four: traded blows, big shuddering, teeth rattling punches. He could bang all right and hit me high on the cheek, my legs folded up like they were spring loaded. I hit the floor with my knees but bounced straight back up as if I were Zebedee! The referee waved us to fight on immediately. No eight count in those days – if you were on your feet, you fought. Looking back on the fight, I should have taken an eight count on one knee, but got up quickly, part from shock at going down, part from pride. No boxer likes the view from the canvas, an embarrassing position to be in. Also by getting up so quickly, I was sending him a message that his punch didn't hurt me.

Course it hurt, they all bloody hurt!

Back on my feet, knew I was dazed and began working on trying to let that fog clear from my head. Had to be sensible for a while, keep the beast at arm's length, box a bit, let the lights come back on. It worked and soon I got back into it and upped the pace.

End of round four; we pat each other again.

In the corner, Speedy Mitchell asks me, in his normal chilled way, if I am alright.

'Yeah, fine!' I answered.

Les just said, in a really calm way, 'Now go out there and give it to him.'

Couldn't wait for the bell to go, to carry on; was so hyped I didn't need the minute's rest between rounds. Mind's clear now, fog's gone. Came off the stool with menace, was on top and punching him with very little return. Caught him a goodun! Big right uppercut and down he goes in front of Harry Holland, his corner man. I can taste victory and want him to stay down for 11, or get up in 2. He does neither as Harry yells for him to stay down, take a breather and signals him to get up at the count of eight. Trevor does as he's told and when he rises, I rush in to finish off the still dangerous, wounded fighter. I get a bit reckless as we exchange a few shots and bang! Am now looking at the ceiling and don't like the view.

Again I drag myself to my feet too quickly; dazed, fragile and pissed right off at being caught. I'm wounded now and he's after me, he's forgotten he's been down and comes to finish me off. I hold on to him. We're both tired and I tell myself if Smith's going to beat me, he's going to have to knock me out. Some strength comes back to me, he's misses with his punches and I deliver a flurry to his head. I throw, duck, weave and he catches me as the bell sounds and my backside meets with the canvas again. Get straight back up. The crowd think it's all over: it's not. The referee sends me to the wrong corner while Trevor is prematurely celebrating a win. His corner men scream at him to get back to them.

The minute's rest is needed by us both and as the bell is rung for round six, the referee signals us to stay in our corner as his pen doesn't work. I'm so grateful for those few extra seconds that help my head clear just that little bit more.

Les pours water over my head and says, 'You okay son?'

I nod.

Round six: we start to box because we're both exhausted. We hold and waltz but then we start again, increasing the pace. I am still there, in his face, his punches, not as strong as they were, still hurting, but not as much. He's no longer the fighter I first got in the ring with… but neither am I. This is going to be whoever wants it most.

'Keep going forward!' I tell myself, 'keep throwing punches and keep your chin tucked up John L.'

Bell sounds for the end of six.

It's not till after the fight I am told by someone next to Trevor's corner, that when Trevor flops on his stool, he tells them he doesn't want to go back out. If that was the case then this is where a good corner man earns his keep. Harry Holland is a great corner man all right, knows his fighter and knows how to get the best out of Trevor. It was not a comforting arm he put round Trevor's shoulder, but a good jolt of the gloves, a side order of expletives and tells Trevor to sort himself out! Seconds out, is shouted by the timekeeper and with what Trevor had experienced from Harry, he'd rather come out to the middle of the ring and face me.

Round seven: my heart tells my head I may have been down three times but can win this. Am in the zone; my head believes I can win, my fists agree and sort out some beautiful shots early in the round. It is fitness and the desire for a title that got me to my feet three times. A little voice in my head tells me, *'Keep going, keep going, head's cleared, you've got a chance, box a bit, use your range, counter. In and out.'*

We have the utmost respect for each other. Have both seen the canvas up close and know that one big shot from either of us can win it.

At the end of the seventh I gave him a beautifully crafted, one-two, to his face, just in time for him to go back to his corner and think about it. Always nice to do that just before the end of the round, can really make an opponent think and get inside his head; make him doubt himself, make him want to stay on his stool.

I get back to my corner and Speedy says, 'That round was brilliant… now just keep boxing like that for the next few rounds… box, Ian, box!'

Round eight: my strength's back; head's completely clear. I forget the advice Speedy gave me and take it to Trevor again. He catches me with two good punches within seconds of each other. He can sense the end. Still I go forward, thinking, *'Keep calm and take your chances.'*

Now trading punches and he catches me again with a beaut. I go down and get up too quick and within seconds am down again before I know it. Get to my feet yet again; the legs are a bit Bambi and the referee says he's seen enough. I lie to him, tell him I'm okay. I'm not and know it and more importantly, so does the referee. Trevor rightly celebrates a great win.

Trevor was a ferocious puncher and the only one who ever stopped me, amateur or professional, by sheer punching power. He was only the second boxer ever to put me to the canvas. After that fight, I couldn't work for three days… Trevor couldn't work for a week.

Trevor said at the end of the fight, that Ian John-Lewis deserves to be champion as well and Ian John-Lewis is one of the best welterweights in the country. Trevor added that I took his left hook that rocks middleweights and just kept coming back for more.

Am proud to have been part of that fight. Thanks Trevor.

Under New Management

After the tear up that was the Southern Area title fight, Les sat me down and told me I needed a manager. Far as I was concerned Les was my manager, and I told him so. He liked my loyalty, which he said was rare in life, but said the Southern Area title fight was about as far as I could go with the setup we had. Les had now let his manager's licence lapse and didn't have the contacts he felt I'd need to progress.

'If you want to realise your full potential and get that title, you'll need a full time manager, current, with contacts, a manager on the way up who can take you with them… like Frank Maloney.'

Reading between the lines, I guessed Les had already spoken to Frank, who apparently would be very happy to get another title challenger in his ever increasing stable. It was an exciting prospect for me as we all knew Frank was climbing and building.

First met Frank a few years earlier in 86/87 when he was matchmaking small hall fights. He was at the Thomas A Becket pub, South East London, developing an eye for fighters who might have that little something extra that would take them to championship level. Wouldn't be too much longer before he'd be making a name for himself and managing some very good prospects.

I was training at the time in the popular Lonsdale gym in Carnaby Street, and had the time slot before the brilliant Michael Watson and his team. They'd have the gym to themselves in preparation for the upcoming blockbuster with Nigel Benn, which would be voted fight of the year. Les suggested I take a look at the Henry Cooper gym. Took his advice; went there with my good mate, Mark Pellett and liked the setup.

As usual, Les was there to supervise training as Speedy, a 'chippie' by trade and a grafter, couldn't always make Saturday morning because of work. Like me, he had to earn most of his money away from boxing.

Frank was present and after training I had a chat with him which developed into a full discussion about a possible new setup and plan for me. It was important for me to have Speedy on board and Les in my corner. Frank told me that he had no problem with Speedy still training me but wanted me to come up to London to spar more, as he felt it was the part of my game that I was lacking in.

At this time I was ranked number one in the Southern Area and the British Boxing Board had ordered a re-match between Trevor Smith and me. This was great because, plain and simple, Trevor had beaten me up and I wanted revenge. Harry Holland, Trevor's manager, was more than keen, along with everybody associated with the two camps. Later, I would wonder if the only person who didn't want the re-match was Trevor.

We knew the fight would generate interest and ticket sales because of the right royal tear up of the first one. Although I was never in boxing for the money, I'd be more than happy to take my share, avenge the loss and get a title of note. But Frank had other ideas, which proved beyond any shadow of a doubt that he rated me, was interested in my development, believed I had a future, and had thought about and planned for it.

'Ian,' he said, 'that was a gruelling fight you had with Smith. Took a hell of lot out of you. I don't think it's wise to jump straight back in with him just yet.'

'But the Boxing Board have ordered a re-match and I'm itching to get back in the ring with him, Frank!' I replied.

'I'd ease you back in with a few wins. Then we'd go after Smith,' reasoned Frank.

Still wasn't happy with what I was hearing, simply because I was bursting to get even, which is never the best reason to take a fight on.

Frank was happy for me to talk things over with Les, which was good for me. Les was such an honest, loyal guy, which is rare in any walk of life, not just in boxing. Mickey Duff once said if you want loyalty, best buy a dog! Knew I was lucky to have Les, he was a straight talker and what you saw with him was what you got. Now most managers wouldn't have allowed that setup, but Frank had learnt a lot from Les when he was a young matchmaker and didn't mind at all. Les would remain my mentor throughout my career.

Later, I had a chat with Les, who agreed with Frank about Trevor Smith. So I took the advice and later that day wrote a letter to the Boxing Board asking to be withdrawn from my mandatory position. Went to Speedy, all excited, told him about the meeting and discussed the possible new setup. Speedy was fine with it until he heard the part about me sparring more as he had his own ideas about my development and more sparring wasn't part of it.

'All this sparring... leaves your skill in training! YOU, (he really emphasised the 'You') will be warring all the time... will burn you out... it's what happens to fighters that do too much sparring!'

Speedy knew there were only so many big punches a fighter could take before the chin turns to straw. Again, told me I was prone to getting into wars, even in training. Knew what Speedy meant, they're called gym wars and I'd been willingly involved in plenty of them as an amateur.

One I remembered was a favour I did for Gary Davidson at the Thomas A Becket one Sunday morning. His fighter, Martin Smith, a 6 feet tall, long armed, black kid from Tottenham, was fighting Frank Warren's prospect, former 1986 Commonwealth Bronze Medallist, Damien Denny. Gary asked me if I could give Martin a few rounds of sparring. Told Gary I'd be glad to.

In my corner were Mark Pellett and of course, as always, Les. Martin and I were introduced, the bell sounded and I go out thinking we're going to have a light spar; a move around as we call it in the trade. I was wrong and realised it when he started knocking me all over the place, which caused much delight for his mates standing at ringside. The round ended and when I got back to my corner, Les calmly said in my ear, 'You've got to fight back, Ian. He's beating you up in there.'

'I thought it was just going to be a move around, Les,' I replied.

'Well it obviously isn't, so go out and give it to him… and shut his mates up as well! They're doing my head in! ' he said firmly.

With that I came out a different animal, steaming right into Martin, catching him by surprise. He'd had an easy first round but would now know he was in a fight when I banged in lefts, rights, hooks, uppercuts and the so-called 'move around' turned into a right old rumble. After four hard rounds of sparring, I got the respect of Martin and his now much quieter mates. Gary commented, 'Ian, thank you so much for that; my guy needed a hard session. Doesn't normally get hit much and certainly not like that. I tell you what though, Ian: your offence is your defence. Remember that.'

So I knew what Speedy meant, acknowledged his concern about spar wars and took what he said on board – had to, or was going to have a very short career. I kept my sparring at the 'Cooper' to just Saturday mornings and one day in the week. My other sessions would be with Speedy in Strood.

With Frank now in charge I fought and 'lost' to Andy Furlong, which was a shock. It was back at the Latchmere Leisure Centre and another big crowd came up from Medway to roar me on. It was all going to plan; first round, boxing nicely working out Furlong's awkward southpaw stance. Then I threw a straight right bang on his chin which sent him tumbling to the canvas. When he got up, instead of jumping on him like the fans from Kent were demanding, I let him off the hook, because I remembered what happened in the Smith fight when I rushed in to finish him off and found myself on the deck.

In round three, with me still dominating, we got into a clinch and Furlong, while in close, deliberately head butted me. It split my right eye and I complained bitterly to Mike Jacobs, the referee, but because he didn't see it, just shouted, 'Box on!'

Knew it wasn't good when I could feel warm blood run down my face. I chased Furlong to try to finish it quick. It finished quick all right but not the way I wanted it. In my eagerness I walked onto his left hand which dropped me for a split-second. Got straight up, but with blood streaming down my face, the referee stopped it. I sank to my knees with disappointment and could hear the crowd booing loudly. My work mate Rob Elvin told me afterwards that a couple of my more troublesome mates were going to start a riot by throwing some chairs into the ring. Thankfully Rob managed to talk them out of it, saying, 'Come on guys… think of Louie… he wouldn't like that!'

He was right, I wouldn't.

Two losses on the bounce, never good for a boxer. Frank made it clear to me when he said, 'We really have to get you re-established. This is a big setback; need to get a few wins under your belt.'

This was why I needed someone like Frank; he could make the right contests and get my rating back up. To renew my confidence, he laid a plan out in front of me saying that he felt I had what it took to be a British Champion and if that were achieved, then we would be looking at the Commonwealth title. What a motivator, made you believe in yourself, could access and destroy the doubt in your mind. Obviously destined for greater things, he got his big break when he managed to sign an Olympic Champion, under the noses of the top promoters/managers, by the name of Lennox Lewis.

Got back to winning ways, with a hard-fought, points victory over the very tough, Ray Taylor. Gave him everything I had, as was so determined not to lose three on the spin. I tried my best to stop him inside the distance and could hear him groaning, moaning and wincing when my big shots crashed into him. But this short, squat, powerful guy took it all and I nearly punched myself out on him after eight, very hard, rounds.

Next came my easiest professional win; a first round stoppage against the very game Chris Haydon. He was a tall boxer but I was beating him to the jab, keeping Chris on the back foot. As I started to open up with right handers, I caught him with a cracking left hook which opened up his right eyebrow. I sensed the end, poured on the pressure as my faithful fans demanded, and the referee stopped it.

My confidence was returning and I was feeling good again. Next fight was another quick, first round victory, over my first overseas opponent from Mexico. After the fight, Frank told me that one more victory and we could talk eliminators and titles again.

By now Frank had brought in former World Flyweight Champion, Charlie Magri to train his stable. Again, Frank mentioned the need for more sparring under the watchful eye of Magri. Said I needed to discuss this with Speedy and would also need to speak to Les.

Les agreed with Frank saying I needed to change what I did in training to get to the next level. I knew it too, no question, and had taken on board what Speedy had said about the sparring – learn from the sparring; don't burn out because of it.

Speedy wanted to continue the way we were, just me, Frank and Speedy. He was never going to be comfortable with the new setup; not having full control regarding training. Understood where he was coming from and how he felt but said I needed to change some things in training.

Told Speedy that Charlie Magri would be my trainer from now on, which was tough to say to a guy I trusted and who had taken me into the pro ranks. Obviously not happy, Speedy said I was wrong, but added that I had to do what I thought was best for me and wished me luck. We shook hands and he was very gracious about our parting of the ways. He had class.

Charlie Magri was a great coach, a really nice guy, and from the start was just one of the boys; down to earth and modest. I liked and respected that. You'd never have guessed he'd been a former World Champion. He showed me new moves, did different things and yes, the sparring had gone up a few levels, but I remembered what Speedy had said and avoided wars… when possible.

Next fight, another Mexican, and what a tough one. Didn't come to lie down easily. At the weigh-in, I looked at him, *'No problem,'* I thought. Again, got it wrong. Later that evening, in the ring, I looked across at him and thought, *'Is that the same guy I saw at lunch time?'*

He was massive. Looked like he had been pumped up.

Now in boxing we all know what a good Mexican likes… a bloody good ruck! I out-boxed him for a couple of minutes but allowed him to lure me into a punch up. As Speedy had done before, Charlie screamed at me to box, but the warrior in me came out. By round two it was all over, with me pounding my opponent on the ropes, and the referee jumping in to save him from further punishment.

I think the crowd got to me that night, because I wasn't the only Medway fighter on the bill. My former St Mary's gym mate, Johnny Armour, ABA Flyweight Champion of that year (1990), made his professional debut and had brought the whole of Chatham up to roar him on, and these fans from the other side of the river kindly threw cheers and chants my way.

Four straight wins. Frank tells me it's the big bill time and what a bill it was, with the headliner being Lennox Lewis who was fighting for his first professional title, the European Heavyweight Championship against the Champion, the rugged Gypsy Frenchman, Jean Chanet.

I'd seen a lot of Lennox when he was training at the Henry Cooper gym. He'd told me how he loved sparring, how important it was to boxers to spar often and cleverly. When in the ring, you could see his

Olympic class; he moved silently, smoothly and quickly for such a big guy.

Les said to me, 'You're looking at the next Heavyweight Champion of the World.'

'Really?' I replied.

'I'd put money on it,' Les said smiling.

Wish I had, but wasn't a gambler.

Speedy's words were soon to come back to me when I was in the gym, warming up, doing a bit of shadow boxing. In walked the Lennox Lewis clan. His head trainer, the American, the late John Davenport, came over and asked me, smiling, 'Can we have some work?' which from an American means sparring.

'Who with?' I asked.

'This guy.' he replied, pointing at this big American lump who was a Light Heavyweight.

'Naaaah… He's too big for me, I'm only a Welterweight!' I said.

'It's just a move around… light stuff… you know,' he drawled through a convincing smile.

Thinking about what Lennox had told me about sparring and the fact that Davenport said it was just a move around, I said, 'Okay.'

Well, let's just say I did lot of moving around; moving around trying to stop this big lump from taking my head off. It was only thanks to my speed and fighting spirit that I managed to survive the three rounds they required. Longest nine minutes of my life!

When the smiling trainer asked for another three rounds, I just told him to, 'Poke it! He's just too damned big!!!'

Could almost hear Speedy saying, 'I told you you'd be warring all the time!'

My opponent on this big bill was Chris Blake, the former Southern Area Light Welterweight Champion and British Title contender. He'd decided to come up a division and when boxers do that, it is sometimes said that they won't be as strong. The people who say this are also sometimes wrong and definitely were in Blake's case.

My partner Julie was now pregnant and although we knew the due date for our daughter was just a few days after the scheduled contest with Blake, I agreed to the fight. Julie was in full support knowing that this was a good step up for me to be on such a show.

The week before the fight, Julie developed pre-eclampsia and was taken into hospital for observation as it is a potentially dangerous condition. It was the only time I ever thought about pulling out of a show, but Julie told me not to as she was in hospital and there was nothing I could do. She then added, 'And anyway, you're always an arse this close to a fight.'

Despite Julie's condition and my worrying, the preparation had gone well and as always, the nearer I got to the fight, the more of an arse I became. My head was not a happy place to be living in but in the place needed to get my gloves on and get into the ring. Training was going really well and I used the punch bag to release the stress.

I would pop into hospital after training, making sure Julie was okay and keep her company. The evening before the fight I promised I'd make her proud by coming back a winner. As I kissed her goodbye, she whispered, 'Good luck, I know you can do it.'

She smiled, but I could see in her eyes how nervous she was. There was I, about to get into a ring and Julie, with very high blood pressure, about to give birth. I felt very nervous too but consoled myself that she was in the right place if anything were to go wrong. Not the best preparation.

This was a big fight for me, one step closer to a British Title shot. Blake knew it too as he was rated just a few places behind me. The stakes were high; there would be blood and effort over the canvas by the end of this fight.

The show was being aired all over the UK and around Europe, by the new technology of Satellite. Was so pumped up on fight night I was fit to explode; certainly in the right mood for a fight.

That night I was fourth on the bill. This meant there could be as many as thirty rounds before I went on: or just three. As we sat in the dressing room thinking that we had plenty of time, Charlie Magri reminded me of how hard I've worked and what it means to me to win. I got changed and started to limber up, when the ring whip came in and shouted, 'Ian! You're on in five.'

'What? I'm not even bandaged up yet!!'

'The adverts are on, you need to hurry up. First three bouts ended quickly.'

Charlie quickly wrapped my hands. I knew it was the same for Blake but I always liked a good warm up before I got in the ring. I preferred to be hot, sweating and psyched, but when I looked at myself in the mirror there wasn't even a bead of sweat on me. Before I knew it I was being rushed to the ring.

The bell signalled the start and Blake steamed into me. He was immensely strong, had a very good punch and was trying to rough me up. At the end of the round, Magri said, 'Box him, Ian, box him … you're letting him bully you around!'

'I'm not warmed up yet, Charlie,' I replied, but felt I was getting there.

The next couple of rounds, we traded on even terms, punching lumps out of each other with the crowd and commentators loving it. Because the first three fights had all ended in the first round, Blake and I had to live up to the hopes of the TV people by producing fireworks. In those first couple of rounds, Blake really surprised me by just how strong he was, but the pace was getting to him more than it was me. In close, when we traded hooks and uppercuts, I could hear him huffing and puffing, but me; I was now getting into full flow and was growing in confidence.

At the end of round three, when I came back to the corner, Magri was pleased that I was now executing the plan we discussed before the fight. Box, fight, box, was the plan and the fight was starting to go my way. Felt it was just a matter of time before I would wear Blake down and stop him.

Near the end of the fourth round (a round I was winning) what changed the fight wasn't a punch but a clash of heads that left me with a cut – no, a wound to my forehead. As soon as my cuts man, Mick 'the rub' saw it up close, he pulled a face, the type of face that says, *'What the fuck do you expect me to do with that?'*

He wagged his head, told me the fight was over. Another bloody loss from a cut! Sitting on that stool, I could've cried. I pictured Julie in hospital and remembered what I'd told her. I was so upset. Roy Francis, the referee, came over to me, rubbed my head and said, 'Any consolation, Ian, had you both level.'

It was nice of him to say it, but it was no consolation. I had so many people watching the fight on Sky Sports that I was devastated. Wanted to dedicate the win to my baby and Julie, but instead had to go the hospital and tell Julie I'd lost.

The due date was a good guess, but wrong. Babies arrive when they're ready and since her birth, she always has. Our daughter Kelcie (named after the 1988 American Olympian, Kelcie Banks) was born on the 4th of November, and as it was also Julie's birthday, we sang happy birthday. The disappointment of the loss disappeared as I held this beautiful, healthy, baby girl. A stunner from minute one, day one.

The exposure on 'Sky' really raised my profile and it was also my biggest purse to date, which enabled us to get what we needed for our new arrival. Christmas was amazing.

Because Chris Blake won the fight, he was lined up to fight Mickey Hughes in an Eliminator for the British Welterweight title held by Kirkland Laing. Kirkland was now 36 and getting on and all of us young lions started to think we may be able to give the 'Gifted One' a fight. This would be a re-match: Hughes having stopped Blake in five rounds, two years earlier at Wembley. I was ringside that night, keeping a watchful eye, knowing one day I could be facing these guys. I then saw Mickey again at York Hall, Bethnal Green, where he managed to spark Gary Jacobs in a fight he was losing. The knockout punch he delivered was a beaut and it led me to thinking that if I were ever to get in the ring with him, then I'd avoid that knockout punch at all costs.

Fortunately for me and unfortunately for Blake, he took a tough assignment abroad and lost, so I was given the opportunity to fight Mickey Hughes as Blake had only beaten me by a cut.

When Frank rang and gave me the news – an eliminator for the British title and the biggest purse of my career, I was really excited but also a bit apprehensive. The fight, after all, was against the knock out specialist Micky Hughes. Frank reassured me by saying my speed and boxing skills would nullify Hughes' biggest asset – his awesome punch.

Felt better after hearing that and believed it, until I talked to Les about the 'good news'.

'Don't take the fight, Ian,' he said.

'Why's that, Les?' I said surprised.

'Because I think Mickey will knock you spark out Ian; that's why son.'

I really respected what Les told me and admired him for telling me straight.

'I know he's a big puncher but he's slow and one paced. Everyone thinks I'm going to steam into Hughes and come a cropper. I know I have to put my boxing head on and out-box him. I'm up for it.'

This was the first and only time I'd gone against Les's advice.

No one needed to tell me not to get in a war with the big punching Hughes. He had sparked Jacobs and I knew how good Jacobs was, having sparred with him for five days. Boy, did I earn my money that week. It worked out about a pound a bruise!

Before the fight with Hughes, I would watch their match on the video continuously. The class and power of the pair of them was awesome. I knew I had to be careful.

In that Hughes fight, my concentration, movement and discipline for nine rounds had confused Mickey, and he didn't get to knock me out – the ref did. Not going the distance with him hurt me more than losing. Yes, there was one more round to go, but the way I was boxing and the way he wasn't seeing; don't think that knockout was coming.

When the fight with Hughes ended, Les told me again to become a referee. Think he knew, as I did, that I should quit, knowing that a loss in those circumstances can be more damaging than a knockout blow. Although something had gone from me after that fight, boxing is highly addictive and is hard to quit. Soon you miss the applause, the stress and adrenaline mix, the training, that taste of metallic blood when you train really hard, the combination punches that come off and rock an opponent, that left hook that connects sweetly and you know it's over before your opponent does as he folds, joint by joint to the canvas. Thinking about glory days just doesn't cut it like being in the ring, which is probably why boxers come back to try again, convincing an aging body and slowing reflexes that it's young again – that it has one more good fight left in it.

Most of the time, it don't.

Quitting, comebacks or continuing on is hard in boxing. What separates boxing from other sports, though, is that there's no hiding place in the ring. Footballers will go quiet for a few minutes and hide behind opponents so they can't receive the ball, cyclists slip stream, runners go to the front to slow the pace or tuck in behind someone to make them do the hard work. Boxing is one on one, gladiatorial, and if you're not up to it... you'll be found out quickly and painfully.

That journey home from York Hall after the Hughes fight seemed long; always does in defeat. When you win, your body hurts but not as much as when you lose. Happy hormones must contain painkiller. The pain is even worse when you, and everyone connected with you, feels you were cheated. Believe me; I felt every bump in the road on that journey home, down the A2 to Gillingham in Kent. So much so, that I wondered if the car had any bloody suspension.

Once home was met by Julie's Dad, Archie Crane, the 'one armed bandit' as he was known locally. He'd lost the use of it in a car crash when returning home from court having been acquitted for a robbery he'd taken part in. Archie, with his disabled right arm tucked into his waistband, was really disappointed for me in the only way he could show it – 'eff this, eff that', but I knew what he meant and knew he meant well. Looked at him and smiled thinking how much I'd been accepted by him; far from the time when I had to secretly meet Julie at the corner of her street, just a couple of years before.

Julie had been a good sprinter, had mixed with black people early on and had friends from all backgrounds. They were accepted by Archie and were welcome into the house but Archie was 'old school', and didn't think it was right for Julie to bring 'one' home as a boyfriend. He'd brought Julie up to be independently minded so she made her own mind up on that one, telling him to get used to it or she'd be moving out! He was overprotective of his daughter as many of us can be.

When I finally met him, he was a watered down version of the violent, no-nonsense hard man, with a nasty reputation. Age, injuries and two 'near-fatal' car crashes, where he was pronounced dead at the scene of both, had taken their toll. Following one of the accidents, where he lost the use of his arm, he'd gone into a coma and Julie was told that even if he survived, Archie would be almost brain dead. He came back from the brink a few weeks later and continued living. Archie had so many stitches around his neck; it looked like they'd sewn his head back on!

Listening to the stories of him in his younger days, you wouldn't have wanted to make an enemy of him. On one occasion, Archie was told by one of Julie's school friends that she was being interfered with on her paper round by one of her customers. He went to the pervert's house and dealt with him, severely. The man was not seen in the area again. Archie was involved in anything crooked, was also a post office robber and had no conscience about it; justified it by saying that they were part of a big company who could get the money back on the insurance. Any big firms would be looted but he would never ever steal from a house or person.

'I was a professional,' he would always say to me with a smile.

In the power cuts of the 70's he'd have the elderly neighbours in for tea, making sure that none of them froze to death. Many times, Julie would come in from school to find 'Mad Stan', a well-known homeless guy from Gillingham, eating a dinner that Archie had made. There were two sides to this guy and it was a wise move to keep on the right side of him.

My first meeting with Archie was when I brought Julie home from a food shopping trip. She was unloading the car and taking the bags up the stairs to the flat they lived in. I stayed in the car, not feeling welcome enough to enter the place even if it was only to deliver his food.

'Where is he?' Archie asked Julie.

'Sitting in his car,' she answered.

'As he appears to be sticking around, you better get 'im in 'ere.'

On entering his flat he took one look at me and said, 'If he's half caste... I'll eat my fucking hat!'

Which was a strange thing to say – 'cos he didn't have one.

Soon after, Julie moved into my place and invited him over for the evening. I picked him up in my car and after a few minutes he lit up a cigarette. 'Can't do that in here mate,' I told him. He looked at me strangely and replied with a challenge, not that well-disguised, in his voice,

''Errrr yeah, I can.'

'Said you can't... I am not breathing in that shit... I'm a keep fit guy and a professional boxer!'

'You better let me out then, son.'

So I pulled over, leant over him to open the door, he got out and I drove off. A hundred yards down the road I thought of what Julie would say when turning up at our house without her Dad. Drove round the block to find him puffing on his cigarette, wound the window down and said, 'Shall we start again?'

'Good idea son,' he answered, dropping his half-finished cigarette to the floor and stepping on it as he walked to the car.

Later when I told Julie what had happened, she said he was testing me and that I'd done the right thing. Archie liked someone to stand up for himself and from that day he accepted me, thinking I'd take good care of his daughter. He knew how to take care of women: rumour has it he was married five times!

Although feeling beaten and sore about the result of the Mickey Hughes fight, the thought of seeing Kelcie, all tucked up and safe in her crib, lifted me. Peeked in so as not to disturb my beautiful daughter and consoled myself further by thinking I had just earned £6,000 for my family which would help us get on with the jobs that needed doing round our house.

£6,000 was a lot of money in those days and we used it wisely. Whenever I got any prize money, always tried to make it work for me. Les advised me early about looking after these lump sums and told me that I'd never know when my career was going to end, so never factor it in as part of my income. If I were to rely on it I might find myself boxing on when I could no longer cut it in the ring, and that, he said, is when the real damage in boxing can be done. Can end up being someone people want to fight because you're on your way down and may be considered a good trial horse for an up and coming boxer.

Following the fight, local radio and newspaper interviews were requested from me. It seemed everyone who had seen it, heard it or were connected to the fight thought I was winning, except the most important one, the ref. His word was final, his decision unchangeable. It made me think that if I was going to be a referee someday, then I'd better be the best I can be.

It was some weeks later that I ran into Mickey Hughes. I was working security at the Chris Eubank versus Dan Sherry fight in Brighton. Mickey and I acknowledged each other and he came over, shook my hand and kindly said,

'I totally underestimated you. Never realised how good you were… respect to you and good luck in your career.'

I noted that his eye was still bloodshot from our encounter. My 'cut', that caused the fight to be stopped, was fully healed.

The Wheels Come Off

Frank was busy signing boxers and building a bit of a stable. Johnny Armour, another boxer from St Mary's, was destined for great things and received many offers from people who wanted to manage him. Johnny was a very talented guy who went on to be a world champion and had three notable wars with Francis Ampofo from Bethnal Green.

Johnny Armour senior asked me how things were going with Frank, the usual questions from a protective Dad wanting to make sure he signs his son with a reputable manager. I was very happy under Frank's guidance and told Johnny so: let him know what he'd done and the plan he'd made for me. I trusted Frank; they trusted me. Johnny signed with him and went on to become a world champion. It's as easy as that... If only!

With the work at my day job (at ICEL) being rationed and a family to take care of, I had to find more. This also came via Frank, who knew someone in the security game who provided guys for pubs and clubs in and around London. So door work it was to be, at The Globe in Bow Street, Covent Garden. To make up the shortfall of work at ICEL I'd have to work three nights a week: Thursday, Friday and Saturday. Not ideal for a family man in full training, but it was work and work means money.

Peter and Carol were the managers of the pub and they didn't want a huge, scary looking 'bouncer' type on the door of their establishment, as it was a nice, friendly pub with clientele from the city to match. About a minute after us meeting they told me I had a job with them. They used to spoil me, insisting that they made me dinner when I should be working, and told me to pop inside to warm up whenever I needed. Peter and Carol treated me well and were lovely people, as were their customers. Bow Street Police station was just a few yards up the road and quite a few of the officers used to pop in for a pint. I got on well with them to the point that on several occasions they said they'd assist me if anything kicked off. So for the 18 months that I worked there, I had very little trouble to sort out. It was a happy pub and an easy place for me to earn money.

Maloney and his energy were infectious. He was driven, determined to get the best for and out of his boxers. You couldn't help but get swept up in his ambition and passion. After my massive effort against Hughes, I told Frank that I only wanted to fight for titles. Frank said he would deliver this on his next big promotion and organised the long awaited re-match against Trevor Smith. Well, it was long awaited by me. It was going to take place at a hall... The Albert Hall.

My ambition to fight in the big halls was going to be realised, as big halls don't come that much larger or grander than The Albert. I thought of the classic battles waged there over the years, so was really up for the fight, training even harder for this one with my new coach Gary Nickels. Gary and I had bonded well after our first fight together against Hughes; our tactics had been spot on and we planned to do the same against Trevor Smith.

Boiling the weight off was no problem. I was super disciplined and thought about Trevor Smith any time I felt a temptation or weakness come my way. My only problem was I couldn't get in the ring soon enough to fight. I'd felt ready to fight Trevor ten minutes after he beat me, so was more irritable than usual. It would be down to Gary and Frank to make sure I didn't burn out before the contest.

With fight night nearing it was time for me to ditch the roadwork. Long runs are great for burning off the fat when trying to make the weight, but if you run slow, you move slow. Move like that in the ring, you might as well put an x on your chin. So it was sprints time, get those fast twitch fibres firing to their maximum. They put spring in your step, making you that micro second quicker, allowing you to be fast on your feet and hard to hit.

The sprinting I did in an alley, Paget Row, at the back of the garden of our house. I'd begin with a jog and stretch, gradually increasing the pace of the 60 metre sprints until I was warm enough to run flat out. Didn't want to risk a hamstring tear so close to the fight.

The early morning would become light as I jogged down the unlit alley. I would reach the kerb, turn 180 degrees quickly, and sprint as fast as I could to the other end, dodging dog shit, broken glass and the neighbour's terrified cat. One of these mornings, third run in, on leaving the alley and reaching the edge of the pavement, my face changes from one of recovery to one of preparing for business. Just as I am turning away to run, I spy a police officer. For a split second we look at each other and that was it, I was off like lightning, pumping my arms for all I was worth! As I ran I thought, *'Wonder if that copper's chasing me?'*

Even though running flat out, the thought of it made me smile. Sure enough, when I finished sprinting and rolled to a stop, I turned to find he was chasing me. His face was a picture of shock and surprise as I jogged back towards him, smiling. 'Morning Officer… fight's in a couple of weeks… just doing my speed work,' I said.

He bent forward, placed his hands on his knees, and between heavy breaths gasped, 'Oh Fuck!'

Jogged past him to the end of the alley and ran another three sprints before going back to shower and heading out to work.

The sparring went very well as I had an edge in the ring and hurt my sparring partners more than I normally would've. In my mind every one of them was Trevor Smith and they all stood in the way of me gaining a belt, revenge, and a title of note. I looked forward to another war, but this time a war dictated by me. In the first fight I fought Trevor at his own game, gave a great account of myself and nearly beat him. Gary was training me to box, fight, box, but I was to choose when, unlike the first fight where I'd let Trevor pull me into trading blows. That was a big mistake to make when in the ring with such a prolific puncher.

In those days, boxers would also sell tickets to their own shows; some still do. I used to carry quite a few on me to sell to people from my area. Sold a lot of tickets for the rematch, with people from Strood, Gillingham, Chatham and 'The Globe' in London buying them. They sold quickly because people remembered the brutality of the first fight and knew this was going to be more of the same.

Walking around with hundreds of pounds of ticket money in my pocket made me a bit uneasy and I was always pleased to get rid of the money to the person who'd be responsible for it. My support would be good, loud and I was looking forward to hearing them chant, 'Louie, Louie!' as they did when they came to watch. When out doing road work I could hear that crowd chanting in my head. It passed more than a few minutes of running; always made my speed increase on those cold, dark mornings when most sane people were still asleep.

The venue, The Albert Hall, would be a more neutral surrounding. The first fight had been in his backyard and he'd had far more support than me. Even the thought of the name, The Albert Hall, made me smile and train to the maximum.

Just under two weeks before the fight we started to hear rumours that Trevor might pull out. Gary told me to ignore it as he might be playing mind games, trying to upset my discipline and training. This is sometimes done because it can take a boxer's mind off his routine; he can become a bit slack, thinking that all the hard work might be for nothing. I continued to train hard and if anything, was now honing an edge I'd never previously known. If he was trying to play with my mind then he'd got it wrong. It made me more determined.

Enjoyed training. Loved being fit. Did my runs, speed work and sparring like my life depended on it. Still watched my four pre-fight films continually: Rocky 3 and 4, First Blood and Enter the Dragon; much to Julie's annoyance. Had 2lbs to lose which would fall off with the remaining training. I was not easy to live with, being hyper irritable and wanting to get into the ring for the re-match. My usual friendly smile became a stranger to my face in the lead up to that contest.

The bombshell came via a phone call from Gary Nickels.

'Ian, its Gary... Sorry mate... Trevor has pulled out of the fight... cracked a rib sparring.'

I was stunned, felt sick, but answered calmly, 'Don't believe it. Mind you, if I'd won the first fight, wouldn't have wanted to fight him again. Why would he want to get hurt by me again? He couldn't work for a week!'

'Frank is trying to line something else up for you so keep the discipline,' replied Gary.

I put the phone down, devastated. Walked aimlessly round the house picking things up and putting them down, with no reason for doing so. Shortly afterwards the phone rang again; it was Les offering his condolences, telling me to stay focussed and to wait and see what Frank could come up with.

Not for one second did I believe that Trevor had broken a rib. My belief was that the first fight had been so hard that he didn't want to get into the ring again with me. Yeah he won the fight, was the only fighter, amateur or pro, to stop me by sheer punching power. For him to fight me again would mean he had nothing to gain and everything to lose, so why would he put himself through another war? Began to think about the 'what if' and 'if only'. Totally pointless.

The phone rang again; this time it's Frank. By now I am almost in a pit of depression.

''Ello!' I answer annoyed.

Frank is his normal upbeat self, 'Not all is lost Ian!' He almost shouted down the phone.

'I can get you… an eliminator… for the Commonwealth title! Win this and you have a shot!' he said, really excited and probably expecting me to be really pleased.

I knew my boxing and realised the guy who held that title, Donovan Boucher of Canada, had delivered quite a beating to Gary Jacobs, so my heart didn't sing at the thought of that prospect.

Before this eliminator, I would have to beat Razor Ado, a tall, gangly, long reaching, African. I'd been training to beat a small stocky fighter by the name of Trevor Smith and he was the only one I wanted to fight. Again, it wasn't the money; I wanted a title and a belt. Pound notes come and go but I'd see a belt forever. Don't think Julie saw it quite the same way.

'I'll think about it.' I replied, non-committal.

Frank was none too impressed with my reply. Not surprised really, after all, he'd got me a fight at the Albert Hall, on television and had given me the chance I'd always dreamed about and here I was appearing ungrateful.

Rang and talked to Gary, who knew of this guy that Frank had lined up, and he told me straight, 'It will be a good fight Ian, but I think you'd lose.'

Les agreed. I trusted Frank, Les and Gary. Gary was my trainer and was on a percentage of the purse, so it was in his interest for me to fight, but here he was telling me I'd lose.

Got back on the phone to Frank to tell him, no. Frank replied, still trying to sell it to me, 'But Ian, it's an eliminator… big opportunity… Albert Hall… live on Sky!'

He got me thinking that this was the equivalent of playing at Wembley. He was right, it was - and here I was turning it down!

I was sitting listening to Frank, still all guns blazing trying to convince me. He left a pause in the conversation hoping for me to digest what he'd said. I was at home in the kitchen, looking into an open fridge, disciplined, hungry, thirsty and bloody irritable. My eye spied a can of cold Guinness, the condensation on it made it look even more inviting.

'No Frank… made my mind up don't want to get banged up and cut for nothing. Going to give the ticket money back and will bring the tickets back to you.'

Knowing I'd made a decision I wouldn't be swayed from, I reached in for the Guinness. Frank was understandably unhappy and let me know it. We had an 18 month contract which had nine months to run. Frank said we might as well knock our agreement on the head. In the mood I was in, shrugged my shoulders, agreed, grabbed the Guinness, pulled the ring pull and poured it carefully into a pint glass. I had earned it and it tasted like nectar. I thanked Frank and the line went as dead as our contract.

What I should have done is try to negotiate with Frank, keep him onside, but on the strict diet I was on, I was cranky and to say the least, was in arsehole mode and yeah, it didn't take long for me to think I really should've taken the fight.

Frank was going great guns with Lennox Lewis, European and British Heavyweight Champion, and on that night at the Albert Hall, Lennox was defending his titles against Glenn McCrory. It was top billing. The press had hyped the fight up, saying McCrory had sparred hundreds of rounds with 'Iron' Mike Tyson and had never been put to the canvas. That didn't impress Lennox, who as he left the dressing room was greeted by a fan wishing him good luck. Lennox said with the confidence of a future world champion, 'This won't take long.'

It didn't. It was all over within two rounds. That was just how good Lennox was.

Was now in limbo, contract gone and manager less. Les stuck by me, as did Gary. Wondered what I was going to do. Continued to train, because I loved being fit and Les said he was sure something would come up for me. He wasn't wrong as Barry Hearn's match-maker, Frankie Turner; a very likeable, softly spoken, long coat wearing, big cigar puffing, East Ender, rang me up and said, 'Nice opportunity for you Ian, son... Five big ones on the table... Eliminator... British title... against Darren Dyer.'

I knew who Darren Dyer was. He'd been a Commonwealth gold medallist and ABA Welterweight Champion. Big puncher. He'd been knocked out a few times and I felt his chin was suspect. Spoke to Gary and Les, who reckoned Dyer would lose heart if he couldn't get an opponent out of the ring quick. Les said I would break his heart in the later rounds and beat him. Felt he was tailor made for me and with the offer of five grand to take the fight, thought Christmas had come early.

While preparing for the fight that was to take place in February '92, I was working on the door in Covent Garden, London. It was New Year's Eve and Peter and Carol wanted me to work. When you have the responsibility of a family you take the work when it's offered and earn the money. Would've loved to have spent the evening with Julie and Kelcie but had told Peter and Carol that I'd be there and, being true to my word, headed into London.

Wasn't feeling well that night and to be honest was a little fed up having to graft while everyone else seemed to be partying. So I gave my best mate, Dave Still, a buzz to see if he could take me up there. We headed into London, found a parking space and on entering the pub he set himself up at the bar by the door for the evening. The plan was that he'd run me home at the end of the night so I could avoid all the drunken revellers on the train.

It was a great evening, really happy people partied and got drunk, hoping that the New Year would be better than the last one. As usual there was no trouble. The countdown to midnight was under way and I was thinking to myself that in 90 minutes I'd be travelling down the A2, with double money in my pocket, home to my family.

Just inside the door, where I always stood when it was freezing outside, I clocked two big lumps, one of them about 17 stone. They were leaving the pub, saying they were going to get some more money. They were drunk, as expected, but drunk to the point of looking like they had rubber legs. In the ring, if you're not steady on your feet, I'll stop the fight and in a pub if you're not steady on your feet, I'll prevent one by showing you the door. Told them politely they'd had enough and that they wouldn't be welcome back. The bigger one's mood changed very quickly, as it can when a brain is drenched with alcohol. He became really aggressive in his manner, pointed at me and shouted through clenched teeth, 'Be back soon… and I will be coming back in!'

Dave, on hearing this, started laughing and said to me, 'Bet they come back Lou.'

'Naah, don't think so.' I replied, hoping it was a drunken bluff. It wasn't, and ten minutes later they returned. Dave clocked them first.

'Your big mate's returned, Lou.' he giggled.

I looked through the door and thought, *'Shit! Better go outside and turn them away early.'*

Before he reached me, calmly told him not to bother, to turn round and go elsewhere. His face changed to one of anger and with that much drink on board, knew it wouldn't be long before he could be throwing punches. The odds weren't in my favour. There were two of them and combined, weighed three of me. The aggressive one, as he moved toward me, seemed to eclipse everything behind him. He was easily 17 stone, I was 6 stone lighter and would have to react to the violence rather than get in first.

They must have fancied their chances. I didn't fancy mine but I had a job to do and would do it. The pub had a friendly reputation and we wanted to keep it that way. Didn't want fights, in the pub or outside, so I continued to try and talk him down. As he reached me, he grabbed my arms and pinned them to my sides. Held my nerve, trying to talk him into letting my arms go, but instead he got his head in close and tapped me on the forehead with it. It was a warning from him. There was nothing else I could do. All I had left in the locker was something that had happened to me in more than a few fights when my opposition had run out of ideas.

I had run out of 'nice' ideas and had only one option left. Looking at his big nose, well he was a big bloke, it fitted his face, my forehead quickly found the bridge of it and I felt it break. He fell backwards to the floor pulling me down with him. A quick left and right to either side of his jaw, made him let go sharpish. I got to my feet quickly, his mate running to his aid, shocked and shouting, 'You nutted him!'

Dave came running out of the pub, looked at me in disbelief and said, 'Louie... you nutted him!' He knew I wasn't a violent man and was genuinely shocked at what he'd seen.

We made sure he was okay, applied first aid and in spite of feeling I had no other option; felt a bit guilty. Checked he wasn't concussed and sent them on their unsteady way. It wasn't my finest hour and I was glad to see the end of that year.

No One Prepares You To Quit

There was so much riding on this fight for me and Darren Dyer. We'd both had significant losses and if we wanted to keep alive our hopes of a future career and British title then this was a must win fight for both of us. People knew it was a potential war and tickets were selling very well. Many of the regulars of 'The Globe' pub and people from the Medway Towns planned to be at the Alexandra Palace, ensuring I would have great support.

Because we knew this guy could bang, we'd decided on the same tactics we'd used in the Hughes fight – don't stand still, give him angles, be hard to hit, box, take him to the late rounds, frustrate him, break his heart with hard jabs and of course don't get dragged into a war. Seemed like a good plan to me, shame Darren didn't keep to the script my team had written. No, he was somewhere in London working very hard with the classy trainer Jimmy Tibbs, who told Darren straight, 'Ian John-Lewis is a tough bastard and he won't lie down!'

The bell sounded the start of the first round and I was immediately impressed with Dyer's speed. Very quick indeed. Despite this it was an even three minutes of give and take, nothing to worry either of us, as we tried to find a way in to the other's chin.

Second round: kept jabbing, coasting along, keeping to the plan to take him to the late rounds. Must have lost concentration, because he caught me with a sharp jab to my slightly open jaw. As it landed I felt a click and knew the jaw was broken. Should've stopped the fight then, but adrenaline, pride and a fighting heart made me think I could still win as I'd done when I fought Johnny Nanton. Tried to move, give angles, protect the jaw and be hard to hit, but I was badly distracted and not moving with fluidity.

Julie was the first to notice I had a problem, telling our friends Dave and Shirley, 'Something's wrong... he's not moving right.'

She was spot on and could see I wasn't flowing. Dyer then pinned me in a corner, where both of us threw a flurry of punches which left me cut.

'Not again,' I thought as I pawed at my left eye. *'How bad is it? How many rounds have I got?'*

I could feel my career unravelling and in quiet desperation decided, *'Need to finish this quick, John L.'*

I had no choice; the game plan would have to go. I'd have to take it to him and declare war. Just then, the referee, Richie Davis, noticed the cut and called, 'Time out!'

Knew it must be bad and knew I was on borrowed time. This break in proceedings was my opportunity to tell the referee and Gary that my jaw was broken, but I couldn't as this was last chance saloon for a British title and I knew it. The referee was taking a close look at the cut and Gary, like all trainers do in that situation, was calling out, 'It's not bad ref!'

'Not as bad as my chin!' I thought.

Couldn't stop thinking about my jaw, wasn't able to focus and the ring is no place to be if you're not switched on, especially if the guy in the other corner is an awesome puncher with the words 'Ian J' written on one of his fists and 'game over' written on the other. I got angry with the distractions and told myself to, *'Shut up! Shape up! Finish this damn fight quick!'*

The referee waved 'fight on' and to give me an idea of where Dyer's chin was, I fired two sharp jabs in preparation for delivery of a bomb in the shape of my right fist. Shame, he delivered his first and caught me with a beaut of a punch to my slack, cracked, jaw. My eyes shut tight when I felt searing pain shoot up into my ear then roll round my skull. I was now in big trouble, it had fractured again. Two fractures and a cut, and it was only round two. I panicked through the pain, '*It broke again... shit!... No!... Shit! Two breaks!*'

Went to one knee, but rose quickly and he caught me a couple more times. Darren went to come in again. Good sense came to me and I turned my back on him, with my arm outstretched to protect my cracked chin. I would later be told that another half decent punch would have caused all sorts of problems; even a 'light' jab would've resulted in my jaw needing a metal plate. The referee stepped in, told us to stop boxing and asked if I was okay. Told him I wasn't, let him know what had happened. He then waved the fight, my career and my dream, over. The team were shocked as on the outside I looked fine. In the winner's corner, Darren Dyer rightly celebrated his victory with Jimmy.

Darren would later tell me that he came to the fight in tip top shape and had even been swimming daily because he couldn't do the road work. He said the swimming gave him something he hadn't had before, helped him to recover quicker and train harder. This swimming, along with having Jimmy in his corner, pushed him to the point where Darren felt at the top of his game. Just my luck.

Went back to the dressing room, changed and was taken to the Whittington Hospital by ambulance. I sat in the waiting room, knowing I was no longer a fighter. A big black nurse said in her beautiful West Indian accent, 'Dat bwoys in payn but nut sayin' nuttin' 'bout it.'

Truth was, couldn't feel the pain. That would come later. For now I was numb and already going into the pit of depression that most sports people feel when it's over.

The x-ray showed what I knew: two fractures. They would be wiring my jaw in the morning and for the long night ahead I was given strong painkillers. I never slept for more than a couple of minutes at a time and was continually thinking about the poor performance and the fact that I was no longer a boxer.

Morning came, eventually, and I was taken into the operating theatre. I really wanted the anaesthetic so I could just stop thinking for a while. Some hours later I came round from the surgery to see my 'guardian angel', Les Roberts.

There are sharks in all walks of life where there's a few quid to be made. Some of these predators put pounds before people but I always knew Les was and would be honest with me. Les had been true to his word and had never made a penny from my boxing. He came out and asked me in typical Yorkshire tone, in such a way as to let me know I should be hanging up the gloves. I told him that the fire was out… that it was over; then used the line the great Roberto Duran had supposedly said when he quit after the return fight with the 'Sugar man' Ray Leonard, 'No mas, Les, no mas,' which is Puerto Rican for 'No more, Les, no more.'

Les smiled, nodded and said, 'Good! Now, about that refereeing.'

Les knew, but didn't tell me straight out, how difficult quitting would be and obviously mentioned the refereeing immediately in the hope that it would give me another purpose, a replacement for the boxing.

Julie didn't drive at that time and wanted to visit me, so she asked my mate, good old boy, 'Fat Dave' for a lift. Without hesitation he said, 'Come on then. Let's go see the 'black boy'.'

We'd known each other by those names since we were kids. Best mates can; no offence meant; none taken. I was surprised she asked and accepted the offer because she knew Fat Dave was as quick as a rally car driver and after what happened to her Dad, Julie liked a more sedate pace. He took it easy as he'd promised.

Julie was pleased that I was looking a lot better than when she'd last seen me, and when I announced that my career was over, she was really happy and said to Les, 'I always knew he'd know when to quit. I'm very proud of him!'

'Bit hasty, Lou!' Fat Dave said in his big voice, 'Give it some more time before you make a big decision like that mate!'

'It's over pal. The fire's out... gone... I'm done with fighting,'

It was a sentence I'd be using a lot in the next few weeks and each time I said the words, it hurt.

Later that day the doctor checked me over, showed me the x-rays and explained how they'd wired my jaw. Didn't tell him that I'd had the same injury a few years before and that I still had the wire cutters in my drawer at home. As he looked at the x-rays he seemed baffled by the two breaks. One was a hair line fracture on the right side and the other a clean break on the left. I explained the hair line happened first from a good jab and later the second break was from a big right hander. Shocked, he said, 'A very lucky lad, you are. The only thing that kept your jaw together was your wisdom tooth.'

A wisdom tooth holding my jaw together seemed ironic but was too down to think it through and forgot about it when he added, 'One more punch and you'd have needed a metal plate inserted.'

I immediately thought about 'Jaws' from James Bond and didn't much fancy the look.

I was allowed home and told I'd be 100 per cent again in a few months and could continue the career I'd just retired from. The pain in my jaw wasn't too bad and would later realise that I'd been under the influence of the anaesthetic mixed with strong pain killers.

Once home I tortured myself further by watching the fight on video. I got properly beaten and winced when I saw the punches that broke my jaw. I thought the sharp jab to the tip of my chin wasn't enough to crack my jaw but it had and could see I consciously made the decision to box on. Seeing the fight made me realise the decision to quit was the right one. My goal on turning pro had been to become British Champion.

I hadn't reached it and now the battle to learn to live with that would begin. This was the end. Ouch!

The day dragged with me dropping in and out of sleep. The pain was starting to come back with a vengeance and I knew the night was going to be a long and lonely one; the longest and loneliest ever. The jaw now caned, the pain relief not doing what it claimed on the box and not even taking the edge off. It was worse than the first time it'd been broken and I already knew what three weeks of liquidised food was going to be like.

Shouldn't have bothered going to bed that night. Every turn woke me up because of sharp pain. Kept checking the clock to see when the next lot of medication, that still wasn't killing the pain, could be taken. In the middle of the night, minutes go slowly and only a few had passed since I last checked. Every time I woke, I hoped that another hour had gone and was already desperate for dawn to break and the next three weeks to pass.

Felt like shit. My head hurt and felt worse with every heart beat which seemed to thud against my skull. My jaw was wired, my pride needed wiring; felt I had let myself down. People had paid good money to see me box and I hadn't given them a show I was proud of. It had only been one day since retirement and was already feeling lost and aimless. Sounds dramatic, but it was like a bereavement, I was grieving, and yeah, my heart was broken.

Could never imagine myself not boxing. Never prepared myself for it and always thought that when it was over, would have a championship belt to look at in my trophy cabinet. There were lots of trophies but I would've traded them all for a belt and my name, Ian John-Lewis, the kid from Darnley road, to be in the history books as British Champion.

Les taught me lots in life, so did Freddie Ludlow, Jim McCarthy, Speedy Mitchell and countless others. They taught me about boxing, discipline, living clean, winning, losing and learning to get back in the ring after a loss. Les had told me what to do after I quit, become a referee, but I can honestly say with all the fantastic advice that everybody gave me, no one had prepared or talked to me in depth or detail about how it would feel when it was all over. I really understand how athletes can go off the rails when their sport retires them.

The fire and desire to box had burnt out completely now. Thinking about the Micky Hughes fight; realised I should have quit then. Saw that for sure in the dead of night. Les and Julie had mentioned retirement to me then, but now were more vocal about it. Most boxers don't know when to stop and I'd been no exception, thinking I would be boxing forever. But deep down I was sensible enough to know it was over and that I wouldn't be coming back.

I worried that my fidgeting would wake Julie, so went down to the kitchen. Opened the fridge door, the light hurt my eyes and when I leant in to get the milk, my head throbbed loudly and made me wince. Poured myself a glass and ended up wearing most of the milk down my t-shirt when attempting to drink it through my wired jaw without the aid of a straw.

'Yuk!' I said through wired shut jaw. Three weeks of mushed up food that occasionally would block the straw was not something I was looking forward to. But at least it wouldn't be like the last time when I had to suck up my Christmas dinner through a straw not designed for the job. Sprouts just don't get through!

I came across the wire cutters that were kindly provided by the National Health Service. They were given to me in case of emergency; the wire could then be cut easily in case of vomiting. Went to the lounge, turned the telly on to get distracted from thinking about what might have been. I sat down and felt the darkness surrounding me, I thought, *'Best get up and turn the light on then!'*

Lights on, I tried to get to thinking about the good things: Julie, Kelcie, nice home, small but nice. Thinking about Julie and Kelcie made me feel bad about feeling so low. Went to smile at the thought of them and found my whole face hurt. This in turn got me to thinking of when I'd first met Julie all the way back in 1980, 12 years earlier:

It was Christmas Eve, snowing and me and a mate were out drinking in the 'Ash Tree' pub. I saw a group of girls. Didn't know them but thought this would be an opportunity to break the ice and jumped into the photo that Julie was about to take. Doing that didn't break the ice and I think she mouthed the word 'Pillock' in my direction.

About a year later, met Julie again at the 'Regency' night club where she was a dancer. She had the tiniest waist, the wild hair of the 80's and the big shoulder pads. Very nice indeed, I thought. We got chatting, said we would meet up and exchanged numbers.

At work I told a mate about the potential date and he suggested that I take her to a pub called the 'Hook and Hatchet' at Hucking. The name sounded like a joke but after checking, heard it was a lovely pub in the middle of nowhere. Took Julie there and we had a really good evening, full of laughter.

Now, the thing was, in the 80's, it seemed everyone was getting loads of sex except me. Turning up on a Monday morning after the weekend the blokes would brag about their nights out and the girls they'd pulled and the sex they'd had with yet another willing woman. Thought to myself I must be doing something wrong. So, Julie and I had a lovely first date and we're now in the car park, in the dark, having a kiss and a cuddle. I decided to be more forward than I would normally be on a first date and Julie gave me a full blooded slap round the face, told me where to go and it definitely ruined the evening. The drive home was a quiet one, with her being annoyed, me being embarrassed and thinking that what the lads were saying on the site must be shite. Needless to say, I didn't get a second date.

A couple of years later on New Year's Eve 1983, bumped into Julie and we arranged to meet at the Regency. Hated going to places on my own but was keen on her and turned up full of hope. When I saw her,

I smiled a friendly smile and she just blanked me, in front of all her mates. I was fuming, made a quick exit and headed for home.

Three years later I was with someone else, had bought a house and within a couple of months of moving in, was made redundant. In order to sign on, which I hated and only did twice, I had to go to Chatham. In the part of Gillingham where I lived, there's a short cut across the massive fields, known as the Great Lines, and I used this to get to the dole office. I saw this woman with short hair, walking her two dogs, sneaked a quick look, as you do, and walked past.

'Aren't you going to say hello, then Ian?'

Shocked that this girl knew my name, I asked, 'Who are you?'

'Julie.'

'Julie?' I replied a bit unsure.

'Yes, me, Julie Crane you wally!'

'Damn! Didn't recognise you with that short hair, it was big and wild last time I saw you.'

We had a hug and a nice chat, said good bye, good luck, and didn't see her again until 1989, when I suggested to my mate Chris Hallett that we go to Spatts, which was a very poplar pub down by the Strand, Gillingham. The music was great, loud and the place packed. The reason for going was my old St Mary's sparring mate, Chris King (Kingie), had got a job as a security guard at the yacht club over the road from it. Hallett thought it a good idea to 'shit the life' out of him in his new job, at about midnight.

Hadn't been to Spatts for months, and the only reason we were there was to frighten Kingie. I hadn't been out for a while as was on a downer following the loss to Trevor Smith. Never took losses well. We battled our way to the bar, got a pint and were moving through the crowd, complimenting the women who'd made such an effort to look beautiful. Well, back then, it was rude not to.

I then noticed a very attractive, no… stunning girl, wearing a brown trilby hat, sitting at the back of the pub with her friends. It was Julie. Told Hallet I wouldn't be long and went over to say hi. Julie introduced me to her mates, we chatted and found we'd both just split up from long time partners. Because the music was so loud, we arranged to meet up again on a quieter night. Julie had moved back to her Dad's place in Parkwood, Rainham, which was miles away and because she didn't drive, we arranged to meet at the Cherry Orchard pub, in Parkwood. Went back to Hallett and told him the history behind myself and Julie. Unknown to me, when I'd walked away, Julie said to her friend Amanda, 'That's the guy in the photo I showed you last week.'

They had been going through some old pictures, and found the one of me in the 'Ash Tree' from 10 years previous. She explained to Amanda, that I'd come out of nowhere to be in that shot. Then mentioned the time she slapped my face for being a bit too fruity. 'He looks kind of cute though Julie,' she said with a smile.

When the evening ended, Hallett and I sneaked over to the yacht club, to give Chris King an unannounced visit. We climbed the fence, tip-toed our way to the security hut, made some scratching noises, then a little bit of tapping and when he came out to investigate, we jumped out on him, screaming. He nearly left his skin and called us every name under the sun. When he finished his rant we took the piss out of his ill-fitting starched security suit. His hat was so big that if he hadn't got ears he would've been blind!

When going to meet Julie at Cherry's I remembered on our first and last date (ten years previously) that she'd slapped me. So it crossed my mind that she might not turn up. I thought about how she'd been when she snubbed me at the Regency night club. Needn't have worried though, as at eight p.m. on the dot, in comes Julie looking lovely. We really enjoyed ourselves and arranged to see each other again. It came to the goodnight bit and all I did was kiss her on the cheek, not wanting to overstep any boundaries and get stung again. In boxing you always remember the big shot that gets you on the chin, believe me, you don't forget a hard slap either! Behaved like a total gentleman.

At this time, was training hard for the Andy Furlong fight which would occur in three weeks, so told Julie I'd not be seeing her until after the fight. Well, after that contest, I was in no mood to see anyone. I didn't ring her and Julie wouldn't ring me, thinking that I should make some effort as she was worth it. Julie's mate said, 'Have you heard from that Ian, lately?'

'No, nothing. Don't think he's interested,' Julie replied.

'Thought you fancied him.'

'I do.'

'Well ring him then,' Kay said.

Julie did and I was really pleased to hear from her and explained that I wasn't feeling up to much following the boxing defeat. She cheered me up so I asked, 'Do you fancy coming to Alton Towers, with me, my best mate and his girlfriend?'

We went, had a great time and me and 'Two Amp', (my nickname for her as she is so laid back) have been together, ever since.

It's easy to wallow in self-pity when things don't go to plan. Life can be cruel sometimes. I began to think about my old mate, Chris King. Kingie was really talented and would've been a British Champion at least. In the gym, our sparring sessions always drew a crowd because they were all-out wars. He was such a hard man, good technical fighter, a southpaw and very awkward. We did a lot of sparring together, kept each other sharp and because of him I had my best spell of boxing.

Chris had been a rugby player and came to boxing for a bit of fitness training, fell in love with the sport and quit rugby. He was a very good light middleweight and decided to turn professional in 1983/4. His was a career I was going to follow for a long time… or so I thought.

Turning pro is a big thing in boxing, because if you're not successful, you can't go back to amateur, your boxing career is over. Managers are looking for young lions and you have to be careful of becoming a sparring partner to some of the elite fighters. The plus side of this is you can learn and become a better fighter; the negative, you can get beaten often and badly in sparring, especially if prone to warring. Very quickly the talent you had is destroyed. You take a few pro' fights but burn out quickly. Career over before it begins.

Kingie's Dad was very switched on. He took him to Leicester, to see the well-established promoter/manager Johnny Griffin. Kingie bashed up a couple of old pros when they asked to see what he was capable of. Griffin wanted to sign him there and then but his Dad took him down to London and tried him there. It was obvious to all that Chris had what it took to be a very good pro' and he signed with Frankie Turner.

Couldn't wait to see him box and attended his third fight at the Elephant and Castle. That night he was strange to watch. Chris was always a controlled aggressive type of boxer but in this bout I could see he was holding back and thought his new team had changed the way he fought. What I didn't know was that, in training, Chris was getting short of breath. He thought it wasn't a problem but couldn't lose this feeling of getting puffed out. It wouldn't go away so he had no choice but to go to the Doctor who sent him for further tests and he was found to have a heart defect. Chris was forced to quit just as he was starting out and looking forward to a long and prosperous career in boxing. Boxing ended for him at 23, he never got his shot, never got his chance, but I never heard him whinge about it though. As down as I felt, I decided to try and display the same class Chris showed. How he got over it, I'll never know, but the way he handled himself in the aftermath was amazing.

Chris loved boxing so instead of removing himself as far away as possible to wallow in self-pity, he threw himself into training me and Spencer Cummings. He was a very good coach and occasionally sparred with us... even a 50 per cent fit Chris King was a really good boxer!

We sparred often at our training quarters in Strood, which only had a little ring, so we were in close and able to really give it to each other. This day, we sparred at the Henry Cooper, in a much bigger ring. Chris knew I would come after him, try to bomb him out and get in close where I could get my hooks flowing. Chris showed his class, skill and displayed to me what he might have been as he used his boxing brain to flummox me. He gave me angles, knowing that I liked to box in a straight line. I couldn't, and he wouldn't, let me get my feet set. Every time I almost did, he moved, which meant I had to start again while he just picked me off with stinging jabs. At the end of three rounds he smiled from the other side of the ring and shouted, 'I knew you'd come after me, Louie!'

I was really pissed off as Les Roberts was watching. Chris had retired, had a heart defect, only did light training and was giving me a bloody good boxing lesson. Chris King... pure talent. Whenever we sparred he always made my nose bleed with that left hand of his. He used to love doing that but the one thing he never forgot was the left hook that I landed on his chin. How he stayed on his feet, after it connected, is a mystery. I threw the punch from so low down, about knee height, and accelerated it up to the point of contact. In the changing rooms later, he said, 'Cor Lou; that was the hardest I've ever been hit!'

'Good!' I said all cocky, joking with him but wondering how the hell he stayed on his feet.

He pressed his finger on my bloodied nose as he said, 'Good!? Good!? Might well be, but I made that bleeeeeeeed again, didn't I!'

When he retired, I knew he was devastated but never realised how low he must have felt until the night that I quit. At least I'd had a chance, but no matter what I told myself, I couldn't drag myself out of the pit I was in. I hoped it would pass quickly as it wasn't a nice place to visit and I certainly didn't want to live there.

Although I never scaled the dizzy heights of World Champion or even British Champion, I now understood the boxers who quit and have a hard time adjusting. The adulation they received was greater, the applause for them was louder and the silence, when they quit, more deafening. Difference between me and the top boys was I still had a mortgage to pay as was not financially sorted. I had responsibilities; the bills needed paying, Kelcie needed feeding. A dead end job can still pay the bills, but I was an electrician's mate and the wages weren't great. Pass the boss this, make his tea, carry the stuff to the site. It wasn't skilled work.

We used all the prize money wisely, making our little house in Gillingham a home. The day job paid the mortgage but little else. Money would now be tight. We'd never relied on my fight money, but when it came we'd enjoyed it; now there would be no more.

Les's voice came to me, always did in times of trouble, *'Ian, when you quit become a referee… you'll be a great referee.'*

Didn't give it much thought at the time as even thinking hurt my head. Everything around the house had a reference to boxing. Photos and trophies were in prominent positions along with photos of Kelcie and Julie. Thought about removing the boxing ones but realised quickly that they'd be noticeable by their absence.

Lost myself in the distraction of a late night film, wasn't concentrating on it but not thinking about boxing either. Found I was uncomfortably numb and drifted off to sleep, which lasted until the next time I moved my head. On waking I began taking stock. The first thing I thought which made me wince was, *'No belt! No British Title!'* Tried to comfort myself by thinking of positives, *'Ranked number 6 in a very difficult division though, fought for a Professional title. Not bad. Never totally outclassed in any match, never knocked out as amateur or pro. Made some good friends along the way. Was a bit of a local hero.'*

140

Next came the 'what ifs?' They are nonsense to think of but I did anyway. *'What if I'd won that war with Trevor Smith? What if I'd not clashed heads with Chris Blake? What if I'd beaten Micky Hughes? What if?'* Pointless questions with no answers to comfort me.

A couple of days after the Darren Dyer fight, Kingie came to me and when I told him my decision about quitting he was very forward with his advice, 'Whoa, think about what you're saying Louie. You're a long time retired from this game.'

Told him why I'd made my decision, 'The fire has burnt out Chris. It ain't there anymore. Nothing to do with the broken jaw; had one before and wasn't worried about it. One of the reasons is the dieting, it's so hard to be hungry and thirsty all the time, makes me miserable and not good to live with. The last three days before the fight are hell.'

Chris wasn't convinced, how could he be? The fire for boxing had probably never diminished in him. He'd not had the chance to get it out of his system.

Dieting for fights is hard and as the fight nears, the weight comes down, we drink less. We train hard but don't put the fluid back in. Three days before the fight I only drank little cups of water and as a treat used to suck on an orange and it tasted like nectar. Don 'The Fruit', our local fruit and veg man, was my supplier. After my run I'd cut up an orange or grapefruit and suck the life out of it. God it tasted great but it burnt my mouth, so walked round with red lips for a few days before the fight.

When the weigh-in was out of the way I would always drink deep and long. Would then go home, have a massive spaghetti bolognaise, the biggest bar of chocolate I could find and wouldn't share a square. Good sleep, shower, shampoo, shave and would be ready for action.

One minute I was okay about retiring, the next I'd be down about it. It's hard to quit, a big decision and in the days following you can feel relieved, bereaved, or both, within minutes of each other. You're a 'used to be', and if you're lucky, a 'has been'. There's no need to get up early and train and it leaves a hole in your life. Always enjoyed training but it had to be for a purpose, now it would be just to keep fit.

My job with ICEL was good and things were great at home with Julie and our beautiful toddler Kelcie, but having been involved in Boxing for so long, I now felt an emptiness. Some boxers look for something else to fill the void by going on to become trainers or coaches. I did think about this but having seen the attitude of some boxers, going light in training, not turning up when they should and moaning their way through training sessions, felt it wasn't for me. The only thing a trainer should have to do with a boxer is hold him back.

Other athletes unfortunately hit the bottle, take to drugs and find their marriages falling to pieces as they search in the wrong places for the buzz that boxing used to give them. Some make the mistake of making a comeback, when really not fit or good enough to cut it anymore. It's at times like these that everyone needs someone they can trust, people not on the gravy train, someone that will tell you just how it is. If it's a pay-day pal in your corner, disaster is waiting to happen. The allegiance can be to his wallet and not you. The wheels begin turning, the comeback is announced and once all the fireworks have fizzled out and the hard work begins, they find out that they don't have the ability, desire or discipline to diet and train at such a high level again. Words of advice, don't expect loyalty. It's very rare, but if you are lucky enough to find it, as I was, keep it close, take care of it, cherish it and listen to it.

Having no desire to make a futile attempt at a come-back and be someone else's punch bag while they were on the way to the top, I decided to find out what was required to pass the assessments in refereeing.

Gary Nickels and Kingie made one more attempt to persuade me to carry on. They thought I still had what it would take to make British

Champion but I told them I wouldn't be coming back and in the way I answered, they knew my decision was final and never asked again.

Having that cage in my mouth and announcing my retirement made it a very long three weeks and by the end of it felt I was half way to being a good ventriloquist. I was quiet, bored, felt like I was grieving and was constantly thinking about the belt I'd never won. Couldn't train as running, skipping and hitting the bag all hurt my jaw. Although I missed training, just told myself there was nothing to train for. I felt ordinary.

Missed the sparring, the gym; it was ingrained in my very soul. Deciding to become a referee would give me a point and a purpose and allow me to stay in the sport I loved. I'd throw myself into learning the ring craft of a referee. Knew it was the right thing to do.

Sat down and composed a letter to the Boxing Board of Control announcing my retirement and my desire to go into refereeing. That was a hard letter to write and even harder to post. I stood at the post box and weighed up the plusses and minuses. Decided the letter had to go and when it disappeared into the box, felt almost relief and walking away, knew I'd done the right thing. I had finally quit and now I was going to throw myself 100 per cent into officiating.

After posting the letter, rang Les and told him. Les congratulated me, told me I had made the right decision and said those words again, 'You'll be a great ref, Ian, mark my words, and I mean a great ref.'

His words gave me hope and made me smile, well as much as I could smile with a face full of recycled Ford Escort.

Probationer

Realised the night I quit boxing that I'd have to get a job with more money, as my work as an electrician's mate just didn't pay enough. Could hear myself repeating what my Dad had said (adding a suck on his teeth) about digging holes in frozen earth for pylons,

'Dun't wan' ta be dooing dis fer der res' of ma life!'

I'd been with the company for nine years, my longest job to date, and it would be a hard wrench to leave. ICEL were cutting hours, there was no pension and with a family to support and an eye on the future, I needed more reliable work. A job that would take the worry out of the end of each month when the bills needed paying. Also, I really needed to get out of the cold.

The refereeing was expenses only, it didn't pay a wage, never would, and was something I'd do for the love of the sport and desire to stay in the hardest game.

As a boxer, I used to think the referee was someone who occasionally got in the way, the person you appealed to if the other guy was leading with his head, or the guy who pulled boxers apart if the fight turned into a dance. All I knew about refereeing was that if I hit the opponent more than he hit me, then I should win. Obviously I had a lot to learn and with my letter, stating my retirement and wish to become a referee, somewhere between the post box at the end of my road and the BBB of C, I wrote another to Boxing News announcing my intentions.

'There, done it, no backing out now,' I thought.

The boxing board wrote back with a nice reply.

Dear Mr. John-Lewis,

Many thanks for your letter of 31ˢᵗ March 1992 and for the courteous and correct way in which you have dealt with your decision to retire from boxing.

You have always given 100% plus and have been a great credit to boxing. It is a great tragedy for you that you have been plagued by injuries and without these setbacks I feel certain your career would have gone far further forward.

We hope that your jaw has mended completely and that you will suffer no ill effects.

I have noted your wish to become a referee and I am passing your letter to the Southern area secretary Simon Block, not only so that he can read it but also to take your application for a Referee's licence further.

I feel certain that the first step will be for you to be interviewed by the Southern Area Council but I will leave that to Simon to arrange.

I am delighted that you wish to stay within boxing and I look forward to seeing you in the near future.

Kind regards.

John Morris

General Secretary

Soon after, was summoned to Vauxhall Bridge Road, London, to the offices of the BBB of C. The board had organised an interview with the Southern Area Secretary about my interest. As I sat in the waiting room, thought about Les's advice, *'John L, keep your mouth shut, ears open and learn everything you can. Do that and they'll send you round the world, you'll stay in top hotels and referee top fights.'*

Smiled at that and thought to myself, *'Les... I hope you're right about this refereeing lark.'*

The guy I was to meet was Simon Block, who had interviewed me about becoming a professional boxer when I was 23. He made me welcome, did his best to put me at ease as I was obviously nervous.

Simon kept the meeting informal and relaxed, asking questions relating to work, family and my ability to be able to travel around the country. It would require some juggling, but with the support of Julie, who knew and appreciated that I needed to stay connected to boxing; it would not be a problem.

Simon told me that the British adjudication profession is a serious one that's determined to be among the best, if not the best, in the world. He added that it's a high pressure line of work as split-second decisions have to be made without error. There would be no second chances if you made a howler of a mistake in front of thousands of hyped up fans, who would be baying for your blood. He asked me if I could handle that level of pressure and I gulped out the answer, 'Yes... no problem. It's something I really want to do and can make the necessary arrangements.'

Simon gave me a great piece of advice, the same advice I give to anyone thinking of, or becoming a referee, 'Walk the ring'. This means get into the ring as often as possible and learn how to stay out of the way! A good conductor makes sure the orchestra is perfect in pitch and rhythm, a good referee makes sure the fight is flowing and fair.

As a boxer the thing that used to irritate me and other boxers I'd talked to, was to be constantly stopped during the bout. The fight is not about the referee; it is about the boxers, so best stay out of the way unless necessary. The type of referee I wanted to be was an invisible one. Help the boxers show what they're capable of, that way everybody wins... Well, except the loser.

By going to the amateur clubs, I was 'walking the ring' all the time, clocking up lots of miles and wearing out the boxing boots that I favoured over shoes. As a novice referee I wore shoes just once and immediately knew I wasn't moving the same, didn't feel as nimble in the ring. It really felt alien after 15 years of wearing boxing boots on canvas.

As part of my training I would watch lots of old fights, but observe with a referee's eye rather than a boxer's, looking at his style, good points and mistakes, taking note of them and adding them to the mental library of boxing knowledge that would push me on to fulfil my dream of becoming an expert in the ring, a 'star class' referee.

At night when I shut my eyes to go to sleep, all I could see was a boxing ring, two imaginary fighters throwing jabs, making angles and me moving smoothly around them getting the best view possible yet trying to remain out of the way. Could see what Simon meant, a referee looks at two fighters whereas the boxer only one.

Simon sent a letter, scoring book and booklet which contained the rules of boxing. Because people see things differently, they wanted to know if I looked at a contest as a referee, rather than as a spectator, and if I had an eye for scoring the competition. Went to a lot of shows on my own and checked my scores with the established officials, finding frequently that I scored it the same or similar.

The board was happy with my ability and summoned me. I entered the board room and saw a few inspectors and Board Stewards along with 10 referees who were at the top of their game, referees that I hoped one day to be as good as. Simon Block and John Morris were in attendance and all appeared to be staring at me. God, I was so nervous, terrified, but didn't let the terror destroy my manners or professionalism.

Looked at the round table they were sitting at and thought of Camelot; quickly chased that daft thought out of my head! They introduced themselves and I noticed that Mike Jacobs (ref at my fight with Micky Hughes) was conspicuous by his absence, having been downgraded to an 'A grade' from 'star class.' Enough said.

With introductions out of the way, questions were fired at me. They wanted me to take charge as if I were the referee, no errs, ifs, buts or maybes. This is their profession and they pride themselves on being the best they can be and keeping the standard high. Not just anyone can pass this process.

After the necessary grilling, I say grilling but to be fair it was just a group of top referees asking a novice questions, I left the room and waited outside. Ten minutes passed that seemed much longer. I was ushered back into the room, where they informed me that the vote was in my favour and I could become a novice; a probationer. Nearly punched the air on hearing the news and could barely contain my excitement. When I left the building I almost danced, well, shadow boxed, back to the car.

At this probationer level, the maximum amount of rounds I could preside over was eight. Could score the fight, stop it, but at the end, if it went the distance, how I scored would be irrelevant. A referee outside the ring, watching the contest, pointed to the winning corner and his decision was the result. After the fight my score card was checked and feedback given.

Had three refereeing assessments by Teddy Gardner, Roy Francis and Larry O'Connell. A few years later in April 2000, Larry would have the honour of refereeing the 'Big One', the World Heavyweight Boxing Championship. That's how good Larry was. I was in awe of these guys, considered myself lucky to have them as my mentors. Who else would I want to learn from, as scary as it was?

Having been a boxer in the amateur and pro ranks, I knew the ring, the make-up of boxing, what a hostile crowd sounded like, the tricks boxers played, the comments corner men made and how to deal with and ignore them. May have spent 15 years in a ring, but I won't lie, at the first fight at Bethnal Green's York Hall I was in the men's room for a large part of the pre-fight hours! Was just as nervous as when I was a boxer, but it's easier to pee as a referee as there are no boxing gloves to contend with.

I was putting on my boxing boots, trying to soak up the atmosphere and prepare myself, when Larry came over, shook my hand and said, 'As it's your first fight, you may as well be first on and get it over and done with, Ian.'

This brought back memories of my first time at St Mary's when Freddy Ludlow said, 'Go upstairs, get changed and get in here to spar.'

149

'Yeah thanks, Larry,' I replied, but was really thinking, *'oh shit!'* Then consoled myself with the thought, *'Oh well, at least I won't get punched!'*

Julie wanted to see my refereeing debut and came up with dear old Ann and her husband Eddie, a couple of East Enders that moved to Gillingham back in the 70's. Ann knew her boxing and was a big fan of Frank Bruno's. After my fight with Chris Blake, I was in the bank, sporting a huge shiner, courtesy of Blake, when the cashier, who had seen the fight on Sky, recognised me and asked how my baby daughter was. Behind me in the queue was an elderly lady, who tapped me on the shoulder and said, 'You're that local pro boxer. Read a lot about you in the Medway News. Can I have your autograph please?' And handed me her paying-in book to sign.

'Tell you what. Give me your address and I'll post you a signed photo.'

Turned out Ann didn't live far from me, so I popped round to hand deliver the photo and had a cuppa. It was like being in the company of old friends, and that same Christmas they bought us all presents and continued doing so for the next 15 years. Ann adored my little girl, Kelcie, followed my career, became a very good friend and was over the moon when I became a referee. Time moves on and both have passed away now, so rest in peace, you lovely couple.

When I got into the ring, I was introduced to the crowd by the MC and Ann, bless her, jumped out of her seat to her feet and hollered, 'Come on, Ian!'

Julie grabbed her arm and said, 'Sit down, you silly cow!'

There was laughter from the crowd and inside the ring, but I couldn't help but throw a big smile Ann's way. It felt strange being in the ring in civvies, but forgot this as soon as the bell went for round one.

This fight would be a hard fought battle between two fast and furious flyweights, the unbeaten Darren Fifield, (London) versus Kevin Jenkins (Wales). At the end of the fight, I looked at Teddy Gardner and he raised both hands to signal a draw.

I climbed down from the ring and Barry Hearn asked me, 'Out of curiosity Ian, how'd you have it?'

'Jenkins by a round,' I replied.

'Yeah, agree with you,' Barry said.

It was then that Barry gave me a compliment and a great piece of advice, 'I like your score, Ian... you'll go far. Word of advice... in this refereeing game, be different... stand out a bit... look after the boxers, be your own man, totally honest and tell them you are the referee.'

After the three assessed shows, was told I was a natural and got my B licence, which meant I'd become a fully qualified referee. I was now allowed to take the invisible 'L' plates off and control a boxing competition.

Immersed in boxing again; loved it and was relieved! Was concentrating so much on being a good referee, that quitting boxing wasn't taking a toll on my mind now. When people stopped me in the street and asked how the boxing was going, I didn't mind telling them I'd retired and had become a referee. When I first quit I would find myself on a downer after they asked.

Being qualified meant I now had to have a 'Final Instructions' spiel to say to the boxers when I brought them to the centre of the ring. The Referees' Guide book says,

'There is no need for a long lecture. It should be impressed upon the boxers that when ordered to 'break' they must do so promptly, they must defend themselves at all times except when told to 'stop boxing', under such circumstances they can relax until told to 'box on'. They must be told to punch with knuckle part of the glove, remind them that should a boxer be sent to the canvas the standing boxer must go to the furthest neutral corner and remain there until ordered to 'box on'.

I tried to work out how I was going to condense all that. When digesting all the fights I'd recorded, I came across James Toney, the very exciting World Middleweight Champion defending his belt against the tough, Iran Barkley. The referee, who I admired a lot, was Richard Steele, who, when bringing the fighters together said, 'I'm the referee,' (meaning he's the boss, and he was) 'I'm cautioning you now, obey my command at all times, defend yourselves at all times.'

Now I liked what I'd heard so decided to use it, after all he was a world class referee at the top of the profession. I then played around with some other sentences and finally came up with my own instructions, instructions that many people when meeting me say word for word. I love hearing it and have even had it said to me in welsh.

'I am the referee.

I spoke to you both in the dressing room.

Obey my command at all times.

You both know the rules.

Watch your heads and keep your punches up.

When I shout 'Break!' break clean,

... and remember...

defend yourself at all times.

Shake hands.'

My first appointment as a qualified referee would be on the 15th September, 1993 at the Stour Centre, Ashford, Kent. Told Julie, that morning, to be ready when I got home because I didn't want to be late. I left work early from Purfleet in Essex and was soon in the outside lane doing 69.9mph on the approach road to the Dartford Bridge. I caught up with this motor cycle courier, who was sort of in the second and third lane, and as he didn't have 'wide load' tattooed on his arse, I thought he was a bit on the greedy side. I wanted to get past but couldn't. He looked at me in his side mirror, our eyes met so I knew he knew I was there, and he knew, I knew that he knew I was there, but still he didn't move out of the way. A gap opened up so I went through, and motored on, now crossing the Dartford Bridge. The biker caught me up and decided to ride dangerously close for some unknown reason. He came up by the side of my car and pulled a hard stare at me. Through his clear visor I could see his bruised eye and knowing I wasn't responsible for it, wondered what his problem was. He sped off in front, slowed again and dropped level with my passenger door window this time. He then swerved his bike in towards me, thinking I would react and take evasive action. That was my first instinct but declined the offer as it would force me into the bridge barrier and no one wins against those. The biker ended up falling to the road and part of his body went under my front wheel. I thought I'd killed him as I heard and felt the sickening 'bump, bump' as the wheels of my car rolled over him. I looked into my rear view mirror and saw the rider fly up like a rag doll, crash down to the tarmac and roll to a stop.

'Oh my God!' I shouted. Stopped my car along with all the other drivers on the middle of the bridge and ran back to the writhing motorcyclist. When I got to him, was relieved to see his head wasn't squashed and soon realised that it was his arm that had gone under my wheels. By his complaining, knew he was conscious, well pissed off, but alive. When I appeared in his field of view, he was obviously not happy to see me and tried to get up. Four other people had reached us and thankfully one was a nurse who told him to lie still, in case his spine was injured. The witnesses were discussing the accident and were saying that the biker looked to be staring out to the river, but he wasn't, he was staring me out, don't know why, maybe he didn't like my driving but the bruised eye was a bit of clue to the type of person he might be. Breathalysed, with statements now given to the police by myself and witnesses, I was now late and zoomed home. I opened the door to a fuming Julie, who was ready and had been for some time. As I ran up the stairs I could hear my beloved gently finding out why I was late, 'You said you were leaving work early and to make sure I was ready! Well I'm ready and you're bloody late!'

'Listen, I'll tell you what happened when we're in the car!' I shouted, as I very quickly got changed. I gave Kelcie a quick cuddle, shouted bye to Archie, to which he replied, 'Good luck, son.' Always made me smile, that.

I ran out of the house, jumped in the car to a waiting Julie, then sped off to Ashford, explaining to her why I was late. Managed to get to Ashford just on time and although shaken by the accident, put it to the back of my mind and did really well. I refereed the fight of the night between future British light-welterweight champion Paul 'Scrap Iron' Ryan (what a character and fighter he was), against Shaun Cogan. They went toe-to-toe, with me stepping in to stop it in the third, and Cogan telling me he could've continued. The report about me by the inspector was exceptional, to the point that he even wrote that I'd go far.

Had never previously been in a really good hotel but now found myself refereeing in the Dorchester, Hilton and Grosvenor hotels in London. These places were beautiful and it was nice to get in through the front door and see how the other 10 per cent live. Didn't dare to dream that one day I'd be travelling the world, staying in hotels of equal standing and opulence.

On one occasion, was refereeing a heavyweight fight at the Grosvenor when the up and coming heavyweight fighter threw, what looked to me, an absolute bomb at his opponent but because of the angle I was at, wasn't sure if it'd made contact. His opponent, a very experienced journeyman, went to the floor and stayed there, so I gathered the punch must have landed and counted him out. I helped him to his feet, walked him back to his corner and slightly puzzled I had to ask, 'Did he hit you?'

To which he replied with a smirk, 'No! ... But he was going to!' Couldn't help but laugh.

Spoke to Les often and we discussed the refereeing. He saw me officiate whenever I was in London and after the fight would always give me advice, telling me what I did or didn't do well. Les said time and experience would smooth my rough edges. He saw that in the ring I still moved like a boxer and told me that this would need to be ironed out as I wasn't looking for openings to an opponent's chin, but was making sure a fight was fair and flowing. He saw things in me and my officiating that I didn't notice and taught me how to be self-analytical. Another great bit of advice he gave me was to take one step further back from the action, enabling me to see the 'whole picture'. Told him that I'd be too far away to get in quickly to deal with something, to which he replied that I was fit, fast and could read a fight from all my years in boxing, so would be able to get in amongst it and sort the problem quickly, with minimal fuss. As ever, Les was right.

Les told me to video record all the fights I could, analyse them and be honest with what I did or didn't do well. What I saw today wouldn't necessarily be what I would see in six months as I gained more experience. The recording of fights now, is done for me by long-time friend, 'Click Click' Mick Smith, as he is known in the boxing world. As I was growing up in the Medway towns, Mick lived in Chatham and followed my career from when I was a 15 year old amateur with St Mary's, through to my pro and refereeing career. Mick is a great guy and club photographer for Brighton Ex-Boxers Association and President of Ipswich Ex-Boxers where he now lives.

29 March 1994: York Hall, Bethnal Green.

Con McMullen versus the old warhorse, Peter Buckley.

Peter was a journeyman, and journeymen's managers often say that their fighter is always a couple of rounds down before the bell for round one has even sounded.

155

I understand that journeymen are not meant to win as they are picked for a workout for the hot prospect or the home boxer, but any referee should make sure that in their mind, it is a clean slate with no bias, conscious or unconscious, towards either fighter.

That night Buckley must have fancied it and won by a half point (one round). He won it in my eyes and on my score card so I raised his hand in victory. McMullen wasn't impressed as Peter had won his first fight after about twenty losses in a row. Peter may have lost a lot, but he was a very good workout, difficult to put to the canvas and even harder to keep there.

When I received the news that I was on the big Chris Eubank bill, on the 9th July 1994, I knew I had my first big break. Eubank was on a gruelling but successful run of 14 title defences of his WBO Super-Middleweight belt. Sky Sports had shown them all, and his next opponent was the Brazilian, Mauricio Amaral at the Earls Court, Exhibition Hall, London. I, like most young referees that want to learn, went over and introduced myself to Steve Smoger, a top American referee, who was to be the third man in the Eubank fight. Steve was a really smart and sharp guy, loved boxing and was quite flamboyant. Learnt much from talking to him and like most people that I've met at the top of their game, he was generous with his advice.

Again in this fight, Eubank was pushed to the wire but retained his title with a unanimous decision. I watched very closely how Smoger performed and said to myself that one day, with a lot of hard work, I wanted to be refereeing a world title fight.

With all the cameras around, I was, as always, really nervous. One of the three matches I was to referee that night was Bernard Paul (The Punching Postman) versus Carlos Chase (Cheshunt). This was a fight that had a strange knockout. Bernard Paul was up and coming and Carlos was giving him all that he could handle in the first round and for two minutes of round two. The Punching Postman was looking to deliver the big right hander and record a win. Eventually, he landed it on the side of Carlos's head. Heard the thud as the glove hit and thought, *'Took that well!'*

Two seconds later the punch must have registered as he looked like a leaping salmon. His back arched, feet appeared to leave the canvas and then he fell. He made it to his feet at the count of nine but I could see he was finished. The eyes were glazed and despite his protestations and attempts to reassure me that he was fine, I told him it was all over. Being such a new referee, wondered if I should have let it go on a bit longer but after guiding him back to his corner, could sense his legs were not really listening to his brain and I'd rightly prevented him from having to endure another delivery of punches. Commentator, Ian Darke, said it was a good decision by the referee and as I was new to the game, appreciated the comment.

Next on the bill was Eddie Knight versus Mark Delaney who came out to 'Jump Around' by the 'House of Pain'. As soon as I heard it, I thought, *'What a tune!'* Today, every time I hear it, I'm back at Earls Court.

Delaney was up and coming and was such a tough, hard guy that he broke Eddie down. Eddie must have thought he was in a house of pain with the amount of punches he had to endure that night. This was the first of many contests I refereed featuring Delaney. I really thought he was going somewhere, but then he bumped into an unbeaten Joe Calzaghe for the British Super-Middleweight title. Well, after the beating Joe gave Delaney, stopping him in the fifth, I knew Calzaghe was something special.

Was pleased with how I officiated the match and climbed down from the ring to be met by Julie who wasn't looking too happy. Was waiting for her to congratulate me but all I got was the 'twenty' questions.

'Do you know her?' she said, pointing at a nice looking woman at ringside.

'Not really,' I answered, wondering where the questioning was going.

'Who is she?'

'That's one of the Boxing Board's Doctors… never really spoken to her.'

'Doctor?'

'Yes!' I replied.

'Doctor you say? … Umm, makes sense, because as you swanned around the ring with your tight trousers on, she looked very interested in your anatomy… and I tell you now, she wasn't looking at your face!'

What answer do you give to that?!

On the Monday morning following the televised fight, I returned to work and was having a chat with an old English guy, Roy. He was getting on in years but was someone who as he went through life gained knowledge and was a mine of information. He reminded me of Les Roberts, so I knew to listen.

Roy knew I was a referee and had watched the show. When there was no one in the canteen he said, 'Ian, watched you on Saturday night, son. One of the professions I used to be involved in many years ago was as a talent scout, and I can tell that you are going to be a top referee. Mark my words, Ian. You move well, are in control and you're invisible most of the time. I'll be honest, don't know too much about boxing, Ian, but there's something about you son; you have this presence about you. Keep going with it and good luck for the future.' It was a lovely thing to say; he didn't have to, but took the time to. Meant a lot to me.

However, minutes after, just to keep my feet on the ground, in walked some of my work mates whose comments were more of a piss take at how young I looked:

'Were you on work experience, Ian?'

'Ian, was you saying to the boxers, hurry up and finish quick 'cos I have to be in bed by nine?'

I was 31 at the time... bastards!!!

So much loved the refereeing that on a few occasions I forgot to collect my fee. I'd get home really pleased with the show and my performance, the phone would ring and on the other end of the line would be Larry O'Connell, 'Ian. You forgot your money – again!' Julie would just raise an eyebrow, say she wasn't going to say anything... then would.

I reached the 'A' standard of refereeing after just three years. Les told me it was quick but deserved. I am sure his input, the analysis of the fights I officiated at and the fact that I'd been a boxer helped to get me there. What also helped focus my mind is the fact that referees are assessed every year and at every match there is an inspector and a star class referee observing the man inside the ropes.

23 May 1995: Potters Bar, Hertfordshire.

Spencer Oliver versus Peter Buckley.

We waited so long for Spencer to appear that Peter's flamboyant trainer, Nobby Nobbs, put the stool in the ring, told Peter to sit down and gave him a newspaper to read. Nobby was a nightmare of a corner man. You could always hear him, was very difficult to tune him out as he just had one of those voices that made you listen. During the fight he'd continually offer unwanted advice, such as, 'Phworrr that's a bad cut ref. Need a closer look at that?'

'Oh yeah, ref... that's a good draw, ref... good decision that would be.'

'Need to stop that, ref... stop that quick, ref!'

As the ring girls walked around holding the round card up, he used to flick water from his sponge and growl at them.

The fireworks went off and the loud music started, so we all knew Spencer was approaching. I stood in the ring watching him arrive and thought, *'Hope this boy can fight.'*

Wasn't disappointed. He was a great boxer and later went on to win a European title. In the third round he felled Buckley with a good shot. I wouldn't have blamed Buckley for chucking it in, but as I said before, Peter was a warhorse, a journeyman. He got to his feet, fought on to the end and lost on points.

I really enjoyed the refereeing but was desperate for a new job, a new challenge and more money. Three years had passed since I decided to leave ICEL and was still looking for that job that would get me out of the cold, provide the security I wanted for me and my family and allow me to juggle work and my refereeing. For a guy with just an 'O' Level in Art, that job was proving hard to find.

Rang an old friend, Jim McCarthy, who did a lot for St Mary's as a trainer/motivator. Back in the day he'd pushed me hard. He'd been a police officer, but then went into the Probation Service, so not too many at our amateur club liked him. I thought he was a good guy and didn't care that he'd been 'old bill'. When I was just twenty, Jim said, 'I think you'd make a great prison officer, Ian. I can have a word with someone and you've got yourself a career.'

He gave me some prison brochures, which I read but deep down I felt a bit too young. Told Jim thanks, but no thanks; maybe later. Well now it's later, I'm older and looking for that job, so talked to him about the possibility of becoming a prison officer. Jim told me it wasn't the same as the old days when a word in the ear of someone he knew would get you an interview and a job. Now, it would only get me past the paper sift, which was something, and onto the written tests stage. I spoke to the Governor of Maidstone for 45 minutes. He was keen for me to join, interested in my boxing career and my plans for the future.

160

Was invited to the prison to take aptitude tests. These tests are made up of boxes, squares and patterns which after looking at them for a short time gave me a headache. Gave the tests my best shot and once completed, entered a waiting room that contained 18 people: 16 white, 1 black and me, mixed race. Looking around at the people attending, thought I must be in the wrong place. The black guy nodded at me, so headed for the empty seat next to him. His opening words were, 'You move like a boxer.'

'Good call.' I answered. Tried to guess his previous occupation but couldn't. He was fit and looked like he had done a number of different exercise programs, so wasn't surprised when he told me he was ex-army. He would be ideal for this line of work, just like me.

A big prison officer came forward and spoke to the two of us. After a short time he whispered that most of the guys in the room were the well-educated types, some having degrees. He went on to say they didn't like this type of recruit, not because they were educated, but because the current officers not only had to look after the prisoners and themselves but that they had to look after the new guys as well. Some of these were very young and I wondered how they would handle situations with troublesome inmates, some being very violent.

Was called into a room and informed I had failed the aptitude test, which wasn't a great surprise when trying to work out puzzles through a massive headache. It was upsetting as I felt that this was the job that would allow me to keep going in the refereeing game. Coming home from the appointment, won't say interview as I never got one, I wondered what else I could do. There weren't lot of options.

The next morning I woke and knew today would be a day of banter with me being the brunt of it, as I'd made the mistake of telling everyone at work I was going to be a prison officer. Because of my contact Jim, I was sure I'd get the job, so when I returned, felt really small after explaining that I failed. As expected, they were merciless as was the norm for our place. Next time I went for a job I would tell no one and if I failed, would suffer the humiliation on my own.

Also at this time I was thinking about Kelcie starting school. It filled me with dread and worry. I did my best to put it to the back of my mind, telling myself that she'd be okay and that if she wasn't then I'd go to the school and make sure that she'd be okay. Along with this, I had the job rejection to occupy me and was just getting over it when Miss 'perfect timing', Julie, came straight out with a question that she definitely wanted, not just a positive answer for but a date, 'Ian, when are we going to get married?'

My life didn't flash before me but my legs went a bit jelly like. I tried to gather my senses and do my best to put her off. I had no problem us being together, was very happy and didn't see the need to change this fine set up. Truth is I was a bit scared of marriage as I'd seen good friends who'd been together for a long time, get married and within 18 months it was all over. I wondered what happened to them. Did it change a woman when that ring went on? I didn't know and didn't want to find out, so tried to put her off for a second time and thinking I had succeeded, exhaled a sigh of relief. Julie, not to be outdone, came swiftly to the point and announced, 'If we don't get married before Kelcie goes to school then I don't want to get married, ever!'

There was I, already panicking about marriage and she mentions school. This turned my stomach over. I decided to man up and bite the bullet. I thought we'd always be together anyway and if getting married was the next step then so be it. I agreed to get married there and then. Julie was over the moon, said she would sort it and a couple of days later announced our wedding day would be on the 31st of August, at Chatham Registry Office.

'Nice one! So we've got a year to prepare for it, sounds good to me darling,' I replied, thinking that Kelcie would be safely in school by then, and I wouldn't have the worry of that any more. I should've known my Julie better.

'No, Ian. The 31st of August this year... darling!' she replied.

'What?! That's only seven bloody weeks away! You are joking, love?'

'Ian, if I was joking I would have started my sentence with – I say, I say, I say,' she laughed.

So the race was on, but one of Julie's many talents is organising. She is brilliant at it. She got most of our friends involved, with my ICEL mate, Carl's wife doing the wedding cake. Steve, my next door neighbour, supplied a couple of crates of wine. Rob and Jan, owners of my local, the Napier Arms, said we could use their hall for nothing. Julie's Dad, Archie put a large sum of cash behind the bar and my Dad and his girlfriend paid for the buffet. As ever, 'Click Click' Mick was around with a camera or two slung round his neck and did a great job of our wedding video. Julie made a brilliant music tape for the wedding but only 20 minutes got used so Mick used it as background music throughout the video. Considering wedding videos were quite expensive, Mick, generous as ever, didn't want anything, telling us it was a wedding present.

Julie's friend was a florist, so that was the flowers sorted and lastly, Julie's sister-in-law Alison, had a lovely little outfit that her seven year old daughter, Jackie had worn for a wedding the year before, and that fitted Kelcie. All the measurements were done over the phone but it fitted perfectly and matched Julie's dress.

Because of all the help, our wedding was a brilliant day, cost only £700 and a great time was had by all.

No sooner had I got over getting married, realised that it was time for Kelcie to start school. I was more nervous than she was as we walked to the school gates. It brought back memories of my first day. It came time to let her go and I wanted to say so much to her but couldn't find the words. I needn't have worried about her as she wriggled free of my hand, hugged me, then waved goodbye and floated into school, made friends and enjoyed herself. School was a good time for her, no free school dinners, and I made sure she was able to go on the school trips. I didn't want her having that feeling of loneliness when the coach pulls out with all your mates on it and then coming back and talking about the great time that you never had! Problem was trying not to overcompensate for what I missed out on. Getting the balance is difficult and if you don't get it right you can spoil them and they don't appreciate things. It's not easy this parenting lark.

That was many years ago and I am pleased to say marriage didn't change Julie one bit. No, 'Two Amp' is the same now as she's always been!

We are a larger family now as in addition to Kelcie we have, at time of writing, ten dogs. I've now put my foot down and said ten's the maximum. Bloody food bill's enormous.

The Five Bars Hotel

Euro '96. The ball came to the brilliant 'Gazza', he tipped it over the head of Colin Hendry, ran onto it and smashed it into the goal. Gazza, the team and the nation were ecstatic. He ran to the touchline and the team sprayed bottles of water into his open mouth, which was meant to be a parody of the infamous 'dentist chair' that the papers had reported on in the run up to the competition.

If the dentist was good enough for Gazza, then it would be a good enough excuse for me to miss work and attend an interview that I was trying to keep secret. The banter I'd received the year before, when I failed to get into the Prison Service, had been merciless and if I failed this interview, I didn't want a repeat.

The job description read like that of a prison officer but working out of a police station. It was a new post designed to put police officers back on the streets. So, at almost 35, it was the first job that I had to interview for and I was really scared. Turned up suited, booted with my nails spotless as usual and hoped there'd be no tests like last year that involved pointless boxes, squares and shapes.

To be honest, I'd have felt less nervous sitting in the waiting room of a tooth torturer, as I waited at Rochester Police Station for my interview with the business manager and the area personnel assistant. They asked me lots of questions and although not being familiar with interviews, felt I did well with my answers. At the end, they told me about the pension and paid holidays, so I hoped the result would be positive. The meeting over; they told me they'd let me know the outcome of the interview in a week.

Went back to work in the Purfleet Paper Mill the next morning and the lads ribbed me about pulling a 'sicky' so that I could watch the football. I could take this banter no problem, but not the humiliation of telling them I didn't get another job. Tea break was normally at 10 a.m. but my 'guvnor', Bob, said at 9:15, 'Louie, let's go for an early cuppa.'

Wasn't going to argue with the Gaffer and now sitting down in the warm, drinking a hot, sweet, three sugared tea, reading Boxing News, life was instantly better. The phone rang and Bob told me at first to leave it as we shouldn't have been on a break, but quickly changed his mind, 'Answer it Louie, and if anyone asks, we're just picking up some materials.'

I picked the phone up, introduced the company and a woman said, 'May I speak to Ian John-Lewis please?'

'Speaking,' I answered a little shocked and now wondering if something was wrong with Julie or Kelcie. Needn't have worried as it was the personnel assistant from Kent Police. So instead of worrying about my girls, I was now thinking the worst about the job because they'd told me they'd let me know the outcome of the interview in a week, not the next day.

'I know we told you we'd let you know within a week, but you were the best candidate we interviewed and we'd like to offer you the job, depending on references.'

I was as pleased as when Gazza scored that goal and accepted the job there and then. I was doing a bit of a jig, jumping from foot to foot and the Gaffer, Bob, seeing how chuffed I was, shouted, 'What you so happy about, Lou?'

'It's the Boxing Board, Bob. They've put me on a big show in London next week,' I lied.

Couldn't wait to ring home and spread the good news, so as soon as the tea break was finished I rang Julie, who was really pleased for me.

For the rest of the day I wore a bigger grin than normal. Nothing was too hard and that shift appeared to last only minutes. Once home, got hugged by Julie and told how proud she was. We were like a couple of

166

giggling kids because we knew this was going to change our lives for the better. Kelcie was very happy in school; Julie was now working for a dog grooming company and the extra cash from that was very welcome. A few months earlier I'd been upgraded to 'Class A' referee so was getting bigger fights to officiate at. Finally, for the John-Lewis family, after all the hard work, things were getting better. I looked at myself in the mirror, smiling and said out loud, 'You're doing good kid, you're doing good.'

As pleased about the new job as I was, I was sad to leave ICEL and the great bunch of guys. I'd been there a long time and felt part of the firm. The owner of the place, Tony Day, great fellah, loved boxing and I got on really well with him. The lads said they were surprised I was leaving as the boss liked me, adding that I'd probably have had a job for life. Others said they admired me for leaving to do something totally different. Truth was, I'd spent too much time outside in the cold and was really tired of it, felt it was getting deep into my bones but now could feel the heat at the end of the tunnel.

29 July 1996: I started as a civilian detention officer, or a CDO as we were known, at Rochester Police Station. Even though I thought I had a fair idea of what to expect when going to work for Kent Police, I was very nervous but told myself that the gamble would be worthwhile.

It was a weird feeling going to a police station for work. I'd been into this nick twice before, once as a scared thirteen year old, after thinking that the 'pick and mix' sign above the sweets in Woolworths actually said 'pick and nick'. The whipping I got from my Dad for that made sure I never stole again. The second time was with my Dad when I had to give a statement about the guy who attacked him and died doing so.

I met the 'civvie' driver, Ann, who took me to Kent Police Headquarters in Maidstone to collect my uniform. On returning, was greeted by CDO Callow who took me down to the 'Dungeons' for a tour.

I was then introduced to the custody sergeant who explained the rules to me as we walked the custody block. Next I was put with another CDO, John, and the very experienced police jailer, 'Jock', a Welsh bloke... (no, not really) who showed me the ropes.

I was stationed at Charles Dickens' old manor – Rochester. The detention centre was a grim old place that definitely had a Dickensian feel to it and was worse for us as we did a forty hour week, whereas the guests were in and out in a couple of days or sometimes quicker.

The station contained just nine graffiti covered cells including two for females and one for juveniles. The doors had old fashioned latches, no toilet, it stank and was depressing. The female area had a bath; the male side had a shower. The exercise yard was for both fresh air and a smoke but in those days prisoners could smoke in their cells, unlike now where not even those criminals who reckon that a cell is home from home are allowed. The building wasn't that old but the cells were in the basement and it seemed that as you descended the stairs you also went back in time. The paint was old, peeling and had the colour of heavy tar nicotine. The place smelt but at least it was warm. To be honest it was like a prison down there.

I was given a set of noisy chunky keys, a pair of handcuffs and a first aid pouch, which was all clasped to the side of my belt. When I did the rounds, the prisoners would hear my keys, shout 'Jailer' or 'Guv' and fire all sorts of questions and demands my way. They'd want to know when they were going to be interviewed, fed and be seen by the doctor or their brief. I learned very quickly how bloody needy some criminals in custody can be and to keep those damned keys quiet. It took some time for me to get used to these 'crimms' calling me 'Guvnor' and I tried for a long time to get them to call me Ian. Jock explained to me that 'Guv' is prison talk and ingrained in some of our more frequent guests.

I adjusted to the job well but really found it difficult to understand when CDO John said, 'See that geezer in cell 3, that's Steve; he's a regular.'

'Regular! You mean they come back?' I replied stunned.

'Yeah, lots do Ian, and soon you'll know a few regulars too, on first name basis. Some are very loyal, never get nicked anywhere else but this area.'

When prisoners need to attend court, they're escorted to Chatham Magistrates. Once there, they are housed in the cells below and stay all day until Court ends. I found it weird when first handcuffing someone to me but got used to it. When having the handcuff training, I realised they can bloody hurt when placed on. Mr Duffy, a no nonsense Scot, (are there any other types?) was the trainer. With the rigid cuffs, he quickly put them on me, then shouted, 'Doon, doon, doon!' (Scottish for 'down, down, down) as he pulled my hand towards him. I'd no choice but to go to the floor or have my wrist broken. Even though I was taught this technique, I've never had to use it on prisoners to make them comply.

Next came the Unarmed Defence Training (UDT), which was the first time I met the trainer, Trevel Henry, a fit looking, black, ex-Army guy who really knew his stuff. A nicer guy you couldn't wish to meet. I found the defence training interesting, although a lot of what was shown I'd an idea about from being an ex-fighter and educated on the streets of the Medway towns. After the bruises gained from UDT, we then had to digest the rules of the Police and Criminal Evidence Act 1984, known as PACE, on how to look after detained persons in custody.

The second week was all about first aid. It was brilliantly taught and important for me to know as I would be dealing with drug-addled and drink-laden guests. In their stupor, any of them could die from positional asphyxia or from choking on their own vomit.

Not a shift went by without me seeing someone I'd known or knew from the old neighbourhood. People I'd been friends with, or rucked with, were coming in under arrest for an array of offences from affray to drug dealing or taking.

For the first couple of weeks my mates kept ringing up saying, 'You had a fight yet, Louie? You hit anyone yet?'

I told them that the role was non-confrontational, meaning that it wouldn't be me who'd be rolling round the floor with an unhappy inmate. I went to work that night and thought I'd spoken too soon.

A prisoner was kicking off in his cell, shouting abuse. I asked him to calm down and told him I wouldn't be letting him out to the toilet until he did so. Five minutes passed and although I could hear he was quieter, could sense he was bubbling just under the surface. I opened his cell door anyway and before he appeared, his angry demand did, 'Where's the fucking toilet?!'

I was new to the job and by how starched and bright my shirt was, he knew it too. Trying to calm him, I put my hand on his shoulder and said, 'Just through there mate.'

'Get your fucking black hands off me, you nigger!'

There's that word again. The one that's meant to really hurt me but I no longer let it. He turned and squared up to me, his nose almost touching mine. I repeated calmly, not taking my eyes off him, 'Like I said fellah, the toilets are just through there.'

Half expected him to try and chin me but he turned and headed to the toilet. I waited outside so I could escort him back to his cell once he'd emptied his bladder. He came out of the toilet sheepish looking, head down, and went back to his room. I shut the door behind him and as I was closing the viewing flap he said, 'Sorry about that mate… you're alright you are.'

'Appreciated fellah,' I replied, 'Need a drink?'

'No thanks, Guv,' he replied and we never heard a peep from him all night.

The two guys showing me the ropes, John and Jock, told me I'd done a brilliant job in remaining calm and holding my nerve under the attempted intimidation. My time working security had really helped.

What was strange was some of my mates changed their attitude toward me, almost looked at me with suspicion. They thought I was 'Police' – the enemy. They kept up this suspicion until they were arrested, brought in and found out what my job as a detention officer was.

I may have been on television a lot as a boxer and referee, but at the station there were cameras everywhere, which provided safety to staff and guests alike. It was like being in the George Orwell novel '1984', as you felt 'Big Brother' was watching the whole time. Walked around like a mannequin feeling every move was being monitored and assessed as I found my feet in this new job. After a couple of months I realised that the only time people were interested in the screens, was when there was a potential problem. Began to relax, be my normal self and much to the amusement of my colleagues and guests, began to start singing and shadow boxing my way through the corridors to and from the rooms. It was something I'd done all the time at ICEL to keep warm and thought I'd have to stop when working at the station. Officers asked why I was so happy because the place was pure doom and gloom. Yes it was, but I couldn't let it change me and besides, the place was warm. I soon earned the reputation for being cheerful and having an ability to defuse potentially unpleasant situations. It soon became clear to me that Kent Police was the same as any other firm with people just trying to make a difference and earn a living for their family.

After three months in the role, was called in by two inspectors who asked me about joining up as a police officer. I really appreciated the offer, especially as I was on a six month probation period, and to be highly thought of so soon made me realise I was doing better than okay. I thought about the offer but had just settled nicely into the job and felt it suited me and the developing refereeing career. They respected my decision, stating that I was a welcome addition to Medway's custody team. I appreciated being appreciated.

The strip searches were a bit of an eye opener, so to speak. Nothing in my past could've prepared me for them. This guy had been arrested, had a history with the police for concealing drugs and knew the way things worked. Because the copper was on his own, I had to be present as a witness during the search of the suspect. He was asked to remove his shirt and top, which he did. The search found nothing. He was then able to put these items back on and was asked to remove his trousers, pants, shoes and socks. Next he was asked to squat down and despite his best efforts, we could see he was trying to keep something 'in' by the strained look on his face! It was noted that he had a lighter poking out of his backside, which was retrieved by the gloved-up policeman. When he realised he'd been rumbled, he relaxed and his tobacco, wrapped in clingfilm, made an appearance. Just as I was getting over the shock of that, something else appeared… a mobile phone… with charger! My face must have been a picture. This prisoner had so much stuff popping out of his arse that it reminded me of the conveyor belt on the generation game. The only differences were that Brucie wasn't saying, 'cuddly toy, cuddly toy,' or 'Didn't he do well!'

Welcome to The Five Bars Hotel and I'll show you to your room. It's an all-inclusive stay and no tipping is required. What does make them chuckle is when I tell them the mini bar's expensive. No one's a saint and sometimes people are just unlucky enough to have been caught doing something they wouldn't normally do. The way I see it, they're in the shit, so why make it worse? My motto is – treat people how you would like to be treated; fairly and with respect.

Just before my six months probationary period had finished, a sergeant told me he was concerned because I was on first name terms with so many of our guests. Of course I was, I grew up in the area, some had been neighbours, some were friends and of course I knew a lot of people in the area through boxing. The sergeant's comments made me worry I'd get the sack at the six month point. Spoke to another sergeant who told me not to worry as they were quite happy with my knowledge of the clientele as I seemed to be able to calm things down. That put me at ease.

One day at Chatham Magistrates, Jock asked me if I wanted to take a prisoner up to face the 'beak'. My job was to make sure we didn't lose him. I said yes, escorted the prisoner to the dock and stood next to him, all professional, shoulders back and chin up. His solicitor came over for a chat with him and I was asked to take him down. We negotiated the stairs and Jock asked me what was to happen with the prisoner.

From his question, realised I should have been paying attention to what the Magistrate was saying, instead of people watching. I hadn't been listening to the case because as far as I was concerned, it was nothing to do with me. Already feeling an idiot I was tempted to say he'd been released but thought I'd better come clean in case I got it wrong. 'I dunno'!' I answered.

'What?! You have to listen to find out what they want done with him!'

He sent me back up to the court. As my head popped up, I must have looked like a blushing, black, chad (the cartoon character), as I only put my eyes above the rail. Everyone looked at me as I sheepishly asked what they wanted done with the detainee. They told me he was free to go and I sank back down to be hidden from the court. Never made that mistake again.

On another occasion the solicitor came up with a story that got more and more sorrowful as it went on. All he needed was a violinist in the corner of the court playing music and there wouldn't have been a dry eye in the place. He pointed to the guy's wife in the viewing gallery, who was sobbing on cue and showing just how pregnant she was. When he finished his heart breaking tale he said to the magistrate, 'Can I approach my client to make sure I have covered everything?'

The Magistrate nodded and the solicitor walked toward his client, looking almost sorrowful, as if there was a travesty of justice going on. As the solicitor reached me, he smirked, gave me a wink and said, 'What do you think of that story then? Good eh?'

17 December 1996: Danny Stevens versus 'Kid' McCauley.

With all the fights that I was stopping at The Five Bars, I found it ironic to be in a boxing ring, having to disqualify a boxer, because he wasn't. As far as I was concerned 'Kid' just came to dance, and as this was York Hall, Bethnal Green and not The Lyceum ballroom in the Strand, I disqualified him.

Steve Holdsworth, commentator on Eurosport, who is always quick with a comment, said I obviously didn't have my Christmas head on and that I'd denied the boxer his Christmas money. Thanks Steve.

If there is a disqualification, the Board review the decision and decide if they will award all, half, or none of the purse. The Board reviewed it and I am pleased to say 'Kid' was paid in full. Merry Christmas!

Back at The Five Bars, took a guest to the desk to enable him to check out. I enquired if his stay had been a pleasant one and we said our goodbyes. Thought I may as well get ahead and clear the room for the next guest as sometimes they appear unannounced as 'surprisingly' there is no specified check in time. Donned the gloves and as I lifted the bed I noticed that he had left us a tip, well more of a deposit. He'd taken a shit and smeared it all over the underside of his bed. Went out, told the sergeant that our guest had mislaid an item belonging to him and the guy who was being released said, 'Ian, that was not directed at you, but this place is a shit hole.'

The sergeant went in, saw it and said to the guy he wouldn't be going anywhere until it was cleaned up. It took him about two hours to make it presentable and he was let go.

16 April 1997: York Hall, Bethnal Green.

I had the pleasure of refereeing Gary Jacobs fighting a very tough Ukranian journeyman, Victor Fessetcheko. (Victor is now a referee and I occasionally bump into him on the circuit. Nice guy.)

Gary Jacobs won on points and was still formidable. Preferred refereeing his fight than sparring with him. Seeing his punches land on poor Victor took me back to when I 'sparred' with him back in '89 when I was an up and coming boxer. Between rounds I wanted to go to Victor and say, 'His punches bloody hurt don't they!'

Back in '89, Gary was WBC International Welterweight and Commonwealth Champion. Les had suggested to Gary's team that I'd be a good sparring partner as I had a similar style to the unbeaten George Collins, who Gary was due to fight at the Royal Albert Hall. They employed me for the week and as far as I was concerned, was there to spar with Gary and help him out by practicing various aspects of George's style. Once in the ring I said to him, 'Alright Gary, how do you want me to spar, long, short, inside?'

In his Scottish accent he gave me a short, to the point reply, one that raised alarm bells, 'Just do the best you can do.'

'What the fuck's that meant to mean?' I thought.

Found out what it meant when he threw the first punch, a big left hander. When it landed on my nose it felt like he flattened it to the shape of my face. From that punch I knew I'd be earning my money and for three days went to war with him. In that first 'sparring' session, we were trying to knock each other out. I did four hard rounds with him, was quite knackered and then when warming down skipping, I looked up into the ring to see Gary going another four rounds with a fresh sparring partner. Once those four rounds had finished he then fought another four with another fresh boxer. Awesome fitness and a guy who obviously lived his life in the gym.

After three days of warring with Gary, his trainer, Bobby Neil, former British Featherweight Champion, called us together, read us the riot act and told us to stop trying to damage each other. Gary took notice of his trainer and on the last two days we took it easier and really worked on boxing rather than bludgeoning.

At the end of the week we shook hands and he thanked me for my hard work. He went on to win the fight, keeping his title and gave Collins his first defeat. Jacobs was a really classy boxer and I don't regret never having fought him.

Arriving for the late-turn shift (2pm start), the custody sergeant shouted, 'Good Afternoon, Ian; you're just in time, another pair of hands will help nicely.'

There were a lot of officers in the cell block milling around, so wondered what was going on. 'No problems, Sarge. What's all the commotion about?' I asked.

'The big guy in cell 4 said he's not going to have his fingerprints done, so we're going to take them by force,' he replied.

'Anyone tried to reason with him?'

The sergeant replied that the guest had refused to speak to anyone as he was so angry.

'Who is he? Let me have a word with him,' I replied.

I walked down to the room, opened the cell hatch and recognised him immediately as he had been in custody only a few weeks earlier.

'Hi mate… there are a lot of officers out here just waiting to get their hands on you,' I said.

'Really, let them come in here and try, I'll smash the first one that comes in here,' he replied.

'I remember you. Last time you were in, you were a good old boy. What's your beef, bud?'

'Yeah, I remember you too. You're sound mate, but them out there are fucking arse holes.'

'Well look, if you don't comply, they'll come in here, bend you up and then take your fingerprints. They have to and I don't want to see that happen to you 'cos you're alright.'

'Well, if you take them, I'll be no problem,' he replied. So I did and, as promised, he was no trouble at all. Bruises saved all round

20 May 1997: Black Lion, Gillingham.

Harry Dhami versus Paul Miles; for the Welterweight Southern Area Title.

There was no one free from bruises this night. This was my first title fight as a Class A referee and was the title I fought for against Trevor Smith, which had been voted small hall fight of the year. It was emotional to say the least and just a little walk from my living room to get there.

When the fighters were announced there was a big cheer for them and when I was announced, they nearly took the roof off the place. I was shocked by the reception, especially as many of the cheering crowd I had locked up in custody!

Paul Miles gave him a good fight, but Dhami was just too classy. At that point I never thought that Dhami had the ability to win a British Title but it was nice to be proved wrong. The man from Kent just got better and better and worked hard to improve.

As I climbed down from the ring at the end of the fight, my hand was nearly shaken completely off with local people giving me best wishes and patting me on the back. Neighbours, friends, and guests of The Five Bars congratulated me, asking for autographs and photos. I loved it, to be given that kind of reception from the locals meant a hell of a lot. I was respected.

After another fight at York Hall, I was coming down the A2 on a long downhill stretch and my car just cut out. Ran it to the bottom of the hill and walked into the garage.

Soon after, a tow truck came in. I was dressed in my referees gear and the garage manager asked if the guy in the car transporter could help me out. He looked at me, said yes, loaded my car onto the transporter and we set off. I looked at the guy and realised I had at one time locked him up and did my best to make myself as inconspicuous as possible. While he drove I kept the collar of my coat up, trying to half cover my face. 'I know you,' he said.

I gulped, thinking I may now have my car dumped at the side of the road, maybe with me under it.

'Yeah? I'm a boxing referee... may have seen me on the telly.'

'No, not the telly. You were the bloke who locked me up...' The time he took for him to say I locked him up and his next sentence seemed an age, 'you're alright you are.'

Relieved, out I breathed and was a bit lost for words but we just chatted about boxing. When we got to Gillingham, he even popped the bonnet of my car and told me what was wrong with it! Nice bloke.

I know lots of people in Medway and the surrounding areas, and when Kelcie was little, she would be puzzled by people stopping me in the street. They would refer to me as Ian, John L, Louie, mate, geezer, guv, jailer. When they'd gone, if they'd been guests of The Five Bars, I would look at Kelcie, and make a locking cell sound and pretend to turn a key. As she got older she would look at me and if she thought they'd been a guest then she would make the sound. Generally she got it right but had to tell her once that she'd got it very wrong. The guy she thought was a Five Bars guest was in fact an off duty policeman.

If I meet people on the street who have attended The Five Bars, I mirror what greeting they offer me. If they nod, I nod back, if they say hello, I say hello. Some shake my hand and stop for a chat (usually about boxing) telling me they acknowledge me because I treated them with respect. Isn't that what we all want?

Back at the Five Bars was doing a 'constant'. This is where, if you feel a prisoner is a risk to themselves, you sit outside a cell with the viewing flap down. The prisoner was talking to me, wittering on about not much but then went quiet. The next time I checked on him he was just sitting there. I wasn't happy, he was too quiet and when I looked again, I found him hanging from the sheet of his bed, in the process of trying to kill himself. Rushed in, calling for help as I went, grabbed him, lifting him up to take the pressure from his neck. He croaked at me, rasping through tight vocal chords,

'Let me die! Let me die!'

'Not on my bloody watch you won't,' I answered.

I am glad to say he didn't.

02 May 1998: The Royal Albert Hall!

When I stood in the centre of the ring, Frank Maloney's words came back to haunt me! 'Ian... big opportunity... live on Sky... the Albert Hall!'

'Should so have fought here,' I thought. The guy I was meant to fight was good but I could've played hit and run and that's what I was imagining when I stood in the ring.

It was an honour to referee the undercard here; what a place to officiate in. I was looking forward to seeing Spencer Oliver fight again and defend his European title. He was all 'glitz and glamour' as he was carried into the ring on a Sedan chair with an orchestra playing 'O fortuna'. I went cold when I heard the music and colder still when years later I read the words in English, especially the last three lines.

'Because fate

Brings down even the strong

Everyone weep with me.'

Spencer was carried in on a Sedan chair and left on a stretcher after round eight. That was the end of his career but I'm pleased to say he made a great recovery. After seeing him carried from the ring, I thought maybe I was right not to fight at the Albert Hall.

Back at The Five Bars, two old boxing friends of mine became regular guests and in the end I knew them as Drugs and Alcohol, their favoured poison. Their decline to oblivion was fast. They were booked in and I had a chat with Drugs in the dead of night. As we spoke I could smell something dying and saw that he kept scratching at his leg. 'Let's see that mate.' I said.

He tried to hide his leg behind the other one.

'Ian... don't mate, I'm embarrassed.'

'That don't smell good, let's take a look.'

He pulled up his jeans and his calf was a mess and smelled of rotting flesh. It was the site he was injecting into and it was festering, bruised and dying. Got the nurse to have a look and he was given medical intervention. One month later he was dead: a drugs overdose.

Six weeks later Alcohol came in again. Another chat in the dead of night and we got talking about Drugs, his partner in crime, who'd passed away. Told him that he needed to be careful or he could be going the same way as Drugs.

'Leave it out, Ian. Used to always warn him about sticking that shit in his veins. Just like a drink, me.'

Four weeks later he was gone, drank himself to death, choked on his own vomit.

Different poison, same outcome.

Always discussed the refereeing with Les and always learnt something. One day he said to me, when we were in a café chatting, that there comes a time in life as you get older that your friends start dying. Never heard Les talk like this and was a bit shocked. What I didn't know was that Les's health was failing and he was preparing me for the inevitable: that he wouldn't be around for ever. I was still quite young and didn't think of death and dying. There were people boxing still who were older than me and I still felt fairly indestructible.

Our meetings in the Café lessened and we spoke on the phone more as he was unable to get to shows. He always played down his illness and although I knew he was unwell, still expected him to get better and for us to carry on as we always had. Then one day, the phone rang, it was his wife Cora, telling me that Les had died. Was numb, in shock, managed to offer my condolences although my brain was screaming, 'No!' I managed a bit of small talk, not really knowing what to say as she and Les had been together a lifetime. I'd only known him for twelve years and was devastated.

Can't remember what was said between us but had to put the phone down soon enough. Was raw and found myself sitting down, heart racing, feeling sick and weak. Next the tears came and boy did they come. Kelcie came into the room, looked at me and said, 'Daddy, why are you crying?'

It was pointless trying to dry the tears but I did anyway as I answered her, 'A really good person who always looked after me, Kelcie, has died.'

'What, like you look after me?'

I thought about what she said, nodded as I realised that to me Les was more than just a loyal, wise, respectful friend and mentor. I went to the bedroom and cried like a baby.

Millennium

When starting out refereeing, Les and I set myself the goal of gaining the top grade, ' star class' within ten years, so was really surprised when Richie Davis, (referee at my last pro fight), rang and told me I'd been recommended for the promotion after only seven. In January 2000, I returned to the BBB of C office again, to meet with the 'Knights of the Round Table' once more. This time is wasn't daunting because I was to be told officially of the promotion. What a start to the new millennia.

At the same time, my good mate Mark Green, an Essex boy and a referee for only two years longer than myself, got his star class licence too. We'd first met at a show back in 1994 and hit it off straight away. We're the same age, had the same passion for the sport and like a good laugh. As the chairman, 'Nipper' Reed (our nick name for him after the famous copper who put away the Kray twins) was expressing to us how proud we should be on achieving the grade, I was thinking of Les Roberts and how proud he'd be of me. Although really happy to get the promotion, I was sad he wasn't there to see it and share it. I'd never have thought of going into the profession and would never have been as good a referee without him.

The chairman told us that when travelling around the world, we wouldn't only be representing the BBB of C but also Great Britain too. What an honour and responsibility. Mark and I floated out of that meeting, two very proud youngish men. Later that evening I raised a glass to Les, thanked him for his loyalty, his guidance and hoped that perhaps he was looking down at me, proud of our achievement. Even today, many years later, anytime I travel abroad on a refereeing job, always raise my glass to him with the first drink on the plane.

It was around this time that I decided to do a 'Hagler', before nature did, and shave my hair off. Although I'd always had a Number 2 haircut, it was a bit daunting to go 'shiny' but when I was young, told myself that if I started to become 'follicly challenged', I'd shave it off. Looking in the mirror I could see there was more head than hair and noticed that at the barber's, the time Tom held up the mirror for me to see the back of my head, was getting shorter and shorter, until it was just a flash. The final follicle was after refereeing on television one night. I got back home and Julie said that 'Fat Dave' had phoned and couldn't wait to tell her that he'd seen me on the telly and thought I looked like a black Friar Tuck.

Off it came and my mates and colleagues at the nick called me 'Errol' (Errol Brown) from that successful 70's pop band 'Hot Chocolate'. Some of my mates, colleagues and regulars at The Five Bars, even sang 'No doubt about it' and 'You sexy thing' to me. Sweet! Yul Brynner, the famous actor from the Magnificent Seven, was another name I was known as but the one I laughed the most at was, 'Malteser Head'. Most importantly, Julie said it suited me. She said she liked it and that I looked like my hero 'Marvellous' Marvin Hagler. Before I could get my chest puffed up at the compliment she then added, 'Shame you couldn't fight like him, love.'

Cutting... very cutting.

My good mate Mark Green is a top referee, always in charge when in the ring and the one I always discuss fights with. We use each other for honest feedback. It's important to have someone you trust to tell you how it is and believe me, Mark tells you how it is!

When we can, we travel to shows together as he's just across the water in Essex and if we're heading north then he's on the way. For the six years of travelling together around the country, he also liked to tell me what he thought of my choice of radio station: 'KISS FM Louie... Kiss my arse!'

He hated it and was always telling me to turn it down, miserable git. Then one day when travelling to Manchester, he said, 'Bloody hell

Louie, I'd rather be deaf than listen to this crap any longer. You got any other music in that glove box of yours?'

He opened it and was shocked to see some CDs of that long running and still performing band 'The Stranglers' and the 'Greatest Hits' of the Red Hot Chilli Peppers.

'Stranglers? You like the bloody Stranglers?'

'Yeah, course I do. Love 'em. No More Heroes, Nice 'n' Sleazy, Peaches – brilliant!'

'You mean to tell me you've had this great music in the car all this time and you have forced me to listen to that crap on the radio. Sadist... that's what you are Louis... bloody sadist.'

Now, every time we drive to a show, we start the journey with the Chillis playing, 'Under the Bridge' and 'Californication', as loud as the speakers will allow. Don't know what passing motorists think but we end up looking like that Bohemian Rhapsody scene from Wayne's World when 'No More Heroes' and 'Nice 'n' Sleazy' comes on. Passes the time and keeps us awake on those long journeys.

Being promoted to star class referee would now open up the world for me. The kid from Darnley Road, Strood, who didn't see Big Ben or the Houses of Parliament until his twenties, was about to travel the world...

And the first stop on my World Tour... Leicester, England.

Didn't need a plane.

At the fight I ran into Tony Sibson who came down to see Neil Linford, the new local prospect from his manor. Spoke to Tony and told him I'd watched some of his fights when I was a young amateur and was honoured to meet him.

'Unfortunately Tony, I wanted you to win the 'Undisputed' Middleweight Championship of the World, but your opponent was my hero…'Marvellous' Marvin Hagler,' I said.

He chuckled and replied, 'Ian, he was my hero too… and I can still feel the punches!'

Years later I read in a book that Hagler also remembered Sibson, especially his left hook, a tribute to Tony Sibson's awesome power.

03 March, 2000: Really clocking up those miles now. Unfortunately, not air miles… tonight, Barnsley Metrodome.

This was the first big championship fight for me to referee. Derek 'the Rebel' Roche, versus Harry Dhami for the British Welterweight Championship. 'Rebel' Roche, the unbeaten champion, was on a roll, having defended his title twice in great style. The fight was in his neck of the woods and he was fancied by most to win it.

If I wasn't nervous enough, I had four top referees watching me. Men I respected, admired and dreamed that one day I'd reach their level of expertise and also become world class. The four referees were Roy Francis, Dave Parris, John Coyle and Paul Thomas.

For the pre-fight instructions, went first to the dressing room of Roche. Roy Francis accompanied me to show me the ropes and guide me with what to say to the boxers. He went through his normal spiel, which left no one in any doubt what we wanted from them.

'Okay, Ian is refereeing you tonight. Give us a good fight. When he's in the ring giving an instruction, you don't have to look at him, but make sure you listen! The only words he'll be shouting, will be, box! Stop boxing! Break! Don't hold!'

Sounded good to me and I used it from that day on.

Next we went to see the challenger, Harry Dhami. Looks can be deceiving but it was not the dressing room of a champion in waiting and the corner man made a statement that I thought was more than just a bit defensive, almost accepting that they had little chance of winning,

'Everything is against us tonight, the crowd, the venue. All I ask is that we get a fair shake,' said Terry O'Toole.

Took on board what he said and thought of my answer, an answer given from someone who knows what it is like to be on the end of a questionable decision, in a venue with the crowd for the other guy.

'You won't get a fairer man than me, Terry.'

I stood in the ring waiting for Roche to appear and as if I didn't have enough emotion to control, bagpipes began to play for him as he made his way through the crowd. The pipes made the tiny follicles on my head stand to attention. Bagpipes finished, Ian Darke made the announcements to the crowd. He gave me a great plug, by letting them know it was my first title fight as a star class referee, told them where I worked and reminded me that there'd be a lot of friends and family watching. No pressure then.

The bell sounded the start of the fight. The nerves I'd been feeling left me and I was in the zone. Rounds one and two were good and uneventful and I felt I was cruising along with no problem. In round three, Dhami was put down and was claiming a slip. Ian Darke said my first ever big decision at this level of boxing was a controversial one, but, when they went through the recording, agreed I'd made the right call that it was indeed a knockdown.

The un-fancied Harry Dhami then proceeded to put the unbeaten Roche down six times; once, unfortunately, due to a low blow that really did hurt Roche. It was accidental but Roche could really have played on this. He'd have known he was behind on points and in the year 2000, could've said he couldn't continue, which would've put me in a terrible position as I'd have had to disqualify Dhami. But no, not Roche, a warrior with a massive heart, a man of real integrity; he got off the canvas and decided that if he was going to win, he would win with his fists and on his feet.

In round 12, Roche, knowing he was still behind, went head hunting. Both men were exhausted with not much left in the tank, shots were connecting, not bombs but hard enough to put you on your arse when your legs are rubber. The bell rang out the finish of the fight and we all knew Dhami had won, to become the first British Asian to win the title, refereed by the first, and still only, black British star class referee.

Both corners thanked me, which is easier for the winning side to do. I've always said, when the losing corner gives thanks, you know you've done a good job. It was a great fight and Roche did brilliantly to last the distance. The way he behaved that night was a credit to the sport of boxing and himself. I have so much respect for the man they called the 'Rebel.' Eventually he turned to training fighters and is really highly thought of, not least by me.

Fight over; found I was buzzing because of the quality of the contest and compliments from the corners. Climbed down from the ring, happy with my performance, to be met by the four, star class referees who'd been observing me in my first big fight. They were all smiles, seemed like there were teeth everywhere I turned. Unnerving it was. They gathered round, almost encircling me, congratulated me, patted me on the back, told me I'd done a great job and said I'd done the profession of refereeing proud. It ended with John Coyle, acting as the spokesman, saying, 'John L... that was brilliant... welcome to the elite my son!'

I had to fight the lump in my throat which felt like the size of a boxing glove. Accepted to the elite, by the elite. Meant a lot to me; still does. All those years of hard work... well worth it.

Ian Darke said there was so much that went on in the match that Ian John-Lewis may referee for the next ten years and not get a fight like this! He was wrong.

A few days later, back at The Five Bars hotel, was walking away from a cell where the occupier was busy screaming the obvious, that I was black, and also the not true, that my mum and dad weren't married. Didn't understand his noise as I had brought him a cup of tea, with sugar, well stirred, which is what he'd asked for. As I tuned out the abuse, I recognised a name on the chalk board on a cell further down. My stomach turned as I opened the viewing hatch to see yet another old acquaintance, the son of a really great friend. Any other occasion it would have been good to see him but not like this, not in here. He looked well and when he recognised me, was obviously embarrassed.

My initial reaction was that of a dad and almost said, *'What the fuck are you doing here?!'* But my professional head said, 'Hello mate, want a drink?'

'Yes please, Ian... Hot chocolate.'

Made him a drink and thought about the meeting we'd be having. Read his charge sheet which showed he had been brought in for drug offences. It wasn't his first time, but he was just starting out, dabbling in them. As a detention officer I knew the fall into full-blown addiction can be fast for the drug user and hard for the family. Sensed a 'dead of the night' chat coming on and if I could get him to see sense then it would be worth my hour break.

We spoke for the whole hour. This guy was from a good family, had a really good job but had gotten himself into weekend drugs and the trouble that can go with it. We spoke about the bad old, good old days, about what he was like as a kid and how his parents really cared and worried about him. In those early hours of the morning, thought I'd got through to him and left him to get some sleep. As I went to shut the cell door he said, 'Ian mate… please don't tell my dad.'

Assured him I wouldn't but told him to sort himself out and get some help. Went to go back to my workstation and the prisoner who had given me the abuse an hour before called to me through the closed viewing hatch, a lot calmer, 'Excuse me Guv.'

'Yes mate,' I replied in a friendly manner.

'You, Ian John-Lewis, the boxing ref?'

Answered expecting more abuse but boxing related, or him saying 'I know where you live' type of stuff. But there was no more abuse, just a quiet unreserved apology, 'Sorry about earlier, guv, didn't know it was you I was speaking to. You're all right you are.'

'Thanks for that mate; appreciated,' I replied.

We had a chat through the viewing flap about boxing, found out he was quite a fan of the noble art.

Next morning, let my friend's son out. He looked better than the night before and I hoped our chat would help him somehow. It didn't.

He became a regular, his youth and good looks disappeared quickly and he took on a more tortured expression as he became more addicted. In desperation I even showed him a picture from when he was fresh faced and first arrested. It made no difference and the guy I knew well, just disappeared, 'till at the end he hardly recognised me and didn't seem to care that he was back in custody again.

His job was gone. The crimes to feed his habit were getting worse. He was lost. It was now his way of life and in a matter of weeks he died from a drink and drugs overdose. What a waste. He was such a talented boy, somebody's son, my mate's son. Heart-breaking.

My poor old passport was gathering dust, the bloke in the photo still had hair and I still didn't need a plane for my next appointment as a world class official. I was to be one of the judges, along with the very experienced Roy Francis, at the IBF World Championship fight in Bristol.

07 April 2000: Bristol, England

IBF Super Bantamweight Championship

Lehlohonolo Ledwaba (Champion) v Ernesto Grey (Challenger)

We had only moved into our new home, a week before, so felt a little guilty taking the day off to travel to Bristol but Julie was great about it. What a classy boxer Ledwaba was, completely dominating the experienced Grey, stopping him in the eighth.

One of the lads who was part of a small gang that used to bully me as a kid, was pulled into the station, arrested for drinking while driving and assault on police. The arresting officers had to use pepper spray to subdue him. It must have been twenty years plus since I last was abused by him and of course I could remember his name. Not one to bear grudges, I said, 'Hello fellah.'

He looked at me as if he couldn't believe his sore, swollen, watering, pepper-sprayed eyes. His facial expression turned to one of fear and the first words that came out of his mouth were, 'Is this payback time then?'

Was taken aback but answered calmly, 'Don't be stupid. Water under the bridge.'

I found it strange, I'd been a boxer, a doorman and was no stranger to confrontation, but when I saw this guy who had bullied me as a young kid, the fear came straight back. It also brought back some very unhappy memories of my childhood when I had to be wary of walking past three particularly abusive households in Darnley Road. He was treated no differently than any of the other guests.

06 October 2000: Maidstone, Kent

Dominic Negus versus Gary Delaney

Southern Area Cruiserweight Championship

Could've caught the bus to this one and was starting to think I'd been grounded! Roy Francis, top referee, told me this Southern Area cruiserweight fight could be a rough one and said I'd better be on the top of my game. Thought to myself that if I couldn't handle it then I wouldn't be worthy of being a star class referee.

Was a rough fight by two hard, tough men who continually tried to out-psych each by talking in the clinches. The chat wasn't stuff like, 'Great boots Gary, very flash,' or, 'Looking dapper there Dom.' No, it was a tad more unfriendly.

After ten hard rounds, Gary won on points to become the new Champion. Felt I did a good job, let the fight flow by working hard and keeping them from getting into too many clinches. Boxing is an art, when boxers hold on too long it becomes a bore and a chore, the public don't like it and neither do I.

My new passport remained stamp less. My first passport had only ever received two stamps, so now I had as many passports as trips. Then one January morning I received a call from the IBF.

'Hi there Ian, we have an appointment for you, can you go to Kazakhstan?'

'Kazzak who?! Where the fuck's that?!' I thought, ecstatic, but saying, 'Yes!'

I'd been selected to officiate at the International Boxing Federation Cruiserweight Championship, on the 6th of February, 2001 in Almaty, Kazakhstan. A contest between Vasiliy 'The Tiger' Jorov (Kazakhstan) and Alex Gonzalez (Mexico).

I put down the phone and dusted off the Reader's Digest Atlas that Julie had bought me when I got promoted. I located Kazakhstan and was surprised to find it was a big country that the UK could fit into many times over. Almaty, my destination, was right down the bottom of the country, on the border with China.

'Oh yes!' I thought. I definitely needed a plane as I was going halfway around the World. I rang Mark Green, who was really pleased for me, and a month later, Mark called me, excited about his first appointment abroad, which was at Caesars' Palace, Las Vegas. Lucky sod.

Drove to Heathrow airport, buzzing, so excited, and while waiting at the departure gate I noticed the Puerto Rican referee, Roberto Ramirez. Had seen him referee big fights on TV many times and he was to be a judge at this contest. I was going to be in top company and flew top company too, Emirates airlines. Enjoyed this international experience and for once, instead of me taking drinks and meals to guests, someone kindly brought them to me and they didn't get insulted doing it. The service was almost as good too.

When we touched down there was snow everywhere. Fortunately, I'd checked the weather before leaving and was dressed for it. Couldn't have my head getting cold, that wouldn't do.

The hotel was huge and beautiful. When I got to my room way up in the sky and looked out the window, the view was great, to a point, and then the new build stopped and it became shabby and old. It looked like a shanty town.

Later we were taken for a walk and I wrapped up well against the freezing conditions. All the people had fur hats on and were not bothered at all by the snow and ice. They must have known we were visitors by the way we slipped around.

We were told not to give to beggars and be on our guard. One of the judges for the fight, felt quite sorry for a youngster, gave him a few dollars and instantly we were surrounded by lots more. The Kazakhstani official with us read the riot act, but I knew where the judge was coming from. These people had nothing and when you've had nothing yourself, you know how they feel, because the memory never truly fades.

I was fortunate to meet the world class American official Eddie Cotton here, who had been selected to referee the fight. Learnt a lot from him, gave me advice freely, a really nice, generous guy. Because this was my first time at a press conference I watched how the more experienced officials carried themselves. This fight was a massive event as Jorov was defending his world cruiserweight title for the first time in his home land. Armed guards stood everywhere. Everybody wanted to see the 'Tiger' who had won the Light-Heavyweight Olympic Gold at the Atlanta Games in 1996. He'd also won the Val Barker Trophy for outstanding boxer of the games, which is probably equal to winning another gold medal.

On fight night, the Sports Palace stadium was full to bursting, with 16,000 attending to see their world champion. I felt so proud to be judging a fight of this quality and felt like a VIP as we were cheered by the crowd while being escorted to our ringside seats. I wanted more of this.

After the fight, which Jorov won in the very first round, I congratulated him and explained in my best, most fluent Kazakhstani accent, that it was my first world title fight abroad.

He replied, in very good English, not quite cockney enough to make him truly convincing but very good none the less, 'Here, take my boxing gloves as a reminder.'

What a generous gesture and I have them in my gym at home.

The day after the fight we were taken on a tour of the city in a little old mini bus and then began to drive up a mountain for nearly an hour. When we stopped, China, where a billion people live, was pointed out to us. I thought that surely they must have a few world champions living there somewhere, and with the country opening up it should be an interesting time for boxing. Will be keeping an eye on that one and would really love to officiate there.

It was like being on top of the world, really mountainous views and thin air. Shortly after we jumped back in the van and the joyride began. I say joyride but it wasn't much fun with the van engine screaming for mercy in first gear to help save the brakes from overheating. I was glad to get to the bottom and when I got out of the van my legs were wobbly like I'd been hit by Trevor Smith.

26 March 2001: Wembley

Butch Lesley (Champion) versus Tony Oakey (Challenger)

Southern Area light heavyweight Championship

In 2001, the World Boxing Union (WBU) were new and lightly regarded in Britain but were well established in Europe. It was the creation of Jon Robinson, a huge man who once entered 'Britain's fattest man' competition. Jon spent a lot of time in his wheelchair, knew boxing inside out and liked to have things done a certain way.

I was the referee for this title fight and was the first time I'd met the unbeaten Tony Oakey. I thought he looked quite small for a light-heavyweight, and although chunky, thought he'd bitten off more than he could chew when challenging champion, Lesley. I'd refereed Butch a couple of times and knew he was a handful for anyone brave enough to get in the ring with him. But Tony out boxed, out manoeuvred and out punched him, forcing me to stop a cracking contest in the last round.

Feeling I'd done a good job and now able to relax, I sat at ringside to watch the top of the bill. It was this kid called Ricky 'Hitman' Hatton fighting for his first title, the WBU Light-Welterweight Championship, against Tony Pep from Canada. I'd heard a lot of talk about this Hatton and on seeing him fight, knew it wasn't just hype. Pep wasn't a bad fighter, but couldn't keep the relentless, body punching Hitman away and was crushed in four rounds. Pep found the canvas three times from rib crunching body shots, which would soon be known as Hatton's 'brand'. Hatton now began his long WBU Championship reign and because of his massive following, a fan base not seen since the Barry McGuigan glory days, it made the WBU big business in the UK.

At the end of the night, I saw Reg Thompson, a very good referee, who'd refereed me four times as a pro, talking to Jon Robinson. Didn't know who the big fellah was at that time, but went to say hello to Reg and Jon introduced himself to me, told me he was President of the WBU and would like me to officiate for them.

I was over the moon with Jon's offer. Here I was just a newly starred referee who wanted to get some bigger fights and I was being offered the chance with the WBU. At the time I was officiating for the IBF who the BBB of C had appointed me to, but I wanted to get more coverage, to be able to display my ability and so get the bigger fights. At that time in boxing, I was becoming well known in Britain, which was great, but also wanted to branch out and referee worldwide.

That night I sent my details by fax as requested to Jon so he could contact me for appointments. One month later, thinking he may have forgotten me, I received a fax from Jon asking me to officiate at a WBU Cruiserweight Championship in Liverpool, a show that would be live on Sky Sports. Problem was the BBB of C had also appointed me to referee a Commonwealth Lightweight Championship on the same show. In my naivety I was thinking, *'Good... Double bubble!'*

Double money in refereeing terms is not a lot and I wasn't in refereeing for the cash. I contacted the WBU, thanked Jon for my first appointment, and told him that I was refereeing the Commonwealth title fight also that night. Jon told me that I couldn't work for the WBU that night. He had rules and one of them was that if you were officiating for the WBU, you couldn't take part in any other fight. Officiating the world title would earn me a few quid more so I rang the boxing Board and told them I couldn't referee that night as I had been booked by the WBU. The Board put me straight saying that I was licenced by the BBB of C, not the

WBU, and they'd appointed me to referee a title fight in Liverpool. I got the message, rang and explained to Jon, who told me not to worry and that he'd get me another fight, another time. I thanked him, put the phone down and hoped I hadn't missed my opportunity with the WBU.

At that Liverpool show I did the Commonwealth title fight between Alex Moon (Liverpool) and Karim Nashar (Austrailia). What a good fight. Nashar wore crazy bright yellow fur shorts. They must have weighed a ton towards the end of the twelve rounder, with the water and sweat that had soaked into them. Sure they never helped his movement round the ring. It went the distance with Moon winning fairly comfortably on points. From a refereeing point of view it went well as I didn't have much to do in this very clean fight between two good boxers. This was yet another championship fight under my belt and because of all the televised shows, I was now starting to get noticed walking round the local town centres.

Once back at The Five Bars I knew we had a boxer in a cell. I had just come on duty and was walking to the room where the unhappy guest was kicking off. He was abusing the custody sergeant from the other side of the door and in order for the sergeant to get a face to face, he decided to drop the viewing flap to talk. As he did, a fist that belonged to a bantamweight came out of the viewing flap and just missed a quickly reacting sergeant. Knew he was a boxer as he didn't catch his knuckles on the way out, or way in, of the viewing flap.

'Great accuracy,' I found myself whispering.

That day it seemed some of the guests were more punchy than normal and when I explained to the guest that he'd be going straight to prison, not home first, he looked down at his hands, formed fists and before I could say, 'Don't!', he'd punched the wall. I winced on his behalf but he felt the pain as he broke several bones in his hand. The wall was unscathed and won by technical knock-out. Always does.

03 August 2001: Avezzano Rome Italy

Ferid Ben Jeddou: Champion (Tunis) v Magoma Shabanica: Challenger (Tanzania)

WBU Super-Flyweight Championship

My first world title fight as referee. Jon Robinson rang me and gave me this open air fight, up in the mountains. It was free to anyone who wanted to attend and was televised by Italian TV. Was nervous but got even worse when the cabby, who took us up the mountain, thought he was a rally driver. There were shrines at the side of the road to mark where people had gone over the edge and died. Thought I might be getting one of my very own and when I arrived, stumbled out the cab and whispered, 'Thank fuck for that!'

Fortunately it was lost in translation and I walked off on unsteady legs, anybody watching me may have thought I'd taken a drink.

Was excited about refereeing my first World title fight, but to do it on my first 'open air' show was fabulous. The day before the fight, we checked the already built ring and the surrounding area. They'd done a great job. I asked who was going to guard it overnight in case of theft or damage. The official looked at me strangely and appeared not to know what I was talking about. The day of the fight I got to the ring early, I suppose to make sure it was still there. It was. I told Jon Robinson that if this had been in my neck of the woods that by morning the ring would've been up for sale in some of the surrounding pubs.

Weird feeling, standing in the middle of the ring feeling a warm breeze and the hot sun on my face. It was quite relaxing but shook this feeling from me when I brought both fighters to the centre of the ring. I could see in Shabani's eyes that he was up for this and from the first bell he came swinging, showing the Champion no respect for his better boxing skills. Shabani was hungry for victory, crude in style, but his determination couldn't be criticised as he continued to put the champion on his back foot.

Jeddou tried, and at times succeeded, to make the Tanzanian look silly with his classy footwork, but Shabani didn't appear to be suffering from humiliation and just upped the pace, continued his relentless assault, forcing me to stop it in round six.

The fight went well from a refereeing point of view and as Jon congratulated me he told me that it was time for me to judge on some of Ricky Hatton's fights. Felt I was on my way and gained a lot of confidence as Jon obviously trusted me.

08 October 2001: Metrodome Barnsley

Bobby Vanzie (Champion) v Anthony Maynard (Challenger)

British Lightweight Championship

This was one of the days that I couldn't get off from work. I was let go early by the sergeant to be able to make the fight. Arrived on time, changed, entered the ring, said my spiel and within 38 seconds I had to dive in and protect the sagging Maynard from further punishment from an absolutely smoking Vanzie.

Because I couldn't get the next morning off, I had about three hours kip, showered and was heading south by 3 a.m. to make work by 7 a.m. All that effort to referee 38 seconds of action – well worth it! I knew the day would be long and hard but because of my love for the sport, I took it on the chin and struggled through.

Most of the time I'm lucky as I've a great team around me who do their best to swop days off and cover me when refereeing around the country and world. Thanks guys, much appreciated.

03 November 2001: Carnival City South Africa

Cassius Baloyi versus Philip Ndou

WBU Super-Featherweight Championship

These were two world class fighters from South Africa, competing for the vacant Championship. Baloyi was unbeaten in 26 fights with 13 knockouts, while Ndou had been beaten only once in 25 fights, with an incredible 24 knockouts to his name. No wonder they called him the 'Time Bomb'.

South Africa wanted to know who the best was in this eagerly awaited clash. The WBU wanted foreign officials due to the fighter's tribes having a big rivalry. In my innocence I thought about the rivalry between Strood and Chatham but after a brief chat with another official, realised that this was more than just a postcode problem.

A group of us travelled together and flew into Johannesburg. It was a hot, manic, packed airport with many guys touting their taxis. Thankfully we were met in arrivals and taken, under armed guard, to our complex. I'd seen armed guards before in Kazakhstan, but felt like the guns were for show. This was different, there was an atmosphere and the guards were very serious, almost like they expected trouble. Was glad to get to the safety of the hotel but didn't sleep too well, a bit nervy with all the guns around.

Everywhere we went were mean looking guards with very visible weaponry. The day after we arrived they took us out to a market but told us not to show wealth, keep our hands in our pockets and stay close together. The hawkers in the market were heavy sellers, trying to engage you in chat to buy tat.

On fight night, I was asked to observe Ndou getting his hands wrapped while another official observed Baloyi. Seen hands wrapped many times but watched Nick Durandt take it to another level. He wrapped them in a very different way and I said, with a puzzled look on my face.

'Not seen them wrapped like that before.'

'Impressed aren't you?' He replied obviously proud of his craft. It was like watching a genius at work.

The gloves were put on, taped and I signed WBU across the tape. This is done to ensure the gloves are not tampered with after we leave.

All the officials huddled in one dressing room and were quiet. The noise coming from the packed stadium was deafening. If we'd any doubt about how big this fight was before we got to the venue, we didn't now. There was a knock on the door and waiting for us were armed escorts who took us to our positions and stayed with us for the rest of the evening. I was glad of the company.

It was a very entertaining close fight with the frenzied crowd roaring their boxers on. It could have gone either way but Ndou, the puncher, beat the boxer on points. When the result was read out it was taken very well and we were all escorted back to the dressing room. What a cauldron to be an official in.

On touching down from South Africa I had to rush home, change and head straight to work. By the time I got there I was knackered. The Custody Sergeant said, 'To think Ian, this morning you were in a top South African hotel being waited on after judging a World title fight, that I watched live in the UK. Then, this afternoon, you're in custody bringing a prisoner a cup of tea. Amazing, certainly keeps your feet on the ground, young Ian!'

By 8 p.m. it was my chin that was on the ground, when the jet lag really got hold of me. The Sergeant looked at me all wilted and insisted I went home. I didn't argue.

13 December 2001: Equinox, night club, Leicester Square, London

The first female bout that I refereed was between Kathy 'the bitch' Brown (although to be fair she was really nice), versus Ilina Bonova (Kiev).

It was a busy night, as I refereed four female contests. Three of them were stoppages with only one going the distance. What's weird is when you have to get them to break, you have to be careful where you put your hands. After a refereeing career of getting in and wrestling men apart, it was off putting. Decided I would separate them by placing my hand on the shoulder or stomach. It went well and I didn't end up on a register!

On The Nightshift

This ain't the same nightshift the Commodores sang about, no, this is Chatham Custody night shift. Arrived straight from refereeing a fight, still in my tuxedo and dickie bow, and entered the custody suite to be given a nod and a wink by the custody sergeant. I stood next to a very drunk man who was insisting that he wasn't drunk at all, that he was perfectly sober and that the sergeant was mistaken, a killjoy and not a very nice man. I remained quiet but smiling. The drunk man turned, looked me up and down, then looked up at the television and saw me on the screen refereeing a fight, he looked at me again, then the screen and slurred to the sergeant, 'Sergeant... in this instance I think you're right... I'm drunk... probably very drunk,' he pointed at the telly, then me and added, 'I need to sleep. Could you have someone show me to my room, please.'

I changed out of my refereeing clothes, got my uniform on and was told about a prisoner who was doing a dirty protest.

'Oh shit.' I said.

'Yeah... Literally. He's a bit of arsehole, been swearing, kicking the fuck out of the cell door and abusing everyone who tries to speak with him. He's fuming because there's a warrant issued from the Courts and he's to stay here over the weekend. We've got him till Monday morning. That's what he's protesting about.'

Went to the cell, opened the viewing hatch and the stench hit me straight in the nose. I leant away from the smell, breathed in some 'fresh' jail air and said, 'Hello fellah, what's this all about?'

'Fah koffff!' was his not very original response. I'd heard this endearing term so many times in my short career as a detention officer that I'd thought about changing my name to 'Fah kofff' by deed poll.

Looking round the room I could see the walls were covered in his faeces, his bed was on the floor and covered in urine. It stank. He then stared at and recognised me.

'Is that Ian John-Lewis the referee?' he asked.

'Yes mate,' I answered, still being friendly but deciding that I wouldn't be shaking his hand.

It turned out that we were in the same boxing club as kids. He surprised me further by apologising for the state of the cell and asking for a bucket of hot water and a mop. The cell was spotless by the time he'd finished and once he was cleaned up we sat and had a chat. The guy had been a St Mary's boy and he told me of a black and white photo of the old gym that he wanted me to have. Said he'd get it to me in three months as he knew that would be the sentence he'd receive in court on Monday morning.

The custody sergeant couldn't believe the sudden change of heart the prisoner had.

'That guy has been nothing but a pain for a day and a bit. You're here no more than twenty minutes and you've chilled him right out. Glad you came on shift Ian.'

True to his word, three months later he came into The Five Bars and gave me the photo of the gym taken in 1975. It was sad to see him a few months after, arrested again.

26 January 2002: Goresbrook Leisure Centre, Dagenham, Essex.

Colin 'Dynamo' Dunne (Champion) v Martin Jacobs (Challenger) South Africa.

WBU, Lightweight Championship of the World.

The WBU were keeping me nice and busy and this was my first World title fight in the UK to referee. It would be shown live on Sky Sports.

Colin Dunne was a cracking fighter who always set a terrific pace, hence the nickname 'Dynamo'. I'd seen the challenger fight when I was in South Africa, so knew Colin would have his hands full. Jacobs gave Dunne a torrid time, even dropping him during the fast paced fight, but Dunne managed to win narrowly on points to remain champion.

12 February 2002: York Hall, Bethnal Green, London.

Bradley Pryce versus Gavin Downs.

International Boxing Federation (IBF), Inter-Continental Lightweight Championship (Vacant title).

This IBF Championship fight was a war from the off between these two young lions. They gave their all, with Pryce on top at one point only for Downs to come storming back in this see-saw fight. The York Hall crowd were going crazy as first one fighter and then the other took control. In the end, Pryce pinned Downs in the corner, poured a barrage of punches on a defenceless foe, doing enough to make me jump in and stop this wild battle in the ninth. What a fight which was later picked as 'Fight of the Year' by Boxing News.

11 May 2002: Goresbrook leisure centre, Dagenham.

Johnny Armour (Champion) versus Francis Ampofo (Challenger).

WBU, Bantamweight Championship of the World.

It was said that Johnny and myself were mates. True. That we lived in the same area. True. That we'd trained together. True. That we were from the same boxing gym. True. That Frank Maloney had managed us both. True.

So, there were more than a few eyebrows raised when Jon Robinson selected me to referee this fight. Can understand why but as a referee you have to be professional or you let yourself, the profession and the hard working boxers down. That won't do and won't happen on my shift as I have a conscience to keep quiet.

In Ampofo's dressing room, his Manager/Trainer, Dean Powell said to me, 'A few people have asked why I'm I allowing you to referee, as Armour comes from your manor.' He then added, 'I told them I've no problem with you; you're an excellent referee and won't give Armour anything he doesn't earn.'

That is a nice reputation to have, one I have worked hard for.

The contest was just the same as their first fight, a cracking display from both boxers who were in their 30's, which is old for the lighter guys. It would be one of the fights of the year as voted for by the Sky Sports panel. The result after twelve tough rounds was left to the judges, who decided it was Johnny Armour who came out the winner.

A big crowd had come from the Medway towns to support Johnny and in that crowd was Fred Ludlow, who'd trained the pair of us at St Mary's. With tears in his eyes, he hugged me and said, 'Two former St Mary's boys, being involved in a world title fight and I trained you both when you were young lads. This ranks as one of the proudest moments of my life.'

All three of us were choking back the tears as he brought into sharp focus how far we'd come, what we'd achieved since attending that old, cold boxing gym. We were only there because of great people like Fred Ludlow, one of the many unsung heroes who guided us along the path, offering advice and expertise to help us fulfil our potential. Their importance in the sport and life in general cannot be overemphasised. If there are no people like Fred Ludlow, Sam Mercer, Les Roberts, 'Click Click' Mick Smith and Chris 'Clubber' Langley, then the sport dies and potential is not realised.

Audley Harrison lit up and lifted British Boxing with his Super-heavyweight gold medal triumph at the 2000 Olympics in Sydney, Australia. For his efforts, he was awarded an MBE and in 2001 turned Professional. He was very big business with many believing he was the next Lennox Lewis. The BBC signed him with a £1 million deal and would show his first ten fights. Definitely a good start to his career and when Audley fought his debut, six million viewers tuned in to watch him knock out the U.S. club fighter, Michael Middleton in the very first round. The world was there for the taking.

I eagerly awaited my turn to referee him live on the BBC, as we were informed that only star class referees were to be used. The contest I was given, proved to me I could handle most things in the ring. Us referees believe in our ability but sometimes need something out of the ordinary to test us and boy was I tested on the 10th July 2002 at Wembley Arena. Audley was to fight Dominic Negus and I'd earn every penny of the £100 I'd receive for refereeing unbeaten Audley's, sixth professional fight. The arena was full with both fighters bringing lots of loud support.

Dominic had made some claims that A-Force was over-rated and that he had the beating of the big fellah. Negus had been fighting at cruiser weight, felt the need to bulk up as he wasn't just lighter than Audley, he had less reach and height.

There was no title at stake, so no need to go into the dressing rooms to see the fighters, but I did, mainly because it was a high profile fight. When in Dominic's dressing room I took one look at him and said, 'Bloody hell, look at the size of you Dom!'

'Yeah, had to bulk up for this one Ref, he's a big old boy'

He wasn't wrong. I went to Harrison's room and was shocked at the size of him, 6ft 5 ½ inches tall with weight to match.

Dom weighed in at 16 stone 10 pounds; Audley, 18 stone and me, with a fair bit of loose change in my pockets, 12 stone. Was glad that I still worked out and when the fireworks started in the ring, I was doubly glad.

There was a lot of needle before this match with Dom saying Harrison had been hurt by a cruiserweight and wasn't as good as people thought he was. Dom added that Audley couldn't fight on the inside, which I thought he'd said to try and get his opponent in close where Dom would try to rough him up.

The arena was a pressure cooker coming to the boil with lots of vocal support for both fighters. This had all the ingredients to be a cracker and I had the best view in the house.

For three rounds the fight was fairly easy to referee as Audley was boxing nicely and keeping the aggressive Negus at bay with long shots. As hard as he tried, Dom just couldn't get under the long reach of Harrison. Audley delivered a quick left to Negus's chin which caused Dom to crouch down. His knee hovered above the canvas, so technically he wasn't knocked down. Harrison saw this and delivered another punch while Negus was in this unguarded position. It wasn't an illegal shot but Negus, obviously feeling disrespected, jumped to his feet, spat out his gum shield and charged after Harrison, looking like a man possessed. Negus, wanting blood, attempted to head butt Harrison. I couldn't believe what I'd just seen and fortunately for Negus, Harrison's height and quick reactions meant that his head didn't connect and although the intent was there, no physical damage was done.

I forced my way between these two really big guys and was in danger of being squashed. It was getting ugly, heading out of control with the crowd on their feet, screaming, shouting and adding energy to the fire. I sent Audley to a neutral corner, trying to get some distance between him and Negus. I then went over to Negus who was absolutely furious. He looked right through me as he only had one focus – Harrison.

'You do that again,' (the attempted head-butt) 'I'll disqualify you, do you understand me?!' I yelled, loud enough to be heard above the raucous crowd.

This is quite a threat to a boxer, because you're taking their purse away. I hoped the threat would get Dom to focus on the job in hand, which was to fight, but at that moment in time Negus didn't care, all he wanted was Harrison and replied, 'Go on then, do it. Go on; fucking disqualify me then!'

With that reply, I knew that the eruption was not yet over. The pro-Negus crowd were chanting, 'Negus, Negus, Negus,' and Dom nodded at them in appreciation and roared,

'Yeeeeah, come on!'

Now even though I couldn't see the crowd, because my eyes were fixed on Negus, I could sense that if I wasn't strong or if made the wrong move, the crowd could kick off. My best bet was to get Dom back in the zone and this is where my custody experience came into play. I honestly believe, if I'd shown signs of weakness then I'd have lost the respect of Negus, who I thought would've shoved me out of the way, steamed into Harrison and a street fight would have broken out. The television cameras would have kept on rolling because 'bad news is good news'.

I put my hand on his chest to hold him back, I followed him, as he paced to and fro, then I shouted above the noise of the crowd,

'Dom! You know me! Dom! You know me! Now listen to me! Look at me. Look at me, Dom!'

Don't know why I thought of saying what I did, but it brought him back to rational thinking. I saw his gum shield, near him, so shouted, pointing to the canvas, 'That's your gum shield, innit?!'

He looked at his shield and I guided him to it, I say guided because if he didn't want to go, no one would've made him; picked it up and as we headed to his corner I said, 'Let us get the gum shield put it back in, and then do what you do best; fight!'

Dom nodded to me, the red mist was leaving and I knew he was thinking again. Now calmer, he was able to get back to work. Dom went to a neutral corner as requested and I spoke with Harrison, reminded him that I was in charge and that we were going to get on with the fight. Audley nodded.

The fight continued, went the distance, with Audley winning on points. They both hugged each other as you should do after a tough scrap. When I got down from the apron, the time keeper, Nick White came over and said, 'I don't know what you said to them, Ian, but I can tell you now, you stopped a riot here tonight. I was ready to dive under the ring expecting it to kick right off!'

It made me smile thinking of Nick White clutching his beloved bell and stopwatch and disappearing under the apron to safety.

Dom said later to me that Audley was just too big, too awkward, a good boxer, but a good boxer that lacks heart. Dom added that he thought his mum could hit harder than Harrison! Don't think I'd want to find out if that was true. Audley, when interviewed about the controversy said he felt the referee had done a great job and had handled it well.

Told you I earned my fee!

After that fight, I headed to work for the night shift and was pleased to get there and rest... dealing with drunks and drug abusers.

If ever I see Dom now, I normally find that my feet are off the floor as he picks me up. Saw him recently in his gym, 'Spartan 300' in Chingford, Essex, still working out hard in the ring, training youngsters, helping to keep them out of trouble and providing for his lovely family. You need to get to know him to really appreciate him. He has a big heart and it is definitely in the right place.

The WBU was now big in the UK as Jon Robinson had linked up with top Promoter, Frank Warren. Frank had an exclusive contract with Sky Sports and the WBU flag bearer at the time was none other than the World Class, Ricky Hatton. Everybody knew that Mickey Vann was the WBU's number one referee but they'd been keeping me nice and busy also. Jon Robinson said to me, 'Ian, I'm grooming you to take over from Mickey.'

This was an absolute honour to hear as Mickey Vann had refereed the 'who's who' of world boxing for many years. Jon then asked me to referee a WBU Light-Heavyweight Championship at York Hall, Bethnal Green on 12th October. It would be live on Sky Sports. 'No problem Jon, but I'm in Denmark the night before, refereeing an IBF Inter-Continental Championship,' I replied.

'Ian, I'll only let you referee if you're back on British soil before 1pm. I don't want to take any chances that you'll be late,' he said and I knew he meant it. If I were a minute late I wouldn't be able to officiate at the fight.

11 October 2002: Denmark.

Christian Blandt (Champion) v Christophe Carlier (Challenger).

IBF Inter-Continental Welterweight Championship.

This was my first trip to Denmark. On touching down, I wandered through customs into the arrivals lounge, looking for the driver who'd have been patiently waiting to pick me up. I noticed the sign, 'Ian John-Lewis, IBF' being held up by a big guy. As I approached him I told myself, *'That's me, that is.'*

I was dressed in tracksuit and cap and introduced myself to him. He looked at me as if to say, *'What do you want?'*

Pointed to his sign and in my best broken English, which I thought was a Danish accent but sounded more like Ivan Drago in Rocky 4, said, 'Hello... Yes... that is me.'

'You! You? I look for referee... wait for Ian John-Lewis.'

Now that I've heard his accent, I mimic it, always do and can't help it. Do it because I think it helps them out. Surprisingly, it don't.

Now sounding like a cross between Arnie from 'Terminator' and Tonto I reply, 'Yes... that me... referee!'

'You... but you look like fighter... too young for referee.'

Don't know what he was expecting, perhaps an old boy with a beard and a bit of a belly, not someone as young, handsome and with perfect Danish accent like me. He grabbed my bag and said, 'We go!'

I was still getting used to travelling, the excitement of hotels and being picked up at airports. Seeing a sign held up with my name on it gave me a really good feeling. I was on the rise as a referee and this was part of the package. Les's words came to me, *'They'll fly you round the world to great hotels and you'll see the fight for free!'*

Fight night over and with another good scrap dealt with it was time to get back to the UK for the big championship fight. Thankfully the flight was on time and I got over to Reg Thompson's house (WBU Judge that night) before the 1p.m. curfew. I rang Jon to let him know I had returned and prepared myself for the evening's festivities: the WBU Light-Heavyweight Championship, between Tony Oakey (Champion) v Andre Kaersten (Challenger).

Oakey was dropped by a cracking shot that broke his nose in the very first round. He got to his feet, composed himself and after a tremendous struggle, which saw both men on the canvas, Tony retained his title on points, again proving he was a tough man to beat.

15 November 2002: Kjellerup, Denmark.

Allan Vester (Champion) v Lawrence Ngobeni (Challenger).

IBF Inter-Continental Light-Welterweight Championship.

Was waiting to fly out for my second trip to Denmark, when an announcement informs us that the plane is to be delayed for one hour. Just before the hour was up, they inform us again of another delay, a further two hours, due to fog. Not happy with the wait and because I'd read my boxing magazine cover to cover, twice; was already bored and fed up. My mobile phone rang and on the end of the line was Jon Robinson, the WBU boss.

212

'Ian... Ian... got some good news for you.'

'What's that then, Jon?'

'How do you fancy refereeing Ricky Hatton in Newcastle on the 14th of December? The WBU Championship of the world.'

I could've passed out. Was so excited at the prospect of refereeing a Ricky Hatton fight, that the delay now seemed like minutes as I smiled my way through the whole day. I wanted to announce it over the airport tannoy but settled for ringing Julie and Mark Willougby telling them the brilliant news.

The guy who picked me up at Copenhagen airport had been waiting hours for me. As I left arrivals, he noticed me before I saw him, telling me he knew who I was, having seen me on Danish and British Television a few times. Later at the rules meeting, it dawned on me that I'd moved into world-class officialdom, as present were the Danish and South African trainers, the German match maker, the three scoring judges from around the world and me.

Vester, a very well-schooled boxer, beat the rough, tough South African on points after a fight that had Vester looking uncomfortable at times.

When I returned to The Five Bars, I was in one of the cells with a guest when it dawned on me that hotel maids and career criminals have something in common: they both know how to make a bed really well. You can always tell the guys or girls, who have 'done time' because when bedding is given, there's no fuss, they just make the bed real good, get their nut down and sleep the sleep of the innocent.

14 December 2002: Telewest Arena, Newcastle.

Ricky 'Hitman' Hatton (Champion) v Joe Hutchinson (Challenger).

WBU Light-Welterweight Championship.

What an honour to referee the hottest fighter in British Boxing. Whenever the 'Hitman' fought, the whole country knew about it and in excess of 18,000 fans were in Newcastle to cheer their hero on. I forgave myself the nerves I was feeling as I went to enter the ring that night, and forgive me for saying that I was in fact, shitting myself.

To referee a massive fight in the UK on Sky Sports was the moment I'd been waiting for. My good mate, Mark Willougby said to me on the drive up North, 'Ian, to think I've known you when you were an amateur boxer at St Mary's, when you turned pro in 1986, to when you started your refereeing career in 1993. I am pleased to see that with all the hard work you've put in over the decades to get to this point, that you are realising your dream. Enjoy it, my friend.'

Great words from a great mate. It calmed me and enabled me to get massive pleasure from the fight.

Just before I got into the ring, Jon Robinson called me over and whispered in my ear, 'Ian, do yourself and the WBU proud tonight, son.'

I was really encouraged by those words from Jon and knew he was confident in my ability to officiate at such a high profile contest.

Was well and truly over that blue moon when I got into the ring. Approximately 18,000 screaming Manchester City fans then began belting out 'Blue Moon'. The hair – singular – was up on my head again. Knew I would have to keep focused, keep the emotions in check as this was a big step up for me and what I'd been working for. Nothing less than a great job would do.

Watching Ricky enter the arena, chewing gum, he appeared relaxed, more relaxed than me. Just before the fight Ricky spat out his gum and it was like he'd flicked a switch to put him into fight mode. He meant business.

Hutchinson made it clear from the opening bell that he'd come to fight. He put in a good shift that ended in the fourth by a trademark 'Hitman' Hatton body shot. It was obvious that Ricky Hatton had that something special and extra that would take him far. Great punch, great chin, big engine and outside the ring, with the gloves off; a really nice guy and a gentleman.

That fight finished off a fantastic year for me. Out of the five Sky Sports, fights of the year, I was the referee for two: Johnny Armour versus Francis Ampofo and Tony Oakey versus Andre Kaersten. I also refereed the top boxing magazine, Boxing News' 'fight of the year' between Bradley Pryce and Gavin Downs.

05 April 2003: MEN Arena, Manchester.

WBU Light-Welterweight Championship.

My eleventh world title fight was to be, Ricky Hatton (Champion) versus a former world champion, Vince Phillips, who'd KO'd the current, undisputed World Light-Welterweight Champion Kostya Tszyu. This was a big test for Ricky and the fight would be seen live in America.

The crowd nearly chanted the roof off the place. It was packed with thousands of Hatton fans screaming for their hero to appear. I was called over by Jon who whispered, 'Make the WBU and yourself proud tonight Ian, this is a big night for us all, I've got faith in you son.'

'Will do, Jon. Will do,' I replied.

I climbed into the ring and went to a neutral corner, took a deep breath in, composed myself, got my head in the zone before going to the centre of the ring. I did my introduction, the fighters were ready, I got the attention of each individual judge and once they had acknowledged me, I pointed to the timekeeper, who rang the bell for battle to commence.

The punching power was immense; they disturbed the air around me as the blows were so fast and hard. Phillips hadn't come for a pay day, the man had pride and landed some amazing shots on Hatton. It was a great learning experience, a hard one, but a great one for Ricky. He was cut badly in the first round which kept my old cuts man and mate, Mick 'the rub', busy. As ever he did a brilliant job of keeping the cut under control and allowing Hatton to compete.

Vince Phillips, only a little younger than me, was still quick, had lots of fire, defiance and durability. The only way you'd get me in the ring with Hatton would be as referee, which was as close as you needed to be to know what a ferocious boxer he was and yet, here was a boxer, almost my age, up for the battle.

During the fight Phillips slipped and then Hatton did. Thinking this could potentially disrupt the fight and not wanting a boxer to stumble onto a crashing right hand or left hook, I requested the ring be swept. Looking at the effort put in to the cleaning, I wasn't impressed, so requested the corner to give me a towel and got on with the task of making the ring safe for the boxers. This was a brilliant fight, a pleasure to referee and like everyone else, didn't want a controversial ending.

This fight provided Ricky Hatton with just what he needed to be taken seriously in the USA. After the contest I got to thinking just how good Phillips was when considering his age. An amazing athlete who took Hatton the distance, although Hatton, to be fair, won comfortably on points. For Ricky now, the sky was the limit. What a fighter.

As I climbed down from the ring, Jon Robinson gave me a big hug and said I'd arrived on the world scene.

16 April 2003: Nottingham's Ice Arena.

Top of this bill was a British, Commonwealth and European Championship that I was judging, between Howard Eastman (Champion) and Scott Dann (Challenger). This was how I got onto the European circuit, which I hoped would lead to world-wide officiating.

Jon Robinson had always been good to me and had plans for me, but I'd heard complaints from other people in boxing about him. Things like he was domineering, a hard negotiator who liked things his own way. Just sounded like a boss and a business man to me. As highly as Jon thought of me, his rules were his rules and he abided by them. This is when I found out that if it's not his way, it's the highway.

One of his rules were if you were working a WBU fight on a show, you couldn't do another one on the bill for another boxing body. Another rule was you couldn't officiate for the WBF or other low key championship fights as Jon didn't recognise them. The Boxing Board had requested that I referee two WBF fights on this big bill. I couldn't say no; had no choice.

Had so much enjoyment working for Jon and was devastated when he dropped me but I still thanked him for the opportunities he had provided me and for raising my profile. We headed our separate ways and Jon unfortunately passed away about a year later.

20 June 2003: Copthorne Hotel, Gatwick.

David Louzan versus Schpetim Hoti.

David was a youngster and on his pro debut. The fight was going well and he was holding his own against a very strong opponent. He had taken some heavy shots in the previous rounds but at the end of the fourth, he walked back to his corner apparently none the worse for his experience. The bell went for round five and out they came, both fighters looking able. A few jabs found their way to David's chin and I became aware that something wasn't right with him. Made sure I got into a

217

position to be able to deal with any situation but nothing had ever prepared me for what was to happen.

David looked as though he was trying to find his opponent in the ring, he then seemed to stagger slightly and considering no blows were thrown, I realised he wasn't right. You have to respect Hoti, because instead of taking advantage and landing a punch, he just stood there, looking at his opponent in bewilderment. David staggered on and went to the canvas. I jumped in quickly, trying to catch him on the way down, called for the doctor while removing his gum shield and put him in the recovery position.

David was carried out of the ring, conscious, and taken to hospital for a check-up where they discovered a brain bleed. He never fought again but at least he lived to tell the tale. The Board sent me a letter congratulating me on the care, urgency and professionalism I showed to David.

04 October 2003: Alexandra Palace.

European Light-Middleweight Championship.

Roman Karmazin (Champion) v David Walker (Challenger).

Tonight would be my first taste of European championship boxing and I would be going back to the Alexandra Palace. The last time I was here, I left in a lovely spacious vehicle, worth about £200, 000, that contained a bed, was called an ambulance and took me and my fractured jaw to the Whittington Hospital.

Roman was a world class European champion and Walker was a crowd pleasing fighter, who had been in many tear-ups seen 'live' on national television. His promoter was Mick Hennessy, who at that time had a contract with the BBC, so was very popular. Walker did his best but the champ was just too good with Karmazin stopping Walker in round three. I judged on that fight which is the way they eased me into the European scene. Thankfully, I went home by car that night.

The Green Shirt!

My aim, from the day I stepped into the ring as a novice referee was to officiate for the World Boxing Council (WBC). In my opinion, the WBC is the most prestigious title to fight for as it's the Championship belt that all the great fighters, Ali, Frazier, Tyson, Lewis, Leonard and my hero, 'Marvellous' Marvin Hagler, have fought for, defended and had wrapped around their waists or slung across their shoulders in victory.

18 October 2003: MEN Arena, Manchester.

The former British, Commonwealth and European Super-Bantamweight Champion, Michael Brodie, was challenging for the vacant WBC featherweight title. His opponent was the very durable, brawling South Korean, In-Jin Chi. As this was a high profile Championship, the President of the WBC, Mr. Jose Sulaiman, made one of his rare visits to the UK and I hoped I'd be noticed by him.

The contest that I'd be the sole judge and referee for, was the British and Commonwealth Light-Middleweight Championship between Jamie Moore (Champion) and Gary Logan (Challenger). Gary had been a Southern Area welterweight champion, had not won the big one and at the age of 35, this would be his last chance.

I'd known of Gary for years as he was an up and coming fighter as I approached retirement. In 2002 he made a spirited attempt to win the WBU belt from Takaloo that ended in the tenth, with Takaloo pouring it on and the bout being stopped.

When in Logan's dressing room for the pre-fight instructions, I said, 'Alright, Gary. You're 35 years old now, getting a bit old for all this, although you do look in magnificent shape my friend.'

'I'm going to give everything tonight, Ian. I think I know too much for this young champion,' he replied.

'I like your spirit, Gary.'

He wasn't there for a pay day, believed he could win and looked like he had been living in the gym.

After I gave my instructions in the ring, I heard Sky Sports commentator, Ian Darke say, 'The Referee, Ian John-Lewis was in a few entertaining fights of his own a few years ago!' Nice to hear.

True to his word, the 35 year old Logan took it to Moore from the opening bell, which I think took Jamie by surprise. After the early onslaught from Logan, Moore started to come into the fight, winging in some wicked shots. Gary used all his experience to stay with Jamie, but Jamie, 24 years young, was a class southpaw and slowly but surely, his punches were making a difference, sapping the strength from his elder.

I saw the 'low' blow, which Logan went to complain about. He dropped his hands while turning to me and was put to the canvas by a Jamie Moore right hander. One of my commands at the beginning of every fight is, 'Protect yourself at all times.' He didn't, which is why he ended up on his arse. I gave him time to recover from the 'low blow' that Jamie insisted was a good shot. I thought it was a little on the low side so just gave Jamie a verbal warning and told them to box on. Logan was a bit wound up by the blow and came forward aggressively.

They exchanged hard punches, the older man wasn't going away easy and if he lost, was going to make sure that Jamie would have respect for his elder. He caught Moore with plenty, but the champion, wanting to impress his large home following, started to really drive the blows home. After a brief rally, Moore backed Logan up and smashed in a big left, to what looked like, the groin area. Gary went canvas bound again and 'mugged' me by claiming another low blow, which I thought I saw. Jamie was complaining his innocence, telling me it was a good shot but on first view and the way Logan went down for the second time, I felt docking a point was the right decision.

Obviously annoyed, the Champion came out and put Logan on the back foot, unloading powerful shots for the full three minutes. Moore was now in charge, firing hurtful punches but Logan wouldn't crumble.

This picture was in the Daily Sport.

Future Undisputed Heavyweight Champ Lennox Lewis with baby Kelcie.

Our 1st Family Portrait '94.

Very proud Grandad.

Our Wedding 31st August '95.

Julie, Kelcie & Jackie (Do luv this one).

My 1st Award with Kent Police, I felt really honoured.

My 2nd Award with Kent Police for which I'm most grateful.

My good pal Mark Green.

My mentors Larry O'connell & Roy Francis.

Me & good pal Chris Andrews.

My great pal Mark Willoughby.

Sad day, Grandad Archie's funeral.

Kelcie (on left, holding Granddad pic), me, Julie, Mark (with sunglasses) Julie's brother, his wife Alison & two children Christopher & Jackie (holding pic).

Our re-union at Brightons EBA watched by 'Click-Click' Mick.

Our re-union at Brightons EBA watched by the Author Mark Heffernan.

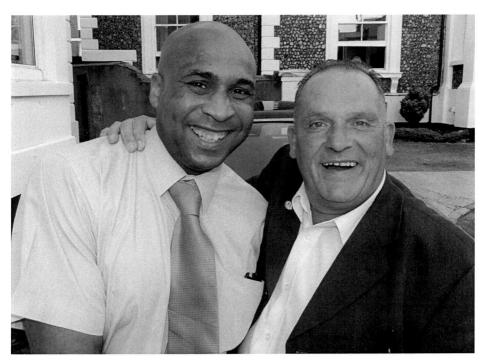

One of my toughest Amateur opponents, Dave Thompsett and the man who put us against each other Ernie Price.

4 top Welterweights, Speedy Mitchell, Rocky Kelly, Me&Sylvester Mittee.

Refereeing the Great Ricky 'Hitman' Hatton.

Reminding Khan of the rules.

Haye's heavyweight debut at Wembley.

無念7回TKO負け陥落

越本引退

El Rudy

親子鷹もラストマッチ…父・英武氏の跡を継ぎ ジム会長として次な

My 2nd time to Japan, the place is amazing.

In South Africa refereeing the 'Greatest's Daughter Laila Ali.

My Modern day hero Marvellous Mavin Hagler in Milan.

Sam Hadfield.
This incredible guy Sam Hadfield runs Caris Boxing Club for the homeless.

Although now cut on the right eye, he tried to stay with Moore, desperately fighting back. This was the exciting scrap that everyone in boxing had hoped for. In round five, after another exciting exchange of punches, Jamie sunk a rib crunching left hook that dropped Gary for the full count.

Although mugged by Logan, I felt he gave a very spirited effort against the talented Moore, who went on to win the European Title. When Moore was interviewed at ringside, I heard him say to Sky's, Adam Smith that the 'low blow' was a good shot. That had me thinking that maybe I'd got it wrong and consequently may have blown my chance of being noticed by the WBC President for the right reasons. As I walked to the dressing room, down and disheartened, having thought I'd lost my chance, I heard a very excited voice, 'Referee, referee.'

I turned and was shocked to see the voice belonged to that of Mr. Sulaiman. With him was Enza Jacoponi, Secretary of the European Boxing Union (EBU). 'You were excellent in there; did a great job and are a very good referee.'

I shook his hand, thanked him for his kind words and told him it was an honour to meet him. He asked my name and requested I fax my details because he wanted me to officiate for the WBC. Enza assured me I would also be getting more work from the EBU. No longer down and disappointed, I floated to the dressing room.

When I saw Jamie at a show some weeks later, told him I'd seen a recording of the fight and admitted that the punch was a good one and that I shouldn't have docked him a point.

'Told you, Ref; told you it was a good one!' he answered.

We had a laugh about it. You have to call it as you see it. Had to take action on what I thought I saw and, of course, Gary's reaction to the not so 'low blow'. You can't always be right and if you're not, hold your hands up and admit it. It shows class.

01 November 2003: Bella Houston leisure centre, Glasgow.

Craig Docherty (Champion) v Abdul Malik Jabir (Challenger).

Commonwealth Super-Featherweight Championship.

This was one hell of a fight which would need every ounce of my refereeing and boxing experience.

Jabir came to destroy the champion and destroy him quick. He cut Docherty badly in the first 30 seconds of the opening bell and followed up with big thumping shots. It was a disastrous start for Craig in the first defence of his belt. I let it proceed to see if the experienced and excellent cuts man, Benny King, could work his magic. I had a close look at it between rounds one and two, saw that Benny had worked wonders and decided to let the fight continue, for now.

The commentators were vocal, that's their job, and although trying to ignore them, could hear them going on about the cut. Because I felt it wasn't hindering Docherty, who was boxing really well under the onslaught; held my nerve and let it go on.

I was well aware that although the fight looked one sided in favour of Jabir, fighters can go 'gung ho' in the early rounds and if they don't get their opponents out quick, they blow themselves out. That is always the danger. If your plan is to get your opponent out in the first couple of rounds, then you'd better do it, because when you're knackered, the slightest tap can put your silk shorts on the rough canvas.

Jabir's attacks lost their intensity and every now and again he would deliver little flurries. Docherty's boxing skill had now contained Jabir and got Docherty into the fight.

I could hear the commentators going on and on about the cut to the eye. For some reason that night, just couldn't tune them out, because normally I can't hear them. I took Docherty to his corner after a time out and was assured by the cuts man that he could control it.

The camera focussed in on Docherty's eye and yes it was a bad cut but under control. The commentators felt that because it happened so early in the fight, it was unlikely that Docherty could last the distance. The African continued to deliver flurries of punches, but less frequent and Docherty was turning the tide.

I put what the commentators were saying to the back of my mind. Round four was phenomenal, which, if I'd taken notice of them, no one would've seen. Three brilliant minutes of boxing saw Docherty keeping Jabir in the corner for the whole round and delivering some cracking punches. The crowd were going crazy, they could see that their warrior had come back in style. At the end of the round, the cuts man got to work on the eye again, importantly, keeping it open.

Docherty continued to box and was getting on top. In round six, I heard the commentators say that the cut was under control.

A cuts man said to me once that they're only as good as the referee allows them to be. If we're going to stop a fight because of a cut then the excitement will diminish. If it is bleeding into the eye and impairing vision then it has to be stopped; no question. When cut in my career I can remember the feeling of warm blood running down my face and the panic that went with it. It can feel like pints yet it's sometimes just a trickle. Whatever, it's a horrible experience. You worry until you see the facial expression of the cuts man and long to hear him say, 'It's nothing!'

In round seven, Jabir remained dangerous but Docherty had the upper hand. It would be difficult to pull him out, as he was not only winning the fight; he was controlling it with his pure boxing skills.

At the start of round twelve, the commentators bellowed, 'Who would've thought that?'

The expertise of Benny King was tested to the full, and he saved Docherty from a certain stoppage. The last round saw two tired boxers exchanging tired punches. The final bell rang out and ended a great fight which I saw as a win for Docherty.

I expected Jabir's corner men to have a go at me about the cut eye, but Jabir's agent came to me and said, 'Ian, you were right to let the fight go on.'

Good enough for me.

After the fight, Docherty gave me a great big kiss (on the cheek I'd like to add) and whispered in my ear, 'Thanks for letting the fight go on and letting me keep my belt, ref!'

'You did the fighting, Craig. Not me, son,' I replied.

20 March 2004: Wembley Arena.

Audley 'A-Force' Harrison (Challenger) v Richel 'the Dutch Sonny Liston' Hersisia (Champion).

WBF Heavyweight Championship of the World.

This was my first taste of refereeing a world heavyweight championship fight. It was live on the BBC and I was pleased to be given the contest. May have been a small Title but as all in boxing know, it could be the stepping stone to greater things, for all of us involved.

The crowd had at times jeered Audley in some of his past fights but not tonight. They got 100 per cent behind him and were treated to a good rumble with Audley winning in four and looking very able as he did so. This was his fifteenth fight in a row, undefeated.

Audley had gone to the States and was training at altitude; had lost weight and several inches off his waist. He looked like he'd made the changes he'd need to be able to fight for longer and harder at world level.

The great Lennox Lewis praised Audley after the fight, even going as far as to say that Harrison had the pedigree and could box better on the inside than he could. Lennox advised him to keep learning and to get the right experience. We all believed he was on the path to greater things.

Although having won this 'World Title' it only pushed Audley's European ranking from sixteenth to eighth, having taken Hersisia's ranking because of the victory. Didn't matter; he was going in the right direction. What I wasn't sure about, was him not having a manager, as he was going on this journey alone. From my point of view I think you should let a manager, manage; a coach, coach and a boxer concentrate on being the best athlete he can be. Audley did state that he would steer his own ship and if it sinks then it would be his own fault.

Earlier in 2003 I had been told by Mr. Sulaiman that he wanted me to officiate for the WBC. Had begun to think he'd forgotten me, but then my fax machine lit up and out came an appointment from the WBC office in Mexico offering me the opportunity to referee a fight, a final eliminator for the WBC Super featherweight division. At last, I was going to be wearing the green shirt of the prestigious WBC.

The fight would take place on the 28th May 2004, Johannesburg, South Africa, between Mzoke Fana (South Africa) versus Randy Suico (Phillipines).

The unbeaten 24 year old, Suico was a formidable opponent for the local, Fana, as he had knocked out 18 of his 21 victims and badly bruised the other three. The 30 year old, Fana had the same amount of fights, 21, and had lost just 2. This was the classic Boxer v Puncher confrontation and I was looking forward to it. Was the first time I had to wear gloves and was insisted upon even though I protested.

Fana was on his toes from the off, pumping out his jab, keeping Suico at bay and cutting him quite badly. He kept hunting Fana, following him around the ring until he found what he was looking for, a big right uppercut, bang on the chin. It froze Fana, his legs stiffened and he dropped to the canvas. It didn't knock his lights out, just made them flicker and by the count of three he was up, shaken, but listening to the mandatory eight count I was giving him. Before I got to say, 'box on', the bell sounded, giving him yet more time to gather his senses.

With his left eye patched up, Suico was again stalking his prey, waiting to strike again. Fana never stood still, pumping out his jab and boxing beautifully. Fana continued the tormenting jabs, the trademark of a boxer, which sting like a slap and irritate the hell out of a puncher. Round 4 and Fana rammed more jabs into the still chasing Suico's blood stained face. Then a big right hand, with a left hook side order, dropped Fana by the ropes. Another eight count and as soon as he was on his feet, Suico tried to finish him, but Fana ran, moved, grabbed and spoiled until his head cleared and his senses sharpened. This was frustrating the Philipino as he was walking onto left jabs that Fana was hiding, so expertly, behind. Suico tried to pin Fana down, chased him, cut corners to keep him where he wanted and in the eleventh round, Suico bit down hard on his gum shield and launched a big attack. Near the end of the round, he finally caught Fana with a sizzling right hand that made him grab Suico like a long lost brother.

The final round: Suico knew he needed a KO to win, but he'd chased Fana for eleven hard rounds and his engine was running on fumes. Then at last he found what he was looking for and turned the South African's legs to rubber after he delivered a big right hander. Fana wobbled round the ring for a whole minute and a half, running when he could and throwing weak defensive punches on the retreat. Suico had him at his mercy but just couldn't find the punch. A great fight was going on and I didn't want to stop it as both fighters were out on their feet and one punch could finish it for either of them. The final bell rang out, Fana got the decision and went on to fight the legendary Antonio Barrera.

Not a bad start to my WBC years.

09 October 2004: Erfurt, Eastern Germany.

Christian Sanavia (Champion) v Markus Beyer (Challenger).

WBC Super-Middleweight Championship.

My first WBC world title fight was a rematch, as the German had lost to the Italian. It was a shock defeat, a loss he would avenge in great style. This was the most amount of pressure I'd felt as a referee, as the two American judges, Chuck Hassett and Dwayne Ford, had decades of experience and I was definitely the new kid on the block. I'd seen them countless times on television when I was a young amateur boxer and when all the big fights from the States were on terrestrial television.

That week I had attended my first WBC Convention which was held in Phuket, Thailand. Met so many top people from around the world in boxing. Managed to have a chat with leading American promoter, Bob Arum; really nice guy. To top it off, met and was given some great advice from Richard Steele, the top American referee, who I'd watched and learnt so much from. What made my night was that when I introduced myself, he told me he knew who I was, having seen me referee on USA cable TV and added, 'You're pretty good.'

After the convention I flew from Thailand to Germany to referee the fight and was knackered. The phone rang at six in the morning. Was jet lagged, dazed, confused and thought I was dreaming that a phone was ringing. Half asleep, I traced the noise and picked it up.

'Hello.'

'Is zat Mister Ian John-Lewis?' asked a voice with a German accent.

'Yah... yes!' I replied, my voice going a little Germanic as I spoke.

'Zis is German TV, vee vish to interview you for zer big fight tomorrow, ya.'

'Ven...When?' I asked still dazed.

'Now, ya. Vee vish to interview you in your full refereeing uniform, ya. Must be smart ya, live on TV.'

My initial thought was, *'Bollocks, I'm not going anywhere. Just turn over and go back to sleep.'*

But then I remembered that this was my first WBC world title fight. Couldn't let them down. Told myself to wake up, shape up and get myself down there. Got up quickly, dowsed cold water over my head to shock me awake. I am dressed and heading down to the lobby within ten minutes of the phone call.

As I come out of the lift I see the two American judges sitting down eating breakfast. They asked me what I was doing as I wandered around the place in my refereeing uniform complete with dickie bow, looking for a camera crew. They said they hadn't seen one so I continued walking around looking for the crew. It was only when I saw the judges chuckling that I realised I'd been set up. When the penny dropped, I disappeared back up to bed for a few more hours kip. The prank reminded me of the time when first working on the buildings. My boss told me to go to the stores and ask for a handful of sky hooks and a long weight. All I got was the long wait.

Later that evening when we were having dinner, Dwayne said, 'You passed the WBC initiation test, Ian. Well done.'

'Well done!' I thought.

Was told that I wasn't the first and wouldn't be the last to be WBC'd.

Fight night. I entered the arena; the place was packed. Beyer was a national hero and the atmosphere was amazing. It had taken me ten years of refereeing to get to this level and to make the night even more special, they played MY national anthem first. Everybody stood quietly and respectfully, as we all should, and I was so proud. The immigrant's son from Darnley road, Strood, was having HIS national anthem played because he was the third man in the ring. Was choked up at hearing it and really proud to be representing my country at this world title fight.

As they announced the judges, it made me nervous, as they had officiated at many of the big fights in the Hagler, Hearns, Leonard and Duran era.

Steve Holdsworth, my old mate, was the commentator for Eurosport in the UK that night and was kind enough to tell the viewers that I was an old friend of his from Gillingham in Kent, and said, 'Yes, that is what he looks like. Not a pretty sight but that is how it goes.'

Thanks Steve… Great coming from someone who spends all his time behind the camera!

Because they had fought each other before, they were very cagey in the first couple of rounds, probing for openings. Then Sanavia was eager to remind Beyer that it was he, Sanavia, who'd won the first fight and began to force the issue.

Rounds four and five were pretty even, with the champion just edging it. Then in round six, a beautiful three punch combination that came out of nowhere, put the champion to the floor with a thud. It took him nine to get up. His legs could hardly hold him and he looked spent. He said he was alright, as most boxers do, but he wasn't able to defend himself, so I stopped the fight and prevented him from further punishment. The champion's corner didn't complain although the champion felt he could've continued.

Most of the time a boxer will tell you he is okay, but on one occasion in the past, a boxer whispered to me, after he was knocked down, 'Ref, get me out of here!'

Waved my arms in the air to signal that the fight was over and then he protested about it, jumping around the ring like he had a wasp up his shorts. He protested and pleaded with the crowd about being stopped and when I got in close to him I said, 'But you told me to get you out!'

'Yeah Ref, but I got fifty-odd mates out there cheering me on. Don't want them to know that!'

After the fight Chuck Hassett said to me, 'You're the best young referee I've seen in the past 20 years.'

'Really!?' I asked, taken by surprise and wondering if there was a punchline.

'Yeah, you move well, you have a presence and you control the fight without getting in the way… you're gonna go far kid.'

'From an expert like you, that is a great compliment. Thank you,' I replied.

Chuck had so many good stories that I could've sat and listened to him for days. Am sure the next referee to speak to him was told the story of the referee who wandered around the hotel lobby dressed in full kit at 6.15 in the morning!

Back at the dungeons, I came in on the late shift for 2 p.m. and was given the 'handover'. The first thing I do is to look in on every cell and it's occupant, say hi and offer a drink/magazine and make sure everything is okay. I got to cell 15 and see this big lump.

'You look familiar, big fella, where you from?'

He sort of looked at me but not eye to eye.

'Rochester, mate!'

'Oh well, I come from Strood which is only a couple of miles away, so may have seen you about,' I replied.

'Yeah, might of,' he said sheepishly.

Later I gave him his dinner; he took it off me but kept his head down trying to hide his face. Still thought I'd seen him before but couldn't think where. He was in for a very serious crime and when the detective constable interviewed him and put him back in his cell, he said to me, 'Something's not right with that guy, Ian.'

'What makes you say that?' I replied.

'Got a gut feeling he's lying.'

When he said that to me it made me think of the time in the brilliant show 'Porridge' when Fletch is in his cell surrounded by several old lags, discussing an item that has gone missing. He makes the 'shock' announcement, 'Gentlemen, there is a thief among us!'

'Well I don't recognise his name but I sort of recognise his face from somewhere. He's not a regular,' I answered.

'I'm not happy. I'm going to interview him again,' he said.

In the interview room the guy came clean straight away saying, 'Louie told you, I know he did. I knew you didn't believe my story or who I was. Knew he'd clocked me'.

'Who's Louie?' asked the detective, not knowing that it had been my nickname at school.

The prisoner was two years younger than me, went to my old school and lived in the same area, just a few blocks away. I hadn't seen him in 25 years and vaguely remembered him but as soon as he said his name, I knew who he was. When speaking to him later he said he recognised my voice as soon as I entered the custody block and thought, 'Shit! That's Louie from school. I'm fucked!'

He was really pissed off when I told him that I hadn't recognised him and that he'd dropped himself in it. He went away for a long stretch for the crime he'd committed.

04 March 2005: Magna Centre, Rotherham, Sheffield.

Clinton Woods versus Rico Hoye.

Vacant IBF Light-Heavyweight Championship.

Half past ten in the morning and I was in my garden watering the plants when my mobile rang and on the other end is Southern Area Secretary, Robert Smith from the BBB of C.

'Ian... where are you?'

'What do you mean, where am I? I'm in my garden.'

'You are meant to be in Sheffield! Tonight is the World Light Heavyweight Championship and you're the referee. It's live on the BBC!'

'What! Didn't get any paperwork and meant to be at work this afternoon. Leave it with me, Rob, I'll make a phone call.'

The custody inspector, Neil Owen was my manager. A really nice guy to work for and a good boss. If he can make it happen for you, he will. He has always done his utmost to accommodate my refereeing by letting me swap shifts and take time off. Rang him at home and told him of the dilemma. Five minutes later he rang and told me he'd got it covered and to go to Sheffield. Everyone needs a boss like Neil. Fifteen minutes later, I was packed and on my way to referee Clinton Woods from Sheffield, versus Rico Hoye from the USA for the IBF vacant world title, light heavyweight division. Our last world champion in this division was the very classy, John Conteh.

Rico Hoye came to the fight with an impressive record of being unbeaten and had won 14 by knockout, a lot of them within the first three rounds. Impressive, and obvious that's what his intentions were before the bell for round one had stopped ringing in my ears. He came out taking it straight to his opponent, but Woods kept his cool, his hands up, and got the better of a very busy first round. He carried on with the good work, mixing up his shots and although Hoye was still chasing, looking dangerous, he was walking onto those shots.

With the home crowd behind their man, Woods fought brilliantly, kept his chin tucked in and hidden away from the knock-out specialist. Each round he was ahead and then in the fifth, Hoye hit Woods low, for which I gave him a stern warning. A minute later he did it again forcing me to take a point away. Hoye looked unsettled by my decision. I thought so and so did Woods, who then launched a very measured attack of intelligent punches to his opponent, while continuing to protect his chin, even when Hoye was obviously weakened. Woods knew that one punch from Hoye could change everything, but roared on by the crowd, Woods forced him back and it was now him doing the chasing. Woods would not be denied, smacking Hoye with some damaging shots. He tried to fight back but Hoye was in no position to continue and I had to stop the fight to protect the boxer.

Thank you gentlemen. That was quite a fight.

No Bias

16 June 2005: York Hall, Bethnal Green.

Johnny Armour versus Tuncay Kaya (France), a former French champion.

A lifetime before this fight, at St Mary's boxing gym, I was in the ring, on the pads with Fred Ludlow, when in walks this tiny cute kid with his dad, wanting to try his fists at boxing. From day one Johnny Armour worked hard and was a front foot, aggressive type, who was lightning fast. He was full of what I called 'Chatham grit' and from very early on we knew for sure that anyone who was going to get into the ring with him would know they'd been in a fight. Sometimes they'd have to wake up first to realise it, but they would realise it.

When Chris King and me sparred at St Mary's it would always turn into a war and one of the excited, wide eyed kids, leaning on the ropes, yelling us on, was Johnny. Him and his little crew would applaud us at the end of the 'sparring'.

But now at 36 years of age, his best fighting days were behind him and he hadn't boxed for about 18 months. The guy they picked for him I felt was not the best for a return. Johnny was in tremendous physical shape, having worked hard in training which was normal for him, but I felt he needed to get some of the rust out by fighting an opponent who would sharpen him up. Johnny had always needed a couple of rounds to warm up as he was used to fighting the championship distance of twelve rounds. These small six round fights are hard to get up for when you're used to fighting for titles and, of course, Johnny had been a world champion.

Just before the fight, Larry O'Connell asked me if I wanted him to referee the fight as he knew Johnny was a good friend. Thanked him but said I was on the undercard and would be alright to do it. I wouldn't let friendship get in the way of how I saw the contest or the result.

The young French guy jumped on Johnny from the off; just came straight for him showing no respect. It was definitely the right tactic. He had obviously done his homework and knew Johnny took a couple of rounds to get into a fight.

Johnny fought as he usually did, on the front foot, always going forward, but kept missing against an opponent eight years his junior. Shots he would normally have landed just didn't connect which left him open to sharp counters, which although he took well, didn't want to be taking at all.

There was a moment of hope when he dropped Tuncay in round two but because John was on the receiving end for most of the round, I was only able to score it 10:9 in Johnny's favour. Again, Tuncay came forward, catching Armour with niggling punches which he would've slipped a few years before. This Frenchman was all wrong for a 36 year old Armour who hadn't boxed for so long.

The fight was tough; Johnny gave his all, as he always had. When the final bell went, my head looked down to the canvas and Johnny didn't even look at me, let alone come to me to raise his hand in victory. He headed straight back to his corner and I went to commiserate and even said, 'Sorry, John.'

'That's alright Ian... didn't do enough to deserve to win it,' Johnny answered honestly.

The next day, a local reporter phoned and interviewed me. He asked how I came to the conclusion that the French guy had won. I replied that Johnny had been outworked and outpunched, something that was very rare in his brilliant career. In my opinion the Frenchman was a bit too lively and a bit too young for him. The way the reporter was talking, I got the impression that he wondered why I'd not given the fight to my mate, Johnny Armour.

'Let me ask you something. Were you at the fight?' I asked.

'Yes,' he answered.

'How did you score it?' I asked.

'For the Frenchman.'

'So if I'd scored it for Johnny Armour you'd now be asking me how I got to that decision?'

'Yes I would have.'

Taught me a lot about how some journalists choose to work.

The John-Lewis household, was doing very well. Julie's business was going great and the refereeing diary was heaving. On the 8th July 2005, I had just flown to Vigo, Spain to referee a European Title fight. This was the start of going to three countries in ten days. Kelcie, now fifteen, was abroad on holiday with a friend and her parents. One evening, they were in a bar having a drink, when Kelcie looked up at the big TV screen.

'Oh, my dad's on the telly,' she said.

'Don't be silly, not out here he's not,' Courtney replied. But she looked up and saw me dancing around the ring refereeing in Vigo, Spain.

The second show was on the 12th July in Hyeres, France, where I had two WBF championships to officiate. I refereed one and was one of the judges for the other.

On the18th July, I flew to Osaka, Japan to referee the WBC Super-Flyweight Championship between Katsushige Kawashima (Champion) and Masamori Tokuyama (Challenger).

Joe Koizumi, whom I'd briefly met in South Africa when he was the agent for Randy Suico, met me at the airport in Osaka. He was there to take me to the hotel and I liked him instantly, a lovely guy and a gentleman. As we drove he turned to me and said in perfect English, 'This is a massive contest here in Japan. You must be very highly thought of to be refereeing this fight in a few days. It is their third encounter and is the equivalent of your rivalry between Chris Eubank and Nigel Benn in the UK.'

Before I could revel in the compliment he added,

'If you muck up, I don't think you'll be welcome back!'

'No pressure then!' I thought.

Once I'd checked in to the hotel, I turned the telly on and instantly saw the fight advertised. For the next three days saw adverts many times and understood the importance of this fight to the Japanese boxing world.

Joe and I spent a lot of time together, with him showing me round the beautiful city. They bought me a lovely sculpture as a gift for my wife and the hospitality was second to none. The food was beautiful, even for someone like me who's not adventurous with other nations' food.

On the train, Joe said, 'You look fit, Ian.'

'I think you need to be in this game,' I answered.

'Agreed... I keep myself fit, also.'

Looked at him and thought that he was too old to be in shape. He then tapped his stomach and said, 'Go ahead.'

Tapped his abs and got the shock of my life. They were like wood!

Joe is the epitome of the Japanese thinking of taking care of yourself. Along with working out often, he is fluent in several languages and I later found out that Joe Koizumi may be a small guy but he's a 'Mr

Big' in Japanese boxing. He knows everyone and anyone associated with the fight game out there.

At the weigh-in, the day before the fight, Joe announced, 'The doctor's ready for you, Ian.'

'You what?!'

'The doctor is ready for you now.'

'What… I ain't fighting,' I replied.

'It is something we do in Japan.'

This is the only country I've been to, where they do a health check on the referee also. It's a good idea as refereeing can be hard, especially in hot conditions under the TV lights. I wasn't concerned, I was fit, trained five days a week, still worked the bag, ran, skipped rope, did press, pull and sit ups. Still do. Passed the medical with ease.

It was at the press conference when I realised just how massive this championship fight was. When Tokuyama had won the WBC Championship back in August 2000, he had become the first North Korean to win a World Title. This fighter was hot property, had made a lot of successful title defences and wanted his WBC belt back. The place was packed with journalists and photographers and I felt privileged to be part of such a big event. They even put me on the top table with the fighters, trainer and promoters. When they announced me, the man who was going to be in the middle of the action, I got a nice round of applause.

Everywhere I went people came to me, bowed and acknowledged me. As the contest approached there was no mistaking how much this fight meant to the Japanese boxing fans and on the night of the fight there was an intensity I hadn't experienced before. Osaka was very hot, the atmosphere was crackling, the stadium full but eerily quiet except for thousands of people fanning themselves. It would be a classic confrontation of the boxer versus the fighter, the purist versus the puncher.

After seven successful defences, Tokuyama put his belt on the line against Kawashima. The first fight had been won by the boxer, Tokuyama on points. After another title defence, Tokuyama gave Kawashima a second fight. This time it was won by Kawashima. It was a big shock with a stunning first round knockout. It seemed everybody, including the boxers wanted a third fight: a decider. On entering the dressing rooms, Joe translated for me. As ever, the boxers were very respectful, stood and bowed as Joe and I approached. Manners cost nothing, yet mean so much.

Tokuyama, the boxer, was the crowd's favourite, although Kawashima had lots of support also. I told him it was an honour to referee such an important fight and wished him well. I then said the same to the Champion.

When I walked out of the dressing rooms, knew it was going to be a war, one worth watching and I had the best view in the house. The whole place was expectant, with millions watching on TV and I later found out, that it was shown live on Sky Sports in the UK. When I watched it on video, courtesy of 'Click Click' Mick, it was so nice to hear Sky's Adam Smith say, 'And the referee for this is our very own, Ian John-Lewis, all the way from Gillingham. What an honour this is for him.'

He was right: it was.

Tokuyama boxed and stayed away from the fists of the fighter. Kawashima, tried to remind him who'd won the second fight as he threw wild punches in the hope that one would connect and do the job of sparking his opponent. Tokuyama wasn't going to let lightning strike twice. He kept his hands up and stabbed his jab into the champion's face and was long gone before the champ could focus on him. Here and there, Kawashima would catch him with a good shot but Tokuyama grabbed, held until his head cleared and was back on his toes. He was piling up the points as Kawashima chased him for almost twelve rounds, relentless in his pursuit, and then, with about a minute to go in the final round, he caught Tokuyama with enough of a punch to put him to the canvas and make his supporters roar. He got up claiming he had slipped, of course he slipped: courtesy of a right hander! After the mandatory eight count, Kawashima flew at his opponent and tried in vain to take him out but had run out of time. Tokuyama regained his precious WBC belt after a tremendous tussle.

After the fight Joe praised me saying I'd done an excellent job. I remember thinking, *'Great, should get an invite back.'*

I did. Been there five times now. Beautiful.

What a show the Japanese put on. They were great hosts and a credit to boxing. Thank you, Japan.

17 February 2006: York Hall, Bethnal Green, London.

Spooky. It was 13 years to the day that I had made my refereeing debut at York Hall in 1993. I refereed my 500th fight on this Sky-televised show. It made me take stock of how far I'd come and how much I was enjoying life.

13 May 2006: Zwickau, Germany.

Marcus Beyer (Champion) v Sakio Bika (Challenger).

WBC Super-Middleweight Championship.

I was a judge for this rough, tough title defence which turned into a fourth round technical draw, as Beyer suffered a very bad cut and could not continue. What I remember mostly about this trip was meeting the famous American Referee Joe Cortez, who refereed this WBC Title fight. Interestingly, he was also the referee in the final chapter of the Rocky series, the film 'Rocky Balboa'. Had a great chat with him and he explained his role with movie star Sylvester Stallone. Said the man was a workaholic. Joe's part took two weeks to prepare and said 'Sly' was a fantastic guy to work with.

30 July 2007: Fukuoka, Japan.

Takashi Koshimoto (Champion) v Rudy Lopez (Challenger).

WBC Featherweight Championship.

My second time in Japan was in Fukuoka. WBC World Champion, Takashi Koshimoto from Japan was putting his title on the line against young pretender, Rudy Lopez from Mexico. Rudy was the WBC Youth Champion, with some saying they thought the fight was scheduled too early in his career. The Japanese camp felt their man would be too seasoned for the youngster.

When the national anthem is played, you can feel the respect and love for their country and it always ends in a polite round of applause. When the Mexicans national anthem was played, the same respect was given.

In the dressing room of the Challenger, I could see the young Mexican was fired up and raring to get it on. In the Champion's room, he and his father were calm and collected.

From the off, Lopez sped out of his corner and took it straight to the southpaw champ, showing him no respect. He backed him up, throwing bunches of punches, which made the Champ fight back desperately. The young Lopez kept up a high work rate which Koshimoto tried to slow with his experience. The youngster had his own plans and ploughed forward, sapping the energy of the older Champ.

In round three, again Lopez poured it on, throwing so many shots that Koshimoto had to grit his teeth and punch back. I could see it was only a matter of time as the Champ was becoming tired while Lopez seemed to be just warming up. It got worse for him in round five when

Lopez, sensing his opponents fatigue, launched a ferocious attack and caught Koshimoto with some wicked shots that made the Japanese crowd wince with compassion for their fellow countryman.

Lopez would not be denied. He just kept backing Koshimoto up; wasn't relentless, just clinical and methodical. In round seven Lopez caught Koshimoto with a number of good shots that had him breaking. I gave him every opportunity to come back into the fight but knew it had become too much. It was time to stop the fight, knowing he'd had enough and that Lopez would be able to pick any number of shots or combinations to finish Koshimoto. I jumped in, grabbed Koshimoto just in time to feel his knees buckle and help him to the floor. I laid him down on the canvas and called for assistance. His father/trainer was there first, as you'd expect, and removed the gum shield. He was checked over and was carried from the ring as a precautionary measure. As he was being taken out of the ring he was telling people around him that he was okay.

I received a lot of praise from the officials and the supervisor in charge. Later, when back in the dressing room, Koshimoto's father came in with an interpreter and thanked me for stopping the fight at the right time and for saving his son from further punishment.

08 October 2006: Palalido, Milan, Italy.

Frederick Klose, France (Champion) v Giovanni Parisi, Italy (Challenger).

European Welterweight Championship.

Parisi was a former WBO Light-welterweight Champion who successfully defended the belt six times and had challenged the Mexican legend, Julio Cesar Chavez, for his WBC belt. But this was now a 36year old Parisi trying to trick his body into believing it was again young enough to take on a very good champion.

I was in the ring, had finished my checks of the 'furniture' and was happy that everything was as it should be. *'Now just need the fighters,'* I thought as I waited for them. I noticed a huge entourage approaching and heard applause that grew louder the closer the group got to the ring. *'Who's this?'* I thought.

Couldn't believe my eyes as my modern day hero was only a few feet away. I broke from my normal preparation and before I realised what I was doing, had already walked across the ring, climbed down off the apron and was standing in front of the bemused legend. I introduced myself. 'Excuse me, Mr Hagler, you are my modern day hero and I've watched all of your fights. It's an honour to meet you.'

Didn't care how corny it sounded; this guy is one of the greatest ever. We shook hands, and he thanked me. I had forgotten that when he retired he had gone to Milan, Italy, loved it and made it his home. He was so passionate about his boxing; cheering on the home favourite and shouting advice to Parisi. Parisi lost the fight and considering he was in his late thirties, had a really good go and had his moments. After the fight he announced his retirement. Giovanni is a really nice guy and despite having lost, had the class to thank me for the way I handled the fight. From then on, whenever I was in Italy, he would always shake my hand and give me a warm reception.

His English was limited and my Italian non-existent, although my Italian accent is brilliant of course. Despite this, we understood each other. He went on to work for Italian television as a fight analyst, so we bumped into each other a lot at the big shows and were always pleased to see each other and chat in our limited way. I was devastated when I read in Boxing News, that on the 25th March 2009, Parisi was driving his car at Voghera, near Pavia, when it crashed head-on with a truck. Parisi died at the scene; he was only 41. Rest in peace my friend.

03 February 2007: Emperors Palace, Johannesburg, South Africa.

Laila Ali (Champion) v Gwendolyn O'Neill (Challenger).

WBC/WBA Super-Middleweight World Title.

Laila Ali had been in South Africa for a couple of weeks before the fight and gave lots of her time to visiting the villages and schools and even met with Nelson Mandela.

She was such a confident woman and would be making history as it would be the first time that women's boxing would be top of the bill in South Africa. The Ali's are still making history.

At the weigh-in, 24 hours before the fight, Laila had to remove all her clothes to make the weight. She made sure that her modesty was intact and with the punching power she possessed would have been able to deal with anyone lacking respect.

On fight night, when giving her the pre-fight instructions in her dressing room, she was truly polite and gave me her full attention. When I'd finished I asked her if she had any questions, to which she replied in her beautiful American voice, 'Yes sir… I have but one… Can you count to ten, sir?'

'Of course,' I replied grinning, waiting for a punch line.

'That's all I need to know then referee, sir, 'cos this won't last long.'

Smiled at her confidence, which she exuded.

Went to the other dressing room and found a fighter that I thought may be overawed. She had been beaten by Ali before in three rounds. I thought her quietness may just be her way of preparing for a fight.

The contest lasted about a minute with Ali being right in what she'd said in the press conference: that Gwendolyn's husband would have a better chance. Gwendolyn was caught cold by a big right hand, bang on the point of the chin. She just beat the count and I knew it wouldn't go on for much longer. Sure enough, the next few punches Laila threw ended it. At the end of the fight I raised Laila Ali's arm in victory. I have that photo and her autograph in a book about her father. I was really hoping that, 'The Greatest' would be there, but due to ill health, the 65 year old couldn't fly. A real shame.

07 February 2007: Wembley Arena, London.

Audley 'A-Force' Harrison v Michael Sprott.

Vacant European Union Heavyweight Championship.

The former 2000 Heavyweight Olympic Gold medallist, who made such a promising start to his pro career, being unbeaten in 19 fights; had a loss of form. He'd just returned from the USA, having had a couple of wins, to take on his bitter amateur rival, Brixton's former British Heavyweight Champion, Danny Williams, for the vacant Commonwealth Title and lost a close, split decision. This snapped his unbeaten record, so Harrison went back to the USA, fought and lost again to Dominick Guinn on points. He rebounded with a good win, again in the USA, and then he stated that he was ready to step up and face world class opponents and get a world title shot.

He got a chance to avenge his defeat by Danny Williams and he did it in style, by fighting more aggressively, decking Williams twice and winning on a third round knockout. Williams suffered a broken nose and severe lacerations. Following the victory over Williams, Frank Warren stepped in and Audley signed a deal with the promoter, whose aim it was to rebuild his career. Warren wanted to get the Olympic Gold Medallist a World Title fight in 2007, starting with the EU Championship against Sprott. From the outset, great things had been expected from Audley, but after so much talk the great things had unfortunately failed to materialise from this boxer who undoubtedly had talent.

When his name was announced as he started his walk to the ring, the boos rang out loudly around the stadium. I thought it was disrespectful, but boxing people always show their displeasure if they feel they are being conned. The big man took it all in his stride, smiling as he approached the ring.

After my instructions, I told them to shake hands, they wouldn't. I said again to shake hands, they wouldn't. So I informed them that, 'The fight won't start until you shake hands!'

With that, Sprott touched Harrison's glove and the game was on. The reason why I'm so insistent on this is it's stated in the rules that you must touch gloves before the start of the contest and at the start of the final round. If you don't do as requested, then you're not respecting me and where does that end. We referees are the guv'nors within the ropes and we will be listened to.

They both came out cautiously in the first, looking for openings, with Harrison doing the chasing. Then a straight left dropped Sprott on the seat of his pants. He got up with a smile as if to say, 'yeah, good shot'. I finished the mandatory eight count and Audley went in for a kill but Sprott fought back and the bell sounded.

Round three: Audley was boxing well, with Sprott trying to get inside those long arms; then out of nowhere, BOOM!! Sprott threw a big left hook that knocked Harrison spark out. It was a beautiful punch that put Audley to the floor and his lights were out as soon as the unseen, fast moving hook connected to his chin. I felt and heard the thud through the canvas when his 18 stone frame landed, very heavily, on it. I waved the contest off immediately, removed his gum shield and put him in the recovery position to protect his airway. The doctors and paramedics were on the scene and administered oxygen.

It was thought by most that Audley would win but Michael Sprott wasn't convinced, to the point that he placed a bet on himself. This third loss left Harrison's future uncertain and Warren suggested that any return to the ring would be for a reduced purse, as the public would no longer show any great interest in him.

On my return to The Five Bars, as I came on duty and was visiting the prisoners, I recognised the name of the guest in cell ten, so looked in to say hello. I'd known him since 1998, when he was already an old regular and a right handful. Thankfully he always respected me and never played up when I was on duty. He was pleased to see me and said, 'Ian! Ian! I was in the nut house when I saw you at that heavyweight fight… Harrison, Sprott; it was on ITV. When you came on the telly, was so excited, I said who you were; told 'em I knew you and they started taking the piss! Told 'em where you worked and everything and they just went "yeah, okay, do you know Donald Duck as well?" I told them you worked at the Chatham fucking nick! They just said, "Of course he does, what else does he do in his spare time?" Well I got so pissed off that they jumped me and sedated me… bastards!… Never did get to see the fight!'

Close… But No Cigar

In March 2007, a new 'Super Nick' was opened in Gillingham, Kent. It would take me a bit of time to get used to the massive police station which amalgamated the Rochester, Chatham and Rainham stations into one.

The custody block was now on two floors and extra staff recruited because of the increased workload. Gone was the very busy but well run Chatham Custody Suite, where we'd been left to our own devices. The Super Nick not only had cameras in the custody suites but in the cells as well. This was very useful as we now knew what kind of mischief the guests were getting up to.

I was now one of the longer serving detention officers and tasked with training the new recruits in how to take care of our guests. One of these 'newbies' took a prisoner to his cell and asked him to remove his shoes before entering. The custody sergeant heard the commotion and called myself and a couple of other detention officers to assist. On reaching the noise the sergeant asked, 'What's up, fellah?'

'I'm not one of the usual druggy scum bags that come here and I'm telling you now, my shoes are staying on.'

Confrontation was in the air and the new officer looked worried as the prisoner did look a bit on the hard side of fair. I whispered to him, 'He's gonna 'ave a go 'ere.'

Negotiations were going in circles, had reached stale mate and a roll round was on the cards. The guest said, 'Look, I told you, they're not coming off. If you touch me, one of yah is gonna git 'urt. Is it really wurf it?'

'Shouldn't have said that; not to this Sergeant,' I whispered to the new bloke.

The Sergeant's response was a huge resigned sigh, a sigh from a man who had been in this situation nearly every day of his working life.

He was tired of it but professional, followed protocol and said, 'Is there anything else I can reasonably say that will make you take your shoes off?'

I knew that sentence was the Sergeants code to jump on the prisoner immediately if he said no, which he did.

'Nah!'

The Custody Sergeant grabbed him round the waist and we all jumped in, wrestling him to the ground. He put up a good fight with us all rolling round the floor with bodies, arms and legs flailing everywhere. It was bloody mayhem. As the action was in full flow, the new recruit jumped up, waving a pair of shoes around and screamed,

'I got his shoes, Sarge!'

The Sergeant yelled back, 'You fucking idiot, they're my shoes!'

We fell about laughing but finally pulled ourselves together and managed to get the prisoners feet free of his footwear. We ran out of the cell, slammed the door and after we stopped laughing the Sergeant told the new boy to pay more attention next time.

27 April 2007: Wembley Arena.

David Haye versus Tomasz Bonin.

Haye's camp had decided to test the water at heavyweight. Moving up from cruiserweight, Haye turned in at 15 stone 7lb. In spite of him bulking up, not an ounce of fat had been gained and none of his speed had been lost. Amazing coaching, nutrition, training and one dedicated athlete, for sure.

Tomasz Bonin, ranked ninth with the WBC, had a good professional record, having just one loss against Audley Harrison. I had seen him fight in the flesh three times in Poland and knew this guy was a credible opponent: no walk over. The contest would be a proper test for Haye and how he performed would leave us all in no doubt that he could fight and beat the best that the heavyweight division had to offer.

Haye didn't look fazed as he stared at his 'no nonsense' opponent, who seemed keen to show David, that this was the heavyweight division and that he wasn't welcome. The fight didn't last long. As Bonin came forward he was met with a ram rod jab that knocked his head back. He took a couple more and then a big 'Haymaker' right hand dropped him. I couldn't believe it, this tough Polish guy who I'd seen have some good fights had been felled in the very first round. He jumped up more stunned than hurt and I gave him the mandatory eight count. Bonin tried to attack, but this left him open for more of Haye's bombs and a big right dropped him again, this time hurting him. When back on his feet, Haye steamed into Bonin, who tried to fight back but was taking some heavy, one sided, punishment, which led me to stopping the contest.

This 'test' was all over in the first. Haye looked magnificent and I thought that all the heavyweights who were watching knew that the 'Haymaker' was a real threat to the division.

With the evening finished, it seemed pointless to drive all the way home, as I'd a flight to catch from Heathrow to Germany in the early hours of the morning. Wembley Arena is not far from the airport so I drove straight there and because it was just past midnight, decided there was no way I was going to pay for a night in a hotel for a few hours' sleep. I kipped in my motor in a car park not far from the airport. At 2 a.m. I woke up, bloody freezing, and thought back to the days my dad used to lock me out if I wasn't home before 11 p.m. I eventually got back to sleep but an hour later decided to get to the airport where it would be warm. When I arrived, had a hot shower and realising I had saved myself £80 by sleeping in the car, I headed for a full English breakfast. Happy days.

16 June 2007: Ankara, Turkey.

Oliver 'Atomic Bull' McCall (former World Champion) v Sinan Samil Sam (Turkey).

These were two very big guys, knew I'd have to be very fit and so upped my normal training regime. I'd need all my strength to make this fight flow if they decided to make it a grappling competition in the heat and humidity of Turkey.

I arrived at the check-in of the magnificent hotel and explained who I was, only to be told that I needed to take the elevator to the 22nd floor and check in at the Executive Suite's reception desk.

I was taken to this beautiful room and found myself saying, 'Bloody hell Les... you should see this... you weren't wrong.'

This was obviously a very big occasion, as WBC President Mr. Jose Sulaiman was present. The day before the fight, he summoned and spoke to the officials explaining how important this event was here in Turkey. This would be the first professional boxing Turkey had seen in 27 years.

The partisan crowd were expecting home wins for all their fighters. I stepped into the ring and noted how hot and humid it was. I suspected the fight may turn into a wrestling match and made sure I was properly hydrated as knew I'd be working hard.

People who know me, know I'm not easily intimidated but this was the most hostile, intimidating place I had refereed up to that time. The crowd, who would only be feet from me, chanted as if they were at a Galatasary football match, where they once had a sign that read, 'Welcome to Hell.'

The two boxers were giants. Oliver McCall, the former WBC Heavyweight Champion (who famously managed to knock out Lennox Lewis), was 42 and allegedly past his best, but even boxers past their prime still have a punch that can win a fight. For me it was a real honour to meet and referee 'Iron' Mike Tyson's former chief sparring partner.

As expected, right from the opening bell, they grappled, waltzed and held continually. I was expending as much energy as they were as I tried to wrestle their 100 plus kilo frames apart. I worked so hard to keep them boxing but when they didn't want to, had to use all my strength to break them up. In spite of being fit I knew I was tiring because when in the neutral corner, I saw the ring girl with the card showing it would soon be the start of the eleventh round and thought, *'Good, just two more rounds… keep going… just two more. Stay focussed John L… stay focussed!'*

I was sweating out, dehydrating and when the final bell sounded I was relieved, took a long drink, some deep breaths and began to relax. The result was read out, a unanimous decision in favour of 'Atomic Bull' McCall to win the WBC International Title. Within seconds a few plastic bottles came in to the ring and the crowd were starting to get ugly.

'Oh shit!' I thought, forgetting how tired and dehydrated I was.

Plastic bottles hurt, especially if they still have some drink in them. Also, when they've run out of bottles, the next thing coming in could be the chairs. Just before the mood turned from ugly to hideous the promoter of the fight and Sinan Sam jumped up onto the apron and waved the crowd to calm down which, fortunately for us in the ring, they did. Soon they began to leave the arena and when enough of them had gone, we felt safe enough to head back to the dressing room.

Gave the after fight dinner a swerve.

25 August 2007: The Point, Dublin, Ireland.

Bernard Dunne (Champion) v Kiko Martinez (Challenger).

European Super-bantamweight Championship.

The promoter Brian Peters and Dunne had rejuvenated Irish boxing big time. The place was packed wall to wall with boisterous, happy, expectant, already partying Irish men, who were eagerly awaiting this fight that I would be a judge for.

Kiko makes the walk to the ring and as soon as I see him, can see he wants this badly. He is sweating from his warm up and is ready to go. When Dunne approaches the ring, the supporters nearly take the roof off the place. He is waving at the crowd, smiling, but to me, doesn't look like he's coming to fight. He's relaxed, too relaxed and I feel someone should have a word with him, tell him there's this Spanish bull-of-a-bloke in the ring who wants to take his head off.

I was concerned for Dunne. Martinez had obviously got his mental preparation sorted as he wasn't fazed by thousands of cheering Irish men. Martinez, a knockout specialist, was ready for war and at that point I felt Dunne needed to get his fighting head on. Gowns off, I expected Bernard to change his expression and prepare for battle. But no, he was still grinning as the referee gave his final instructions.

The bell sounded and Martinez flew at Dunne. Within a minute, Dunne was felled by a big shot, his smile and that of every Irish man in the arena left the building. The decibels dropped from 120 to zero in the time it took for Dunne's arse to find the canvas. You could've heard a pin drop in that arena. Dunne got to his feet, found his smile but the Spaniard came in for the kill and managed to put him over for a second time, removing the smile again from Dunne's face. Again Dunne rose and tried to compose himself. The Spaniard wouldn't allow him the time he needed to get settled and puts him over a third time. Dunne is really hurt. The referee gives him a chance but called the fight over in round 1. The crowd were almost as stunned as Dunne, who was devastated by the loss.

With such a defeat, that can so easily be a career finisher, Dunne must have learnt a lot, as he went on to win the world title and fulfil his dream. A very impressive turn around indeed.

Back at The Five Bars there appeared to be a mismatch of similar proportions shaping up. A huge guy of 6 feet 8 inches and weight to match had been brought into custody. Once signed in he told us he wasn't going to his cell. *'This ain't going to end well,'* I thought.

Our custody sergeant told him he would be doing what he was asked.

'And who's gonna get me in the cell?'

'I will,' replied the 11 stone, 5 feet 7 inch tall, in thick socks, custody sergeant.

'Come on then, come from behind there and do it!' said the prisoner.

The Sergeant went through the door and headed toward the prisoner. When he reached him, it would've looked comical, if it hadn't have looked so dangerous. The height and weight difference was huge but I could tell the sergeant wasn't going to back down.

'Cell number 15. That way please.'

The prisoner laughed and went to his cell. Once he was in and the door locked, we all breathed out a big sigh of relief.

Ten minutes later the prisoner rang his buzzer and wanted to speak to the sergeant. I went to the cell with him and the prisoner said,

'Respect to you.'

'Why'd you go into your cell?' asked the Sergeant.

'I thought that if you had the balls to come from behind the desk, then you must be one hard bastard!'

The sergeant wasn't. But like the rest of us, he didn't like bullies.

14 December 2007: Palalottomatica, Rome, Italy.

Vincenzo Cantatore (Champion) (Italy) versus Johnny Jenson (Challenger) (Denmark).

European Cruiserweight Championship.

This fight was meant to re-launch Cantatore's career and the first round was going to script with him definitely being on top of his opponent. Each time he landed a decent glove the crowd shouted what sounded like 'Olé!'

In round two, Jensen decided to have a go; came forward, unloaded a few punches and caught Cantatori with a big right hander that shuddered him to his boots. He then followed up with another that put Cantatori to the floor. While he was down, Jensen threw a punch which, fortunately for him, didn't connect because if it had I would've disqualified him. Sent Jensen to the neutral corner and began the count. Cantatori got up on rubber legs at the count of 6. Because his legs had gone and unable to defend himself; I waved the fight over. I now had hold of him to make sure he didn't go over again and called for his corner to get the stool which they placed in the ring. The corner man got in and instead of sorting his fighter out decided to have a go at me for stopping the contest. The fighter was still dazed and the corner man was shouting at me saying,

'Standing eight count, standing eight count.'

This is where the corner men and boxers should know the rules. There is no standing eight count in British, Commonwealth and European Championships. Not knowing the rules can cause confusion because if a boxer gets stunned badly and doesn't go down, then takes a few more big shots, the referee will stop the contest. Game over.

Cantatori was still no better as I helped him to the stool and sat him down while his corner man still screamed in my ear. In the other ear I could hear the very upset Italian crowd and thought to myself, *'This is a new experience… don't like this much! Might be needing an escort out of here, John L!'*

Sure enough I got one.

To make matters worse, the Danish underdog and his corner men were jumping around, celebrating the win.

The MC said to me, 'Go with these two guys.'

Didn't need telling twice and walked off between two huge security men, back to the safety of the Danish dressing room till the crowd calmed and left the arena.

My good mate, Mark Green, one of the judges that night, told me later he was a bit worried and wondered where they'd taken me. Could tell he was relieved as I walked in to the after-fight party with my two big minders in tow. Was a bit concerned about attending and almost declined the offer thinking I should just go back to the hotel.

As I headed toward Mark and the other two officials, got some stern looks from the other guests. When I reached them they told me I'd done the right thing in calling the fight when I did. Although a little hungry decided I wouldn't head for the food on the table opposite us.

It was Mark who nudged me to let me know someone was approaching and I turned to see Cantatori on his way over to me. He was bruised, a bit banged up and I gulped a large one.

'Here we go!' I thought, *'What's he gonna' say?'*

Needn't have worried as he was very respectful, shaking my hand and telling me that he knew I had to make the decision to stop it as the Dane had caught him with a really good shot. Happier now, I breathed a sigh of relief and felt free enough to go and get some food, as the spread looked good. Just before I did, Cantatori's beautiful wife, who promoted the show, came to me and said, 'Mr. Lewis… Mr Lewis… you are a very good referee, very good referee indeed…'

Before I could get too excited about the compliment, she took my face in her hands and added, 'But not tonight!'

It was like listening to an Italian Julie.

Obviously she was disappointed about her husband being stopped, as this was meant to kick start his career again which had, in the past, seen him fighting for a world title.

02 02 08: Excel Arena, Docklands, London.

Commonwealth Lightweight Championship.

Amir Khan (Champion) (England) versus Gary 'Superman' St. Clair (Challenger) (Australia).

I'd been waiting and wanting to referee the silver medallist from the 2004 Olympics in Athens. What a talent and when I got the call to say I'd been selected to referee a contest he was involved in, I found myself forming a fist and saying, 'Yes!' very loudly.

Khan had won the hearts and minds of the British public for winning that silver medal and ITV had shown all of his fights 'Live'. This was unbeaten Khan's sixteenth professional fight, his toughest test to date as he was fighting a world class opponent, the former IBF Super-featherweight Champion, Gary 'Superman' St. Clair. Khan would be defending his Commonwealth belt for the third time. That night, millions around the UK were glued to ITV Sport and the Excel Arena was packed. In the crowd also, was my wife Julie and my 17 year old daughter, Kelcie, who'd come to watch me referee 'Live' for the first time. Yeah right! They were both fans of Amir and would be watching him!

Amir, as expected, had his hands full with 'Superman'. St Clair never stopped going forward, cut the ring down well but Khan kept on his toes and moved beautifully. In rounds 6 and 7, St Clair had his moments, catching Khan with some good shots flush on the chin that got his

258

attention. Khan was starting to look a little tired, having only gone 10 rounds once before, so between 7 and 8, his corner told him to stay focused and keep his concentration, which he did. He used his fast, snapping jab into Superman's face to keep him at bay.

Amir had to fight the full 12 rounds and boxed superbly off the back foot. His hand speed was phenomenal and I thought he'd go on to be a world champion, as that night I saw the pedigree of the boxer from up close. What an honour it was for me to referee him and what a nice polite gentleman in the dressing room when I went to give him my final instructions.

When I met up with Julie and Kelcie after the fight, a few boxing fans came over and asked me to sign their programmes and have photos taken with them. As we stood doing the boxers' pose, I noticed that Kelcie was staring at me in amazement. When we walked to the car she said, 'Dad, that was unbelievable, you signing programmes and having pictures taken with them fans.'

I think it shocked her, because at the end of the day I'm just plain old Dad.

08 03 08: O2 Docklands, London.

The O2 was packed with 20,000 fans. Top of the bill was the eagerly awaited showdown between World cruiserweight champions, David Haye (WBC and WBA) and Enzo Maccarinelli (WBO). As they were very big punchers, fireworks were predicted and expected. The crowd would not be going home disappointed. It was being beamed out across the pond as the fight captured the imagination of the American boxing fans and was scheduled late to suit their viewing habits.

The fight I was refereeing was the eagerly awaited clash between Carl Johanneson (Leeds) versus Kevin Mitchell, (London) for the British and Commonwealth Super Featherweight Championship. The fast boys!

This was the unbeaten, Kevin Mitchell's toughest test to date. When Frank Warren was asked about this fighter, he said that Kevin was the best signing he'd made since Nigel Benn. That could mean only one thing: the boy is very, very, good.

He was... but so was Johanneson, who was tough and experienced.

They were both big punchers and there was needle in this match after Mitchell had said some unkind things about Johanneson.

People were looking forward to this fight as much as the main event. The match reminded me of the fights between Francis Ampofo and Johnny Armour, the work rate was high and they both delivered brilliant shots and took them too, throughout the whole fight. They hit each other so hard at times, even I winced.

Frank Maloney had told Johanneson to take Mitchell into the trenches and he did. Mitchell seemed to like it there and the fight ebbed and flowed in each boxers favour, sometimes in a matter of seconds. No glass jaws or weak wills in this fight with both men saying they would knock the other out and with the bombs they threw, they could've been right.

Round 9 began at the same pace as every other round. The fitness was amazing and it took a brilliant left hook to drop Johanneson in a heap to the canvas. I counted the mandatory eight, rubbed the boxer's gloves on my shirt and let the fight go on. Thinking that the fight could soon be over I moved in closer to stop it should I need to.

Mitchell delivered five cracking shots with no reply and I literally jumped in between them to prevent Johanneson being knocked out as he was not defending himself. The match was a referees dream, both had come to fight, both had come to win, I had very little to do and had the best view in the arena.

Quite rightly, this was voted fight of the year.

When I am ironing my work shirts, I put that fight on. Shouldn't really as I've burnt my shirts a couple of times as it's so good. Never tire of watching that one. It's one of my favourites.

Following that cracking fight, I took my ringside seat to see the blockbuster, the 'Battle of Britain' Haye versus Mccarinelli. 'Haymaker' was devastating as he destroyed a very able Mccarinelli in two rounds to unify the Cruiserweight Championship of the World. Knew it wouldn't be a dull fight.

11 04 08: PRIZEFIGHTER TOURNAMENT

The birth of Prizefighter. A great idea by Barry Hearn and rightly taken up by the BBB of C. This was a 'knockout' competition with each fight over 3 rounds. There would be a total of 8 fighters for the quarter finals, 4 for the semi-finals and then the last two standing, battling it out in the final. Waiting in the wings, gloved up, would be two substitutes ready to step in if someone was cut too badly to carry on. Instead of wearing the usual black trousers, white shirt and black dickey-bow; we were given black polo shirts for a more casual look.

We were all nervous that night as it was a new format and hoped that everything would flow well. I was first to referee in the competition and from the opening bell we knew we needn't have been concerned. Two big heavyweights came flying out and were fighting at a fast tempo for the full three rounds. It was an exciting night at York Hall, live on Sky Sports. All the contenders fought at a high work rate as there was only nine minutes of boxing. It appeared everyone came to win the Prize Fighter Trophy and purse, which was finally won by the Northern Irish taxi driver, Martin Rogan.

Prizefighter was a great idea with excellent fast paced boxing and never a dull fight. Also by winning, the boxers profile was raised and gave the fighter a platform to get to bigger fights.

04 07 08: Everton Park sports centre.

Couldn't get the time off work for this one. Began work at 7 a.m., finished at 1:30 p.m. Picked Mark Green up on the way and had to travel via 'A' roads due to a lorry crash that closed the M6. This is when the 'Sat nav' came into its own. It took us through all the 'B' roads and kept us crawling along, which was better than sitting in a gridlocked, M6. Arrived at the venue just in time and fifteen minutes later Mark Green's in the ring, in charge and looking composed as he always does. I was one of the judges for this British Light Welterweight clash between classy champion, David Barnes and rugged challenger, Barry Morrison. Barnes boxed really well, keeping on his toes and led Morrison a merry dance to win on points.

As soon as the evening finished, I had to jump in the car, drop Mark off in Essex, then drive straight back to work for the next early turn! I was knackered to say the least, but sometimes that's the way it goes. I fell into bed that night but was awoken by the police at 1:30 a.m., who informed us that Julie's dad, Archie, was close to death in the local hospital. We drove straight there, entered the room to find a frail, but still stubborn, Archie. The first and only thing he could say when he saw us was, 'Oh fuck!'

He hadn't told the nurses who his next of kin were and he'd been there for nearly two weeks. We'd been going to his house but no one was in. It was only when the police did a bit of digging that they found Julie. We believe he didn't want his daughter to see him like this.

We both held his hand and spoke to him. He couldn't speak as he was too weak. We stayed until 3:30 a.m. and decided to come back later that morning. We went home, put the kettle on and before it had boiled the phone rang to tell us that Archie had passed away.

I was out on my feet but couldn't sleep. Despite our rocky start we'd become mates and shortly before his death, he paid me the biggest compliment. Archie pulled me aside and told me he could die a happy man knowing that I'd take care of Julie. As if that wasn't enough for me to get my head round he finished it off by saying, 'You're a good man Ian.'

27 09 08: Hamburg Germany.

Final Eliminator for the WBC Heavyweight Championship.

Vladimir Virchis v Juan Carlos Gomez.

Had a very bad start to this journey with a big delay at the airport after my flight was cancelled. Boarded another to Hamburg as the one planned for us had mechanical difficulties. It was chaos, with people having a right old moan to the German airline, Lufthansa. My flight was meant to be early morning, but I didn't leave until late evening. We were given meal vouchers due to being at the airport all day. Thankfully the contest was the following night otherwise I would've been having a moan as well.

Virchis was a giant and looked a right handful. I'd refereed Gomez before but thought that Virchis could take Gomez's head off. He didn't. Gomez boxed like a dream, bamboozling the big guy with neat footwork, great movement and in fact dropped him with a cracking left bang on the chin. He won a one-sided point's decision and the right to challenge WBC Heavyweight Champion, Vitali Klitschko.

On the 3rd of March, 2009, Robert Smith of the BBB of C rang me to relay the best news I could have wanted.

'Ian… have some good news for you. Congratulations and well done… You've been selected to referee the WBC World Heavyweight Championship fight between Vitali Klitchsko and Juan Carlos Gomez that is due to take place on the 21st March, 2009… Ian… Do Britain proud.'

Was numb, almost in tears, couldn't believe it and wondered if I was awake, as I had dreamt this moment on more than a few occasions during my refereeing career. This is the one we all want.

Once I put the phone down, couldn't wait to tell anyone and everyone I knew. The first person to hear from me was Mark Green. As expected from a great mate, he was really chuffed for me. Next was Mark Willoughby who told me it was well deserved and inevitable that it would someday happen.

I then rang the local papers and spread the word that the boy from Darnley Road, Strood, was on top of the world! Kept going cold, choked and almost in tears. Thought back to my first day at school and never dreamed that the guy who didn't want to be different would be on a world stage.

I was going to be only the fifth British referee to officiate the Heavyweight Championship of the World! It's the biggest honour in boxing and they gave it to little old me. I floated for the whole week.

14 March 2009: MEN Arena Manchester.

Matthew Hall versus Bradley Price.

Commonwealth Light-middleweight Championship.

A really good standard domestic fight. I had one week to wait for the WBC Heavyweight Championship and although excited had to focus on this one first. Every fight deserves the referee's full attention. Went through my normal preparations for the fight and thought it would be a nice warm up for the 'big one' the following week in Stuttgart, Germany. Was having my pre-fight nap, when a couple of hours into it, my mobile phone rings.

'Hello, is that Ian John-Lewis?'

'Yeah, Speaking,' I reply.

'It's Tito Gonzalez from the WBC office in Mexico here.'

I jumped out of bed, expecting him to tell me something about the heavyweight championship fight next week, maybe the flights had been booked, hotel details, that sort of thing.

'Oh yes Tito, how are you? What can I do for you?'

'I have some bad news for you, Ian.'

'What's the bad news Tito?'

My heart was racing, I knew it wasn't going to be good but didn't think it would be as bad as what he told me next.

'You WERE referring the Heavyweight Championship of the World in Stuttgart next week... unfortunately through boxing politics you have been taken off that and you will be refereeing the WBC Cruiserweight Championship on the May 16 instead, in Rome.'

Devastated, I had to sit down. I wasn't floating anymore but wide awake in shock.

'Why?' I asked.

He was very apologetic.

'All to do with boxing politics.'

Found it hard to speak but did manage to say thank you for the Cruiserweight Championship in Rome. We said our goodbyes, the phone went dead and the tears came as I sat on the side of the bed; gutted.

Getting fights cancelled is just one of those things that can happen in boxing but I'd done nothing to deserve having the greatest prize in boxing taken from me.

Went back to a fitful sleep and when I awoke, prayed that I'd just had a bad dream, but no, I checked my mobile and the last call was Tito. I felt like shit, like I had the flu but knew I'd have to be professional, I had a big Commonwealth title fight to referee tonight and would have to be on my game as normal. Couldn't let this devastating news affect me. Wouldn't let the boxers down; they had dreams they were trying to fulfil and I had to play my part and play it well. Told myself to pull myself together and drove it home with a few insults.

Followed my usual preparations for a contest, showered, shaved and headed to the venue which was within walking distance. It gave me time to get some air, to clear my head and remove any traces of the disappointment that had been dealt me just a few hours before.

Knew this news would come back to plague me after the fight, but not now, not for the next few hours at least, wouldn't let it. Once in the venue, the nerves I normally feel entered my body, I felt strangely relieved by this, knowing I'd be on top form for the upcoming contest. What a contest it was for two rounds, with the title changing hands to the guy from Manchester, Matthew Hall.

The night over and the stadium empty, made excuses to my fellow officials about why I wouldn't be meeting them in the bar. Walked back to the hotel on my own and went to my room. The adrenaline now gone and the fight over, the nightmare returned,

'Yeah... I did get a call and yeah, it was taken off me and no, I would not be referring the richest prize in sport.'

I kept asking why it had to happen to me. Felt really sorry for myself. It was like the night of the Micky Hughes fight and the time when I quit boxing after Darren Dyer broke my jaw. Tried to sleep, but it kept playing on my mind. Now I've got to tell everybody that I haven't got it. Fell into an uneasy, non- refreshing sleep; waking many times and felt awful each time I woke. I got up, went for breakfast which would normally have been welcome but tasted bland and realised that today would be the day I would have to start telling everybody that I was no longer doing the World Heavyweight Boxing Championship of the World. God it hurt just to think of it.

I thought that it could be ten years or never to get that opportunity again.

Once home, the first person I told was Julie who was upset for me and asked me how they could do that to me. Then rang Marks Green and Willougby, who were equally as disappointed for me, as they'd been happy when hearing the news.

I contacted Paddy Gearey at the local radio station and he asked me if I wanted to come in and do an interview about it. Although I was dreading it, it was the best thing to do as I received so many kind texts and messages of support from the listeners.

Never watched the fight, would have been too hard when knowing how close I'd been to refereeing it. Klitchsco won the bout by knock out to retain his title.

As with everything in life, the feelings pass and become less raw. This one took a bit of time though.

16 May 2009: Rome Italy.

Giacobbe Fragomeni (Italy) v Krzysztof Wlodarczyk (Poland).

WBC Cruiserweight Championship.

Everyone expected the young Pole to win the fight, and win it convincingly. He was on the climb and this was his shot at the title. It was a good fight with the Italian, the world champion, on home turf, obviously up for the challenge. He boxed superbly, trading good hard punches, managing to stay with the younger man and sometimes out muscling him on the inside.

Fragomeni took the stance and attitude that if the Pole was going to get the title from him, then he was going to have to earn it and by the end of it, would know he'd been in a fight.

It had been a really easy contest to referee until round nine, when the Pole had got on top and floored Fragemeni with a nice combination. I thought he had caught him late with the final punch but not enough for me to do much about it but give him a little warning to be careful.

The pole thinks he has it now and goes in for the kill, the Italian is dropping his hands and looking like he is running out of gas. Fragemeni goes down again and while on the canvas he gets hit by an over excited Pole who can sense the end. I call it a no knock down and make hand gestures to indicate this to the judges. Because it is a 'no knock down' the Pole does not gain the point for it and in the end this would prove costly to him.

The Italian regains his feet, uses his experience and boxes superbly to the end of the fight. The fight over, I congratulated the fighters on a great display and felt that the Italian had just shaded it. The judges saw it different with them announcing a draw and me raising a hand of both fighters to signify this. The Poles were disappointed as to win the title you have to win, not draw. He fell to his knees in disappointment.

The polish team were not happy and felt they'd been robbed. I explained to them later that I could've taken an official point away from him or disqualified him for punching his opponent while on the floor. He'd been lucky to finish the fight.

Later, the supervisor asked me to explain my actions wondering why I hadn't started the count. Replied that once you start the count you have to continue and if the Italian had not risen then I would've counted him out. A foul had been committed and the best way to handle it was to give the Italian time to recover. The reason I didn't take a point from the Pole was because he didn't get a point from the knockdown.

Didn't read blogs then, but I was alerted to one that had been written saying that the Mafia must have got to me because of the result.

Did have a laugh at that.

'The Richest Prize in Sport'

THE

WORLD BOXING COUNCILS

HEAVYWEIGHT CHAMPIONSHIP

OF

THE WORLD

Vitali Klitschko 'Dr. Iron Fist' (Ukraine)

Versus

Shannon 'The Cannon' Briggs (USA)

As it turned out, I had to wait just 18 months before being given the 'big one' again. It was to take place on the 16 October, 2010 in Hamburg, Germany. This time I kept it quiet as there was no way I wanted a repeat of the devastation I'd felt when the fight was taken away from me. I told only a few good friends and decided it would be something to celebrate after the event.

When sure the fight would go ahead I informed the press officer at Kent Police and soon after was requested to see the new Chief Constable, Ian Learmonth. I'd heard about the Chief with many officers saying he was just a copper like them but with a lot of braiding on his shoulder. That is such a compliment to a man in that position. I met him at headquarters in his office and was expecting to have a 15 minute chat and be on my way. But no, nearly an hour later he said, 'Ian, I've got an appointment to attend now so we have to end our very interesting talk. Come back from the fight and see me. It will be great to talk again.'

As we shook hands he said, 'It's good to see nice things happening to nice people.'

This title fight was the USA's last opportunity to get some pride back as the Europeans were winning this particular battle. Briggs was the USA's brightest hope and was the last American heavyweight to rule the world. When seeing Briggs at the weigh-in, I knew he'd come to win as he was in top shape and prepared to war. The fighters came head to head and Shannon roared in Vitali's face. It looked very intimidating but the huge world champion just smiled.

Prior to going to the rules meeting, which Vladimir attended on Vitali's behalf, there was a row of photographers snapping away. I was suited and booted as always and I recognised one of them. We acknowledged each other and he said, 'Alright, Ian... I remember you fighting way back in '87; you were a pretty good fighter.'

Vladimir heard this, turned to me and said with a surprised look on his face, 'What year was that?'

'1987,' I replied.

'How old are you, then?'

'48.'

'48! No way!' he shouted.

'Yeah, I am. I've got a 23 year old daughter.'

'You're in great shape.'

He then shook my hand. Doesn't everyone like a bit of respect?

At the rules meeting, where claims and counter claims are made about the other camps fighter; the supervisor, Charles Giles, obviously having heard enough of the moans, made an announcement to all in the room.

'Look, we have a very experienced referee in Ian John-Lewis. Do you want to say anything, Ian?'

I answered briefly and to the point.

'I am prepared for anything and everything, so neither camp should be concerned.'

That seemed to quieten everybody down.

On fight night, went to Klitschko's dressing room and told him it was an honour to be the referee and showed him the respect the Heavyweight Champion has earned and deserves. I then told him what I expected, 'You are The Champion of the World; now give us all a good fight!'

'I will!' he replied.

'When you are in the ring you don't have to look at me... but you do have to listen and the only words I'll be saying will be, box! Stop boxing! Break! Don't hold! That's it... plain and simple.'

He nodded his understanding of my words.

Next, went into Shannon Briggs dressing room and found a ready fighter, with a manner indicating that he was here to take the Heavyweight Title back to the United States. He gave me his attention and a hard focussed stare. I knew he felt he could win it.

The Germans know how to put on a show and the stadium was packed to capacity. The television work was spectacular, with the adverts all about power. The evening was running beautifully with typical German efficiency.

When in the ring I ran through my usual checklist. Once happy with the furniture and checks done, I began to get into the zone. The ring filled up with people from both camps and as fight time approached they melted away again to leave about six of us. The anthems finished, I called the boxers to the centre of the ring. As they met in the middle, the one and only Michael Buffer, ring announcer, put his arm around me and kindly wished me good luck. I have a low heart rate normally, but that night there was a world-wide audience of well over 13 million, and my heart was beating faster than some of my coked up customers in custody on a Saturday night. The fight would be the seventh highest rating for any fight in Germany's history. I made my announcement:

'This is the Heavyweight Championship of the World

And

I am the referee…

I spoke to you both in the dressing room.

Obey my commands at all times.

You both know the rules.

Watch your heads and keep your punches up.

When I shout break!

You break clean,

and remember,

defend yourself at all time,

Shake hands!

They ignored my request, went to go back to their respective corners. I told them to return to the centre of the ring and made the request to shake hands an order. They touched gloves and I showed I'd take no nonsense and would be in control.

From the very beginning I was impressed at how Klitschko could, for such a massive guy, move so well. Briggs took some really good shots, took them well and just kept coming, looking to land his own right hand which he and Vitali knew could down an elephant. Klitschko was boxing brilliantly and at the end of round seven, caught Briggs on the chin just as the bell sounded. I jumped in to separate them as I thought the boxers may not have heard the bell above the noise of the crowd. Briggs thinks I've stopped the fight and glares at me. I tell him it's the end of the round and as he goes back to his corner men, who are already telling him loudly that he's way behind on points and that he needs to let his right hand go.

The bell begins another round then another. Briggs is losing but keeps coming forward, so there's no way I can stop this. He may be taking shots but is still going after Klitschko and looking able. It's very unlikely that a fight will be stopped if the fighter is still chasing and so obviously up for the job.

Briggs' team were getting frustrated with him and started to swear from the corner, getting louder and louder as their frustration grew. I'd heard enough, shouted, 'Stop boxing!' and ordered the corner men to stop cursing. They apologised and quietened down.

Klitschko looked like he had a couple of more gears but respected that wrecking ball of a right hand that Briggs was hunting him with. (Previously, when fighting for the WBO crown, 'The Cannon', way behind on points, had landed a punch in the twelfth and final round to knock out Sergei Liakhovich to take the title).

In round ten it was becoming more and more one sided and I thought about calling it off but the bell sounded to signal the end of the round. I felt concerned for Briggs so went to his corner to check on him.

'I'm watching you, Briggs. I'm close to stopping this!'

Looked for his reaction to my statement. The corner men assured me he was okay, but it's easy to be brave from behind the ropes.

'Hell, no way you stopping this fight man!' He answered.

The way he said it, the look on his face, proved to me that he was still up for the task. In the past I'd been asked by boxers to finish the fight, wave it over. But not this guy, not Briggs, he wanted to continue, believed he could still win.

In round eleven, Briggs found Klitschko's chin with a very good right hand which made him wobble and stopped him throwing further shots until he found his legs again. This was the punch Briggs was trying to land all night and was the reason why, in my opinion, Klitschko never went in to finish Briggs off.

The final bell rang out with Klitschko winning on points.

After the fight, plenty of flack came my way. Referees are used to it. The fight doctor allegedly stated he would've stopped the fight in six rounds. If that was the case, why didn't he? He never once came to me voicing or showing concern and can override any decision if he feels it's necessary, but he didn't, so I didn't understand the alleged comment. The judges, however, told me I was right to let the fight continue as Klitschko never did enough to get the fight stopped.

Briggs went to hospital after his courageous effort in trying to take the World Title back to the USA. Until recently I always believed that Shannon Briggs suffered substantial injuries. It was reported that he had a left cheek fracture, broken nose, with some reporting that he had been comatose.

Mark Heffernan (writer) suggested that we speak directly to Shannon about the fight and Chris 'Clubber' Langley organised it though twitter. Shannon replied to Chris that he would be more than happy to speak to us. We huddled around the laptop as Maggie, Chris's wife, sorted out the connection and dialled the number. Shannon answered his phone and was genuinely pleased to hear from us. After some warm introductions, I told Shannon about the book and put him on to Mark who asked Shannon, 'With hindsight do you think the fight should have gone all the way to the end?'

There was not a pause from Shannon.

'Of course! The fight should definitely NOT have been stopped. It was The Heavyweight Championship of the World… the biggest prize in sport… and Ian did a phenomenal job. I was still competitive, still in the fight. I took some shots, he's a decent puncher. At the same time, I know for a fact the injuries were over played. I had a fractured face… that's not true. All the things they were saying were lies. The media were putting out I was in a coma… that's not true. None of that was true. Nothing was broke. If you look at the fact that seven days later I was on the Kerner Show. I did a press conference in the hospital where you could see all the swelling was gone down after two days.'

I told Shannon that I was really pleased to hear that because the highlight of my career had been tarnished when I'd heard about the reported injuries.

Shannon continued, 'In that first round I go to throw a left hook and he blocked it and my arm popped. Still trying to use that arm is what hurt me the most. But that's in the past. Where I am at now, Ian… I feel great… I want to thank you for not stopping it.'

'That means a lot to me,' I replied. 'I received some stick over the decision to let it go on and when I thought you'd been badly injured I felt I should've stopped it earlier. Now I know I was right but I needed to hear it from you, though.'

'No, you did a phenomenal job… it was great. I was okay then and I'm okay now. I'm coming back. I'm looking forward to it.'

We wished each other the best for our respective careers and thanked him for his time. Shannon said to keep in contact, wished us every success with the book and thanked me again.

It seemed fitting and natural to end the conversation with a round of applause.

Shannon Briggs is a warrior, a modern day gladiator.

In my own boxing career, I've had two broken jaws, a broken nose, and suffered bad cuts, it is after all the 'Hardest Game' and as Ricky Hatton has said on more than one occasion, 'It's not a tickling contest.'

That night, on the 16 October, 2010 I became only the fifth British referee to preside over a WBC World Heavyweight Boxing Championship and at 48 years of age: the youngest. What an honour. Have been asked many times how I celebrated that monumental achievement. I didn't because I thought Shannon had been injured beyond acceptability, but after speaking to him, that night I raised a glass to Briggs, Klitchko and of course – Les Roberts.

At work we were told that the documentary 'Coppers' would be shown on Channel 4. Our line of work can be boring but the producers were very interested in the unusual, such as strip searches and Danny Mcintyre's 'Rap', thinking it would make good TV.

It did and almost won an award.

When they were filming the series they came to my station and asked for an interview. I sat in front of the camera and was asked to explain what is involved in a strip search, tell them why we do it and what we sometimes find. I explained that a strip search can only be done by a police officer but detention officers can sometimes be present as a witness. The guy behind the camera kept saying yeah, and looked at me as if he wanted me to say more. Was getting to the place where I was going to have to describe where prisoners hide things. Because I knew this was going to be aired, instead of saying, 'arsehole', I just came up with the term 'Chatham pocket'. Thought they'd never use it as everything we said had to be cleared by the superintendent. I thought he'd veto it but instead came out of the room laughing hysterically and said, 'Ian, that's comedy gold. Chatham pocket... where'd you get that idea from... viewers will love that.'

Shortly after, on a Saturday evening, my phone kept ringing. I couldn't answer it because I was in Cancun, Mexico at the WBC Convention. After the meeting I checked my phone and found that Julie was trying to get hold of me. I rang her back.

'Luv, I was in the bath and Kelcie was watching Harry Hills TV burp in her room. She shouted to me that you were on it. Ian; Harry takes the micky real good, you've got to see it.'

I couldn't wait to watch it and yes, it was hilarious. (Type it into the computer's search engine, and the clip comes up.)

Danny Mc (Mcintyre), as I knew him, came into the custody suite. Danny was, like me, from Darnley road. He was quite a regular and used to attend with his younger mate; always in trouble they were. They were also a right handful but they never gave me any hassle when I was on duty. Full credit to Danny's younger mate, after years on the drugs (and trust me there's been times he's been completely out of it in Custody), he took up mixed martial arts (MMA) and has never been in trouble since. Danny liked me because I boxed, was a referee and came from the same area. He often said that it was great to have a guy do good from our street and was proud of me because if anyone asked, I'd tell them where I came from. Didn't hide it.

Spent many a night chatting to Danny, trying to get through to him when the drink and drugs wore off, and his head was clear. He, like so many of our guests, was quite different when drug free. I'd say to him, 'Look at your mate Danny, he's cracked it. Come on, it's your turn now.'

He'd nod his head in agreement but I knew that's where it ended.

Danny once told me that when he was a guest of Her Majesty at Elmley, some inmates would create a racket when I appeared on the television, with some of the prisoners shouting, 'Ian the jailer, from Chatham nick is on telly!'

Danny happened to be in custody when the production crew were filming. He was good TV and the producers of the show knew it. He told them about the 'rap' he'd written, when put in solitary for a week after he'd kicked off. He wrote this ditty to pass the time and get his own back on the 'Screws'. Danny was asked to perform it for the camera.

I stood next to the camera man out of view. Danny, realising that I was staying kept telling me, 'Ian, I have respect for you… you know that… this is not about you, honest Ian it has nothing to do with you. It's about some of the prison officers… screws inside… I know someone has to 'turn the key' here, and Ian, its better it's you, mate.'

He then rapped a really explicit song about prison officers and as he performed it I can remember thinking, *That's bloody good that is… Won't make the cut though, way too graphic.*

It did make the show and was quite a local hit. It's on YouTube.

Couple of months later I ran into Danny and his mum in Darnley Road post office. I was in there with my mum and we got chatting. He introduced me as, 'the guy who looks after me at the nick when I get into trouble.'

Strange really because no matter how drugged up or drunk he was, he was always embarrassed when I saw him in custody. The cell can be a lonely place to be and we've had some late night chats. People can get clarity in the early hours of the morning and I always hoped he would.

We chatted for a while in the post office. He was in the best shape I'd seen him for a long time. Had hope for him, thought he might have a chance, might have turned the same corner that his mate had. I was sad when the news came through that he'd died from an overdose. I'd known him half his life: the criminal half. What a waste.

Danny was someone's son. I knew whose son he was; had met her, knew she loved him and when he died she must have been broken hearted.

21 May 2011: Bell Centre, Montreal, Canada.

WBC Light Heavyweight Championship.

Bernard Hopkins (USA) v Jean Pascal (Canada).

The news came via e-mail that I'd been selected to be the referee. Did a double take when I saw it. This was a return match, ordered by the WBC because of the controversy over the result. Pascal had received a majority draw decision, which left him still Champion.

With the result being controversial (with some claiming that Pascal was given the nod over Hopkins because the fight had been in Canada), I decided to steer clear of watching the fight. If I didn't see it and was questioned by a journalist about who I thought had won, I wouldn't be able to answer.

Had only seen Pascal fight once and that was against Carl Froch for the vacant WBC Super Middleweight Championship, which Froch won on points. They gave a brilliant display of boxing and punching power that reminded me of the Benn/Eubank fights. I had seen Hopkins many times and thought that this would be a thriller for the boxing world.

This fight was huge, a chance for Hopkins to make more history as he was already in the books as having defended the World Middleweight Championship 20 times. If he won, he'd become the oldest champion at 46 years old, with Pascal having almost two decades on him. Even the referee was only three years older than Hopkins!

The weigh-in was attended by so many people that the conference centre was filled to capacity and then some. A very lively Hopkins was telling Pascal that he would beat him this time, but Pascal didn't allow it to get to him. Hopkins is great at getting under his opponent's skin and into their heads, seems to be able to trigger the little voice in a boxer's mind that makes him doubt.

The rules meeting was straight after the weigh-in and not attended by either boxer. It was no different than any other rules meeting, with both sides suggesting that I might want to be aware of certain things the other boxer may be guilty of.

'I am the referee and I'll judge on what I see. Any problems and I'll deal with them,' I told them.

That dealt with we moved on to the issue of the gloves. The make of gloves are decided when the contract of the fight is being discussed. Gloves are tried on by the trainer and once they have been decided on, are signed for and the gloves go back to me and stay under my care till fight night.

The morning of the fight I went out for a long walk. I do this in every country that is safe enough, as part of my pre-fight preparation. Had been walking for about 30 minutes when I spied a large building with Montreal Police Station written on it. Decided to go in and introduce myself to the guys behind the desk,

'Hi, I'm Ian, I work for Kent Police in England as a detention officer.'

We discussed how each force deals with their guests. He then asked, 'What is the purpose of your visit to Canada?'

'I'm the referee in tonight's big fight.'

'Not the Pascal versus Hopkins fight?'

'Yes, that's the one.'

'You can't be doing that, that's a massive fight!'

'Yeah, think I am… they flew me all the way from England to do it.'

I then took my cap off and said, 'Have a good look at my face, my hairstyle and watch tonight.'

As soon as they realised I was telling the truth it seemed like half the station came out to meet me, wanting autographs and photos. They wished me good luck, we said our goodbyes and I walked the 30 minutes back to the hotel, where I had dinner and the usual afternoon nap to prepare for the nights event.

The stadium, the Bell Centre, was a five minute walk away. I left the hotel and joined the ever increasing crowd on the way to the stadium. The atmosphere was amazing, the crowd in good spirits and I could sense they were really looking forward to the fight. People spoke to me and asked if I was the referee for tonight's main event.

Once in, I sat and watched some of the undercard to get my head in the zone. The inspector told me that the fighters had arrived and we went to do the pre-fight instructions. Nerves were building for me now; it's good to be nervous and I tell anyone in this game, 'Not nervous? Quit!'

Went to Hopkins dressing room first. Told him it was an honour to be the official at the fight. He had a chance to make history by being the oldest World Champion ever by eclipsing the legendary George Foreman, who regained the Heavyweight Championship of the World, at the age of 45. But first he would have to overcome the strong, brilliant and 18 years younger World Champion that was Pascal. Hopkins was in amazing shape for a man of 46 and I thought that although I might be giving him three years, felt I could take him if I had to… Yeah right!

Went to Pascal's dressing room, and as soon as I entered he acknowledged me. There was not an ounce of fat on him and he looked as if his skin had been stretched over his muscles. He was in top shape and had obviously not underestimated the class of the much older Hopkins. As I left the dressing room I was really excited, feeling that it was going to be a cracker.

The atmosphere was simmering nicely. I'm in the ring with the MC, the flag bearers and the supervisor, awaiting the fighters. Hopkins, the challenger, comes in first to Eminem s 'One shot' recording, which

281

then goes into 'My Way' with adapted lyrics that basically said Hopkins would destroy Pascal and do it Bernard's way.

Hopkins walks the ring with a balaclava on, looking menacing, like an executioner, which I would imagine is the point when your fight name is 'The Executioner'. His opponent Pascal, is the undefeated Champion, 18 years his junior, on home turf and has 17, 495 of the 17, 500 fans screaming for him. Pascal is in no rush to get into the ring, making Hopkins wait and by doing so, letting him know that he, Pascal, is the reigning World Champion.

Gowns and balaclavas off, the anthems finished, I call them to the centre of the ring and give my usual instructions. Have to tell Pascal that the fight doesn't start until he shakes hands. He doesn't want to, but touches gloves with Hopkins. That's good enough for me.

Round one: Pascal gives Hopkins respect and allows Hopkins to come onto him. Hopkins takes the pace out the fight, he may be in great shape, but a fit 46 year old won't be in as good a shape as a fit 28 year old. Hopkins knows it and will let the wisdom of his years benefit him.

Between the rounds I hear Hopkins trainer say to him, 'Don't go being dragged into that young shit. Don't get into a war. Out box him. Teach that young boy some lessons.'

Round two: Pascal tries to up the pace; take it to him; make the 'old boy' work but as many opponents before him found out, Hopkins is a master of controlling a fight with slick moves, feints, blocks and holds. Try as he might, Pascal just couldn't land his big punches or get a grip on the fight. In round three, Hopkins caught Pascal with a cracking right hand that hurt him and made him even more cautious.

It was a privilege to watch this old fox 'school' this young gun in a fight that had now become typical Hopkins. It saw him holding, mauling and catching Pascal with plenty of shots that kept him wary. All this made me work real hard for the first five rounds to keep the fight going. Then in round six, I got really fed up when they just wouldn't break when told to. Called a time out and read them the riot act. At the end of the round Hopkins said something to Pascal that really upset him and he tried to follow Hopkins back to his corner. I guided Pascal away from Hopkins and his mind games.

Time keeper shouts, 'Corners 10 seconds.'

Pascal's corner signals to me he's not ready, a problem with his left glove tape. I call 'time out' to the timekeeper and while I'm looking at Pascal to see when he is ready, the crowd begin to laugh. I look over my shoulder and for a split second, wondered where Hopkins had gone. I look down to find him on the canvas doing press ups, couldn't believe it! More mind games.

It's going Hopkins way, he's dictating the pace of the fight and it's not until round twelve, when Pascal, who knows he's losing, rallies and fights the way he should have from round three. Too little too late and Hopkins wins by unanimous decision to become the oldest world champion ever at 46 years of age. Only three years older than Hopkins, I'd felt the pace and no one was punching me!

Climbed down from the ring, put my jacket on, and found a well-deserved drink. Job well done, time to relax and calm down from the high I was on. As it was a 'Golden Boy' Promotion, I was hoping to get to meet the great fighter Oscar De La Hoya and shake his hand. But he didn't attend, his business partner Richard Schaefer did and I had nice chat with him at ringside.

A night of many records: Hopkins age, his 60th professional fight and a record crowd of 17,500 spectators for the Bell Centre.

Got a lot of praise for the way I handled the fight, and was told that the Canadian Commission were pleased they had a strong referee controlling the contest.

Life's been good.

A new detention officer was to be assigned to our team. I was pleased to hear he was Scottish because all the Scots I'd worked with had been no nonsense types, who'd back you in a crisis. So when my colleague and old school mate, Kim Matschas, said to me, 'Here, Ian, you see that new guy Richard, well he's already causing concern.'

'Really. In what way?' I replied.

'Well, he's demanding to wear his kilt and sporran instead of trousers. He was right kicking off when they said he couldn't. He was saying it was his human right and all that stuff,' she said, seriously.

'Bloody hell, Kim, sounds like he's going to be a right pain in the arse. But thinking about it, I suppose he's right because who are we to say he can't wear a kilt thing. Just hope he wears something underneath it, if you know what I mean, Kim!'

She then started giggling, which I was pleased with as I thought she'd found what I said amusing. It then turned to laughter and although I thought what I'd said was funny, I knew it wasn't that funny.

'What you laughing at, Kim?'

'I can't keep it going, Ian. Can't keep a straight face anymore. Was only joking but boy did you fall for it! Your face!'

He wasn't a pain after all, remained kilt less, was one of the good guys and we hit it off right from the start. Richard was very well educated and had left a high powered, well paid job through boredom. I asked him why he'd become a detention officer as the money wasn't great and a real step down for him. He replied that he wanted to be a police officer but joined us to get a feel for the profession. He settled in well and soon found we had a common interest, 'The Stranglers'. He was a massive fan having seen them all over the UK. Richard told me they were playing at Hammersmith so we booked tickets as I'd never seen them live.

I drove to his house in Bromley, had a pie and a pint then headed to Hammersmith. Once there I saw the huge crowd outside and noticed something he didn't – that I was the only black guy there. I then noticed all the 'skinheads' waiting to enter and felt that all eyes were on me. I said to Richard, 'Am I gonna be alright here… you know… with all these skin heads?'

'Ian, they're not skinheads… they're like us; old blokes and bald, mate,' he laughed.

'Oh,' I replied, relieved.

While we listened to the warm up band, a few blokes in the audience recognised me, came over, said hello and made me feel really welcome. It was time for the main event and the one and only Stranglers were just about to hit the stage. It was packed with us all chanting, 'Stranglers, Stranglers, Stranglers'. They appeared to a roar, the music started, the crowd jumped up and down, me with them and they began their first number, a song written about the time they spent in another country when they were treated very badly. The singer belted out the first line, 'I feel like a wog!'

Richard turned, looked at me and said, 'Sorry, Ian.'

'Don't worry about it,' I shouted. My mind went back to 1979 when I was working at the old paint factory, TKS. Andrew Nicholson was 23 and a massive Gillingham FC supporter. I was 17 and had never been to a football match before because back in the 70's football hooliganism was a national past time and my Dad wouldn't let me anywhere near it. Andrew said I'd have to see a home game with him and his mates, so I took him up on it.

Gillingham versus Colchester and we are at the Rainham End, shouting our support, when the Colchester striker, a big black guy, got the ball. The Gills crowd, including Andrew's mates, screamed out monkey chants! Andrew looked at me and said, 'Sorry, Ian'.

'Don't worry, I'm used to it,' I answered. I'd learnt not to let it get me the way it did when I was really young. Every time this guy got the ball and caused havoc with the Gillingham defence, all you heard was 'ooo! ooo! ooo!' To be honest, some of the crowd that were chanting, looked like they'd be the ones happy playing with a rope and a tyre. The ironic thing was, a few years later, that same black striker, Trevor Lee, left Colchester and played for Gillingham FC. Yeah… the fans adored him and the only 'ooo' he heard from them was when he shot and narrowly missed.

30 October, 2011: York Hall, Bethnal Green.

Liam Walsh (Champion) v Paul Appleby (Challenger)

Commonwealth Super Featherweight Championship

Leading boxing promoter, Frank Warren, with his sons, had been working on a new channel on Sky purely for boxing fans. It was called Box Nation and this night they would broadcast for the first time.

It was very hot in the hall already, then they added the TV lights and the centre of the ring became scorching. As the battle was in full flow, the commentator John Rawlings noticed my sweating, glistening bald 'Hagleresque' head and shouted loudly on air, 'It's so hot in there, just look at John-Lewis's head… The shine is on!'

Despite my concentration I did crack a smile.

Box Nation couldn't have asked for a better start as the boys gave their all and as ever, the vocal York Hall crowd played their part by almost screaming the roof off the place and the sweat off my head. The fight was a classic, with fortunes swaying from one boxer to the other. Both fighters found the canvas but at the end of eleven gruelling, absorbing rounds, Appleby's corner pulled him out.

It became the Fight of the Year and yet again I was fortunate to be the referee. I was alerted to the fact that I'd been the first referee to begin the careers of both 'Box Nation' and 'Prizefighter' and both have rightly gone on to be very successful and established indeed.

06 November 2011: Yoyogi National Stadium, Tokyo, Japan.

Shinsuke Yamanaka (Japan) (Champion) v Christian Esquivel (Mexico) (Challenger).

WBC Bantamweight Title.

A great fight: with Esquivel, relentless, and Yamanaka, pure class. Try as he might, Esquivel's bursts, just hit thin air as Yamanaka put on a classic boxing exhibition.

Then at the beginning of round ten the lights went out. Now every referee knows what to do when this happens, it's in the rule book. Up to this point I'd been refereeing for 18 years and this was the first time it had happened. Despite my experience my first thought was, 'Shit!' but quickly went into auto pilot. I called a time-out, sent both boxers to the neutral corners and went to the supervisor. Fortunately the lights were out for only 60 seconds, but it was a worryingly long minute, wondering if they would be able to get the power back on for the fight to continue.

In round eleven the Japanese World Champion's spiteful punches finally caught up with the Mexican and after taking a few will shattering shots, he turned his back on Yamanaka and went to his haunches by the ropes in defeat. I quickly realised the stuffing had been punched out of him. He had no more left to give and nothing left to take. I stepped in and waved the fight over.

I also judged two more world title fights on this big championship bill: WBC Flyweight Champ, Toshiyuki Igarashi, outpointed the game Wilbert Uicab and WBC Super featherweight Champ, Takahiro Aoh, outpointed a very tough and tenacious Italian challenger, Devis

Boschiero. At the weigh-in I could see the Italian meant business as he stared down the Japanese World Champion. He made a great start too, taking the fight to Aoh and putting him on the back foot for a few rounds. The champ clawed his way back into the fight, and just when I thought Boschiero had blown himself out, he found another store of energy. For me he won the last 3 rounds to snatch a fantastic victory in Japan, but the other two judges thought otherwise. Mind you, the Japanese crowd were very quiet when Aoh's hand was raised which I thought indicated they might have agreed more with my decision.

23 March 2012: Civic Hall, Wolverhampton.

Shane McPhilbin (Champion) v Enzo Maccarinelli (Challenger).

British Cruiserweight Championship.

McPhilbin had won this title two months before against Leon Williams at York Hall, Bethnal Green. Maccarinelli was the former WBO Cruiserweight Champion of the World, so a strong favourite to take the very well supported McPhilbin's British belt.

I received some criticism after this fight with some saying I shouldn't have let Maccarinelli continue after he was put down very hard in the first round. It was no secret that Enzo had suffered four bad knockouts/stoppages in recent times and I thought that Shane's corner would be planning to draw him into a brawl and catch him on the chin. That's exactly what happened. McPhilbin came out all guns blazing and the warrior in Enzo willingly obliged. They both swapped big punches with Enzo actually getting the better of it, hurting McPhilbin and causing him to tie Enzo up until his legs regained strength. Then, 'BOOM!' a huge left hook from McPhilbin dropped and hurt Enzo badly. Upon rising, he was still hurt and heard the command of his trainer, the late Dean Powell, telling him to, 'Take a knee!' which he did. It was a wise call from a great corner man because if Enzo had gotten straight up, he'd have been on wobbly legs and I'd have called it over. Those extra few seconds and a good look at Enzo, were enough to convince me to let him continue. I told them to box on and Shane came in to finish the job but before he could, the bell went and I sent them to their corners.

During the one minute rest, McPhilbin's trainer came over to the neutral corner where I was standing and said he thought the round was short. I took no notice of him; I'm not the timekeeper.

Round two: McPhilbin again hurt Enzo but Enzo used his experience to survive. Enzo was again put down in round three but it was more of a stun than hurt. McPhilbin was getting tired and Enzo took full advantage, out boxing him to take the next few rounds.

Round nine: Enzo repaid the earlier onslaught and dropped McPhilbin with a hard shot smack on the button. Both were now tired but Enzo had more in the tank and came away with a hard fought points win, to fulfil his and his father's dream of him winning the British Title.

Found out after the fight, that the first round had been short, by a whole 47 seconds.

27 October, 2012: Japan

Takahiro Ao (Japan) versus the unfancied Gamaliel Diaz (Mexico).

WBC World Super Featherweight Championship.

Diaz was outside the top ten and was probably picked as a sharpener for Ao who was preparing for a future clash between himself and Takashi Uchiyama for the World Title. This would have been a massive domestic fight in Japan but upsets happen in boxing and did this day.

On entering the challenger's dressing room, they may have been polite and respectful but I knew that the whole Mexican camp were up for it. They'd not come to Japan for sight-seeing. An opportunity had been given to Diaz and despite being thousands of miles from home, he was going to do all he could to take it.

Diaz was on a good run but was 31 and with the record he had on entering the ring: 35 wins (KO's 11), 11 losses (KO's 7) they must have thought he was a calculated risk.

I asked the interpreter, 'Please tell him, I am honoured to referee him tonight… tell him I want him to give me a good fight. He's challenging for a WBC World Title.'

Diaz replied, respectfully, 'I will give you a good fight!'

In the Japanese dressing room the interpreter told them I wanted to give them the final instructions. There were bows of respect all round.

Some camps try and draw your attention to areas they want you to look at. For instance, they may say the opponent has a history of his protector riding up or that he leads with his head. I always tell them that any rule infractions will be noted and dealt with. Some know I have been a boxer and those who don't, on finding out, seem more at ease as I know the games boxers play. However, on this particular occasion, neither camp made any claims about the other boxer's style. Both were just eager to get into the ring and get to it.

The bell rang and the twelve round, bloody encounter began with the Mexican challenger fighting like his life depended on the result. The onslaught began in round one and would continue to the very end. They'd given this Mexican an opportunity, may not have underestimated his ability, but had underestimated his desire to win.

The Japanese World Champion came out in round three with a different attitude, realising he had a fight on his hands. It was difficult to keep it flowing as they were like rutting stags with their heads continually colliding. Both boxers were cut; small cuts but the type that bleed and look worse than they are. As I went in to separate them, I kept getting their blood on my shirt. After the fight it went straight in the bin.

I had to deduct two points from the Mexican for low blows but he always seemed on top. Both camps knew it was close and in the rest between rounds eleven and twelve, I prepared myself for war.

Wasn't disappointed!

In round twelve with only 40 seconds left, Ao received a gaping wound on his forehead, due to a clash of heads. I had no option but to call a time out and have the doctor see the cut. There wasn't long left and know it's every boxers pride to go the distance, so hoped the doctor would allow it to carry on. He did.

The end of the fight saw both fighters walking around the ring with their arms raised in victory, but that decision would be up to the judges, who went for Diaz, a decision I agreed with. The crowd were very respectful to the new champion. At no time did I or the judges feel threatened by the home spectators. There was not even a hint of trouble and I walked back to the dressing room through the crowd.

Joe Koizumi, told me I'd done a great job and to have that said by him, made my night.

09 November, 2012: Olympia, Liverpool.

Orvill McKenzie v Enzo Maccarinelli.

British Light Heavyweight Championship.

Refereeing is never plain sailing. One fight you're on top of the world and the next people are telling you the decision you made was diabolical. Sometimes you're damned if you don't and damned if you do. To be a referee you need a thick skin, selective hearing, faith in your ability and be able to dissect the information thrown your way and learn from it. If you're too sensitive, the mistakes will pile up one after another until all your confidence is gone and they stop inviting you to shows. If you've made a decision and you felt it was right, live with it. It doesn't matter what anyone else says, you have a duty of care to the boxer and even though you may have saved him from unnecessary punishment, he may not thank you for it. Referees are not there for thanks but to protect the fighter at all times, even when they don't want protecting.

This was Maccarinelli's next fight and again I received criticism, but this time because I stopped it. Enzo had decided to drop down from cruiserweight to light heavyweight. When I went into his dressing room to give my instructions, he looked different, still fit but very gaunt. How he got his 6 foot 4 inch frame from 14st 4lb to 12st 7lb must have taken an amazing amount of will power, hard work and dieting. In contrast, in McKenzie's dressing room, he was heavily muscled and looked very strong indeed.

It was no secret that McKenzie starts fast, slinging his big knock out blows in the hope of taking his opponent out quickly. It is also no secret that he has a tendency to fade early.

I heard a few whispers with people saying they feared for Enzo's well-being. He'd survived a heavy first round knockdown in a punishing cruiserweight fight and had now dropped a division to fight a big puncher at light heavyweight. To get these whispers from my mind I decided, as I always do, to act on what I see: simple as that.

From the start McKenzie bullied Maccarinelli to the ropes and as expected unloaded with his big punches. Even though he was under fire, the wily Maccarinelli would catch McKenzie with the odd good counter to keep things interesting and honest. When McKenzie did get through with hard shots they worryingly hurt Maccarinelli and made his legs stiffen. The same again happened in round two, with McKenzie trying to pin Maccarinelli to the ropes so he could land his powerful punches. McKenzie got him to the ropes near Maccarinelli's own corner, threw some shots that were blocked but then caught Maccarinelli with four massive punches, all landing to his head. Even though his hands were up, they were snapping his head back and forth and the last one that landed made his eyes roll back. I jumped in to stop McKenzie hitting him again, got between them and was expecting to see Maccarinelli's eyes still rolling but they weren't. He appeared to be okay but remembering why I jumped in, to prevent him getting seriously hurt, I waved the contest off.

Maccarinelli claimed in his interview that I said, 'I'm sorry, Enzo.' meaning that I'd made a mistake. I did say sorry but as part of a longer sentence, which was, 'I'm sorry, Enzo; I didn't want to see you get hurt!'

I was also surprised by the comment made by the respected commentator, John Rawlings, 'I've seen some bad stoppages but this one takes the biscuit.'

We see more in the ring and he didn't see the worrying eye roll and from that point I was convinced Enzo was finished and not protecting himself well enough to warrant the fight continuing. In the end I have the boxers' welfare and safety in my hands and when people asked me about the decision I made, I always answered, 'Enzo's pride's hurt but not his health.' I can live with that.

24 November, 2012: MEN Arena, Manchester.

The return of the 'Hitman'.

It was great to be officiating on this bill featuring the eagerly awaited return of Ricky the 'Hitman' Hatton. Just the year before at the WBC Convention in Las Vegas, Ricky Hatton was one of the many boxing stars to attend. He hadn't boxed for quite a while, was 15 stone and out of shape. We had a few drinks together and he told us some of his boxing stories. Ricky Hatton is one funny guy and had us all in stitches. I asked him what it was like fighting super star Floyd 'money' Mayweather.

'He was so fast, couldn't have hit him with confetti!' he answered.

A couple of months before his comeback fight I saw him at ringside in Liverpool for Prizefighter. He was in amazing shape and must have worked so hard to lose that amount of weight and get back to the level of fitness that he'd previously known.

On fight night, the 18,000 fans came alive when they saw a glimpse of the 'Hitman' shadow-boxing. Then there was an almighty roar as he made his way to the ring. Everyone hoped he would make a successful return to boxing.

Unfortunately, Vyacheslav Senchenko hadn't read the script properly, and after taking the early onslaught, he hung in and dug deep. He was cut in round seven but was now starting to catch Hatton with some full-bloodied shots. Senchenko's determination finally paid off and ironically, he put Ricky to the canvas with his own trademark punch, the body shot, which had him counted out in round nine. I'd wished he'd taken on a tough journeyman before tackling someone like Senchenko, after all, Ricky had been out of the ring for three years. But Ricky's a proud fighter and always took on the best.

The next morning, after breakfast, Mark Green and I drove to Manchester airport to fly to Mexico for the WBC Convention. This was a double anniversary, as the WBC was celebrating being 50 years old and so was I. The conventions are held all over the world and on this special year it happened to be at the home of the WBC, Mexico.

It's great to catch up with the other referees from all around the world in a relaxed environment as normally we are professional and business like. We share stories and play 'What if?': a game where a referee will tell a story about something strange that happened in the ring and we are left to decide what we'd do if it happened on our watch.

I told the one about the poor boxer shitting himself between rounds and asked what could have been done in this situation. A couple of serious answers came first but soon descended into toilet humour and jokes about nappies, talcum powder and corks!

I was told by Tito Gonzalez to be at a certain place at 5 p.m. and with that deadline approaching, I was basically manhandled through some large doors to find myself being approached by a large birthday cake, carried by none other than Gamaliel Diaz, the Mexican World Champion, who'd won his title in Japan shortly before.

Was taken aback and was almost speechless when I looked to my left to see a cameraman pointing his camera at me. This was to be, only the third birthday cake I'd ever received, (how sad!) but this one, live on Mexican television, made up for all the times I never got one. Nice way to mark my 50th.

Diaz was such a humble guy and as he delivered the cake to me he thanked me for his world title, to which I replied, 'You won it mate, not me.'

The Mexicans love their boxing and I was recognized at the all-inclusive complex by guests and staff, even though I was a long way from home.

Convention over and back to the day job. It dawned on me how long I'd been a detention officer when a kid, brought in under arrest, said, 'Hey, you know my dad. When he sees you on the telly he always says he knows you.'

'Really, what's your dad's name then?'

He told me and I realised I'd first met his dad when he was his son's age when I had to lock him up. On a couple of occasions I've had dads ask me to have a word with their wayward son to try and straighten them out. Not sure it helps but you do what you can and I often direct them to the idea of boxing. It gives you discipline, fitness, a purpose and when you are knackered from the training, you tend to be laying on a sofa recovering, not getting up to no good.

15 March, 2013: York Hall, Bethnal Green.

Matt Skelton versus John McDermott.

The English Heavyweight Championship.

A very good fight that went the distance, was well-balanced with lots of energy and a high work rate by two heavyweights who obviously wanted to win.

John was rightly, in my view and the judges, given the verdict with gentleman Matt Skelton congratulating him on his win. John can now go forward, build on this and get his shot at a decent career. He was given a good fight by the 42 year old Matt Skelton, who has had a good shot, fighting for a world title and losing on points. The crowd were very appreciative of the show put on and were treated to some really good boxing. The Title meant a lot to both boxers, as it should. It is a title from which you build a career.

The fight over, the York Hall crowd begin to leave. After a chat with fellow officials I head home with my co-writer in tow, still asking questions as he has done for the last 6 months. I am buzzing from a great fight and from a refereeing point of view it went well and I was pleased with the job. As I walked the quarter mile to the car among the crowd of boxing fans, a few people recognised me and shouted well done. It's appreciated.

Going through the Blackwall tunnel, Mark makes me think back to the night I lost to Micky Hughes.

'Does that decision still hurt?' he asks.

Twenty plus years later it doesn't as much and I think if it hadn't happened, then perhaps I wouldn't be the referee I am today.

Once home I watch the fight on Loaded TV, to see if there was anything I could've done better or anything I missed. I leave the recording running and see Frank Maloney being interviewed about York Hall.

It had been threatened with closure and the council and boxing promoters got together and raised the money to save it. York hall is, in my view, English boxing heritage and should now be safe and kept that way. It's known as one of the best places in the world to box, in the top ten, not a bad seat in the house, with the crowd, upstairs and down, really close to the ring. It's a special place and despite what happened to me there, I love it. The crowd are loud, appreciative, love their boxing and really do play their part.

And Frank is still Frank, by name and nature. Leaning on the apron of the ring and still not a man to mince his words, he says, 'A lot of great fighters have fought at York Hall: Benn, Eubanks, Lewis, Haye... In fact the referee Ian John-Lewis over there was cheated out of a British Title here by another referee, Mike Jacobs.'

That was 20 odd years ago and in my mind, can still see a younger Frank getting up on the apron that night, telling the ref that he'd taken a fucking liberty! It makes me smile.

Time for bed, tomorrow is another big day in boxing and I have the honour of handing out the trophies to excited and nervous kids who will be trying to sleep at the moment, but thinking about their fight.

I will need to be up early for a workout to burn off the big bar of chocolate I just ate! Weights in hands when training and shadow boxing as I run, no army boots now but comfy trainers and the use of a headset. No zoot suit to sweat out in, but still always wear a hat. Then into the gym: shadow box, use the speed ball, work the bag, skip, warm down, shower, then onto Strood Sports Centre. Never know, but I could be meeting a future champion, could be another Johnny Armour, Chris King, Nigel Benn or Chris Eubank in the making. Who knows, I may be the referee at their world title shot in the future and tomorrow could be where it all starts.

Really am going back to my roots; it's my old back yard. The sports centre is less than 200 metres from where I was born, fifty plus years ago in a cold council house, 113 Darnley Road, Strood, Kent. The streets there are littered with memories of rucks I had while growing up, fighting to earn respect and acceptance. I felt I got that respect and some great mates and neighbours as well.

Looking back at those early days hasn't been the most comfortable. I've experienced real meanness in people but also great kindness and weighing one up against the other, I find the kindness shown to me beats the meanness by about 10 to 1. All in all... seems like it wasn't so bad being different... but I really would've liked that belt though!

Ian John-Lewis
AMATEUR BOXING RECORD

CLUB: St Mary's, Chatham, Kent.

Manager: Ernie Magog.
Trainers: Fred Ludlow and Harry Shannon

Received Boxing Licence: 31ST January 1979

Junior Contests

1.	20 03 79: I.Vizzard	(Margate)	won points
2.	12 10 79: K.Fenwick	(Horton Lodge)	won points
3.	16 10 79: L.Bird	(Bulian)	won points
4.	03 11 79: A.Smith	(White Oaks)	won KO 2nd
5.	15 11 79: M.Gaunt	(Junior Army	won KO 3rd

Senior Contests

6.	09 01 80: S.Williams	(Romney Marsh)	won KO 2nd
7.	25 01 80: L.Waters	(Seven Oaks)	won KO 2nd
8.	02 02 80: T.Eastwood	(Bexhill)	won KO 2nd
9.	07 02 80: J.Carvin	(Margate)	won KO 2nd
10.	18 02 80: J.Tsansarides	(Marvels Lane)	won KO 1st
11.	04 03 80: S.Payne	(Beccles)	lost points
12.	12 05 80: A. Lawrence	(Horton Lodge)	won KO 1st
13.	03 11 80: S. Kendall	(Westree)	won KO 1st
14.	10 11 80: K.Bernard	(Danson Youth)	lost points

Kent Welterweight Championship

15.	06 12 80: T. O'Brien	(White Oaks)	won points
16.	06 12 80: I. Mc'Cartney	(Margate)	won KO 3rd
17.	06 12 80: G. Louther	(Faversham)	won points

At 17 became Welterweight Champion of Kent

18.	02 02.81: G. Louther	(Faversham)	won KO 3rd
19.	14 03 81: Belusa	(SSVS)	won points
20.	24 03 81: E. Wilson	(Battersea)	lost points
21.	03 04 81: H. Roberts	(Devon/Dorset)	won points

Essex v Kent Tournament
Kent Captain
22. 10 04 81: A. Wells   (Berry Boys)   won KO 1st

23. 29 10 81: M. Mills   (New Addington)   won points
24. 05 11 81: J. Harvey   (Sandwich)   won points

Defended Kent Championship
25. 05 12 81: R.Maggs   (Faversham)   won KO 1st

Kent v Police Force
26. 25 01 82: C. Neil   (Met Police)   won points

Southern Counties Championship
27. 06 02 82: F. Lyons   (Crawley)   lost points

28. 11 03 82: L. Greenidge (Ramsgate)   won points

Kent v Navy
29. 15 03 82: M.Thackeray   (Royal Navy)   won points

30. 20 10 82: M. Mills   (New Addington)   won points
31. 11 11 82: D. Tomsett   (Patcham)   won points

Defended Kent Championship
32. 04 12 82: D. Williams   (Romney Marsh)   won KO 2nd

Southern Counties Championship
33. 05 02 83: J Elie   (Basinstoke)   lost points

KENT v FRANCE
34. 09 04 83: Owoutoh   (France)   lost points

35. 26 04 83: J. Harvey   (Sandwich)   won disq
36. 07 10 83: R. Connor   (Fitzroy Lodge)   lost points
37. 09 11 83: C. Graham   (Chadwell/Tilbury)   won points

Kent Championship
38. 19 11 83: D. Francomb   (Westree)   won points
39. 19 11 83: S. Smith   (Gravesend)   lost points
Lost Kent Championship

40. 10 01 84: R. Edgar   (Islington)   won points

Southern Counties Championship
41. 18 02 84: D. Francomb   (Westree)   lost points
Lost in Semi-Final

42. 06 03 84: R. Harper   (Berry Boys)   lost points
43. 20 03 84: D. Francomb   (Westree)   won points
44. 19 10 84: L. Hughes   (Legionnaire)   won KO2nd
45. 22 11 84: J. Smith   (Golden Horse   lost points
46. 11 12 84: P. Barley   (Lyn)   won KO2nd

Southern Counties Championship
Quarter Final
47. 09 02 85: N. Logan   (Woking)   won KO2nd
Semi-Final
48. 15 02 85: D. Sharpe   (Canterbury)   won disq3rd
Final
49. 15 02 85: J. Laundon   (Portsmouth)   won disq3rd
Southern Counties champion

Zone Finals
Southern Counties Champion v Eastern Counties Champion
50. 02 03 85: S. Kyriakrides   (Ipswich)   lost 2nd

51. 01 04 85: S. Smith   (Gravesend)   lost points

Southern Counties Championship
Quarter Final
52. 07 02 86: S. Small   (Fareham)   won points
Final
53. 15 02 86: S. Smith   (Gravesend)   lost points

Amateur Boxing Career
53 Fights: Won 40 (KO'd 20) lost 13

Ian John-Lewis
PROFESSIONAL BOXING RECORD

Town: Gillingham, Kent.
Managers: Les Roberts, Frank Maloney.
Trainers: Achille 'Speedy' Mitchell, Charlie Magri, Gary Nickels

Date got Boxing Licence: 8th September 1986.
First Fight:

1.	04 03 87: Kesem Clayton	Dudley	Lost 4th.
2.	09 04 87: Ray Golding	Weston-Super-Mare	Lost points
3.	27 04 87: Willie McDonald	Glasgow	Won KO 1st
4.	08 06 87: Dave Heaver	Glasgow	Won KO 5th
5.	25 06 87: Rory Callaghan	York Hall	Won points
6.	17 09 87: Tony Britland	Gravesend	Won points
7.	04 11 87: Nick Meloscia	Gravesend	Won disq 5th
8.	09 12 87: Johnny Nanton	Greenwich	Won points
9.	13 04 88: Jim Beckett	Gravesend	Won KO 3rd
10.	18 05 88: Tony Baker	Gillingham	Won KO 8th
11.	30 09 88: Paul Seddon	Gillingham	Won KO 4th

Vacant Southern Area Welterweight Championship:

12.	24 01 89: Trevor Smith	Wandsworth	Lost KO 8th
13.	16 05 89: Andrew Furlong	Wandsworth	Lost 3rd cut eye
14.	15 11 89 Ray Taylor	Lewisham	Won points
15.	23 04 90 Chris Haydon	Crystal Palace	Won KO 1st
16.	22 06 90 Martin Garza	Gillinghan	Won KO 1st
17.	24 09 90 Alejandro Barbosa	Lewisham	Won KO 2nd
18.	31 10 90 Chris Blake	Crystal Palace	Lost cut eye 5th

British Welterweight Final Eliminator

19.	06 02 91 Mickey Hughes	York Hall	Lost cut eye 9th
20.	19 02 92 Darren Dyer	Alexandra Pavilion	Lost 2nd

My Professional Boxing Career
20 fights, won 13 (KO'd 9) lost 7